Constructing the User
Interface with Statecharts

CONSTRUCTING THE USER INTERFACE WITH STATECHARTS

IAN HORROCKS

Addison-Wesley

Harlow, England • Reading, Massachusetts • Menlo Park, California
New York • Don Mills, Ontario • Amsterdam • Bonn • Sydney • Singapore
Tokyo • Madrid • San Juan • Milan • Mexico City • Seoul • Taipei

© Addison Wesley Longman Limited 1999

Addison Wesley Longman Limited
Edinburgh Gate
Harlow
Essex CM20 2JE
England

and Associated Companies throughout the World.

Cover designed by Designers & Partners, Oxford

Typeset by 30

Printed and bound in the United States of America

First published 1999

ISBN   0-201-34278-2

British Library Cataloguing in Publication Data
A catalogue record for this book is available from the British Library

Library of Congress Cataloging-in-Publication Data
Horrocks, Ian, 1971–
              Constructing the user interface with statecharts / Ian Horrocks
                          p.   cm.
              Includes bibliographical references and index.
              ISBN 0-201-34278-2
              1. User interfaces (Computer systems)   2. Statecharts (Computer
       science)   I. Title.
       QA76.9.U83H66   1998
       005.4'28--dc21   98-34482
                                                                                          CIP

CONTENTS

14 Testing statecharts

15 Evaluation

PREFACE

For a long time I have been concerned by the apparent informality in which user interfaces are constructed. Typically, developers create the objects that appear in a user interface screen and then add the code related to those objects in a largely ad hoc manner. User interface software tends to be written in a bottom-up way, rather than being designed as a whole before the code is written. In other words, user interface code tends to be written without there being a clear understanding of how it will all eventually work together.

When I first started writing user interface software, I wanted a book that would explain how to design such software before starting to code it. I found there were broadly three types of books: user interaction design books which focused entirely on the external behaviour of the software; software design books which did not address user interface software directly or did not address it in sufficient detail; and programming guides which explained the syntax of particular programming languages without considering the overall structure of the software.

I began to think about the nature of user interface software and experimented with different ways of designing the software. The technique presented in this book is a result of those thoughts. The technique is not an academic theory, but a highly effective practical technique that has been used on real projects. I hope it will go some way to filling the current void in the literature on user interface construction. I also hope it will stimulate some debate on improving the way user interface software is developed and tested. Inevitably some readers will disagree with my opinions and such disagreement is healthy in helping fuel the evolution of software engineering techniques. I hope that those who disagree with the approach will offer an alternative design technique rather than criticism alone.

Who should read this book

This book is primarily written for professional software engineers. Much of what is written will be of little interest to readers who have not experienced the enormous difficulties of producing large, complex user interfaces that must be continuously enhanced over several years. It is not intended for developers writing software that will never see the light of day with real users.

Structure of the book

Chapter 1 clarifies some terminology that will be used in the book and answers a few basic questions about the technique. Chapter 2 provides an overview of the nature of direct manipulation user interfaces, the tools used to develop them and the nature of the application code written with such tools. Chapter 3 describes some of the problems associated with the majority of user interface code and provides a clear diagnosis of the root cause of the those problems. Chapter 4 presents the UCM architecture, a three-layer architecture for structuring user interface software, and explains how it solves the problems identified in Chapter 3.

Chapter 5 serves two purposes. Its main aim is to use a case study to demonstrate that statecharts are a viable way of realizing the UCM architecture. As a by-product of this, an argument is presented in favour of using statecharts to specify the behaviour of user interfaces as opposed to natural language specifications.

Part 2: Chapters 6 to 9 provide a detailed description of the statechart notation and ways of using statecharts to design user interface software. Part 3: Chapters 10 to 12 go on to demonstrate the use of statecharts by using three case studies that are built up step by step.

In Part 4, Chapter 13 presents a way of converting a statechart design to code and Chapter 14 is concerned with testing user interfaces constructed with statecharts.

Finally, Chapter 15 provides an evaluation of the technique and looks at the future of user interface development tools.

Acknowledgements

Thanks to Sarah, Oliver and Tom for their patience and understanding over the past few months.

Ian Horrocks
Ipswich, May 1998

Part 1
Concepts

Chapter 1
Introduction

What this book is about

There is a widespread belief throughout the software industry that user interfaces are easy to develop; a belief that has been strengthened by the proliferation of user interface development tools. Yet despite the obvious power and sophistication of such tools, the user interface part of a system is typically the most problematic. User interface code often contains more bugs and is usually more difficult to test and enhance than other types of code in a system. It is true to say that user interface development tools can make the initial coding of a user interface very rapid, but they don't make the long-term maintainability of the software easy.

The problems associated with user interface code stem from the way the software is constructed. Almost without exception, user interface software is coded without an overall software design. In this respect, user interface software is unique. No other type of software is constructed without there being at least some initial design work. The lack of a design for user interface software results in code with an intricate structure that is difficult to understand and enhance.

This book is concerned with establishing why it is important for user interface software to be designed and more importantly it provides a proven design technique that has been used on several real business applications. The technique is concerned with raising user interface development from a coding task to a software design task. It is concerned with creating abstract representations of user interface software and then converting those representations into code. The basic philosophy of the approach is to design the software so that it can be changed repeatedly throughout the lifetime of the system, rather than simply coding the software to behave in a particular way for the first release. The result of using the technique is user interface code that:

1   can be written quickly and easily;
2   is easy to test using white box techniques;
3   is easy to enhance repeatedly over the lifetime of a system;
4   can be modified without introducing unwanted side-effects;
5   can be regression tested without the need for full re-tests.

3

These are bold claims and I expect many readers will approach this book with a degree of scepticism. That is a healthy attitude to adopt and I hope I will be successful in convincing such readers that the technique lives up to these claims.

What this book is not about

User interface design is composed of two distinct types of work: user interaction design and software construction. User interaction design is concerned with the 'look and feel' of the interface and the behaviour of the software in response to a user performing tasks. Software construction, on the other hand, is concerned with designing, coding and testing the software that realizes the user interaction design. These are two closely related types of work but they demand very different skills. They are best performed by different people working closely together.

A user interaction designer is concerned with understanding the tasks that users will perform and then designing a user interface to support those tasks. The design includes the general form of the user interface, how the user will interact with the software, how the functions of the user interface will be organized, how the user interface will support different levels of user expertise and so on. To be successful, a designer must have a good understanding of what is feasible to develop within the time and budget available.

A user interface developer must work closely with a user interaction designer in order to understand the user interaction design before designing, coding and testing the software that will realize it. Developers should understand the principles of good user interaction design, without necessarily being responsible for producing the design.

User interface design is not a simple two-stage process; it is an incremental, iterative process. Inevitably users will provide feedback on the successes and failures of a user interface and there will be requests for changes to the software. The user interface design process continues throughout the lifetime of a product and is best visualized as a spiral, rather than as a simple two-stage process (see Figure 1.1). Clearly, user interface design is part of a larger software development life-cycle and the spiral shown in Figure 1.1 is intended to fit in with the iterative, evolutionary development processes of many software projects.

This book is about software construction. It is about designing, coding and testing the software that controls a user interface. It is *not* about the visual design of user inter-

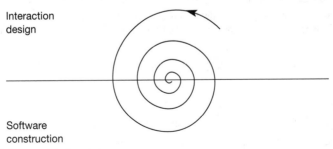

Figure 1.1 The user interface design process.

faces. User interaction design is very important and there are a number of good books which more than adequately cover the subject. Throughout this book, there is an implicit assumption that the user interaction design is completed before the user interface software is constructed. Little is said about user interaction design, not because it is unimportant, but because the book is intended to be focused on improving software construction.

About the technique presented in this book

Types of user interfaces

In simple terms, the design technique is concerned with ensuring a user can only supply valid events to a user interface and that the correct actions are executed in response to each event. Thus, the technique can be used for any type of user interface. All the examples used throughout the book are based on traditional windows applications, but there is no reason why it cannot be used to design the software that controls a web-based user interface. As web pages become increasingly interactive, the complexity of the underlying code will increase and will need to be designed in just the same way as conventional user interface code.

Development languages

The designs that result from applying the technique can be implemented in any programming language or user interface development tool. For instance, it can be used with Java, Microsoft Visual Basic, C, C++, Oracle Forms, Borland Delphi and so on. Furthermore, the technique should transcend the current range of languages, development tools and even the style of user interfaces themselves.

User interface software components

Software components are an important part of user interface construction. The technique is intended to be used to co-ordinate user interface objects and components so that they work together as an application. There is no reason why the technique cannot be used to design the components themselves.

DSDM and traditional life-cycles

The technique is concerned with improving the quality of user interface code by designing software that can be changed quickly and easily. User interfaces constructed with the technique can have large changes made to them without reducing the quality of the code or introducing unwanted side-effects. It is therefore particularly appropriate for use with iterative development processes such as the dynamic systems development method (DSDM) as well as more traditional development processes.

Tools required to support the technique

The technique does not require sophisticated design tools. A word processor and a reasonably good drawing package are all that are necessary to use the technique success-fully. It is best to use a drawing tool that allows arrows to be connected to other drawing objects, so that when an object is moved the arrows remain connected. A good drawing tool will also allow templates to be created, so for instance a set of standard design components can be created.

The impact on user interaction design

Most practitioners know that the choice of development tool can constrain the user inter-action design quite severely. It is therefore valid to raise a similar concern about the design method presented in this book. I strongly believe there is no reason why the method should influence or constrain the interaction design of a user interface. The design notation is extremely flexible and does not influence the behaviour of a user interface from a user's perspective.

Terminology

The lack of consistent terminology in the computer industry has great potential to cause unnecessary confusion. To help clarify matters, I will define some basic terms that will be used throughout this book.

Design

To a software engineer, the terms 'user interface design' and 'software design' are clear cut. 'User interface design' refers to the design of the screens and how the users can interact with those screens. 'Software design' refers to the internal structure of the software – the things the end users will never be aware of, such as the database design, the data structures, the objects and so on. However, this distinction is not recognized in all branches of the industry. In particular, user interface designers tend to use the terms user interface design and software design synonymously because they usually have little interest in the internal structure of the software itself. To help clarify matters I will use the following terms:

- **User interaction design**, which is concerned with the 'look and feel' of a user interface and the behaviour of the software in response to a user performing tasks. In other words, it is a reference to the design of the external, user-visible aspect of the software.
- **User interface design**, which is the two-stage process of interaction design and software construction.

In general, any other form of design referred to in this book is concerned with the design of the software that controls a user interface. In other words, it is a reference to the abstract representation of software entities and not the user-visible aspect of the software.

A technique or a method?

A mathematical method is a strict sequence of steps that, when followed correctly, will always give the same result. For instance, consider the method for long division. No matter who follows the steps of the method, if the same two numbers are being divided and the steps are followed correctly, then the answer will always be the same.

In software engineering, the term 'design method' is a misnomer. I don't like to apply the word 'method' to software design because it suggests a well-defined, repeatable procedure that will result in a good design no matter who applies it. No software design method can claim this. Designing software is a skill, and like any other skill, it requires a lot of practice to become good at it. There are many so-called design methods which often seem be little more than verbose descriptions of notations. Frankly, most engineers don't care about differences in notations because the notation is just a means to an end. Instead, engineers want books that will help them become proficient in designing software.

This book offers more than yet another design notation with a few woolly reasons for using it. Indeed, the notation used is not mine and I have not attempted to modify it. Instead the focus is placed heavily on design heuristics, standard techniques and case studies. Although I use the words 'method' and 'technique' to describe the information contained in this book, I do not pretend that there is a sequence of steps that can be followed to produce a good design. Design is a creative process. There is no one way of producing a design and there is no such thing as a correct design.

Chapter 2
User interface construction

This chapter provides a broad overview of user interface construction. It considers the nature of direct manipulation user interfaces in contrast to command line interfaces, the development tools that are necessary to create direct manipulation user interfaces and the nature of the code that is written using such tools.

The inherent complexity of direct manipulation user interfaces

Command line interfaces

Before the advent of direct manipulation user interfaces, all users had to interact with systems via command line interfaces. A command line interface allows users to enter commands at a prompt in a scrolling display. The user enters commands *about* an object which cannot be seen. For instance, in a command line interface that gives access to a database, a user may enter an SQL[1] query that retrieves information from a database table. The user interface does not provide a representation of the table for the user to interact with directly. Instead, the user must understand the nature of database tables and enter the appropriate commands to manipulate the data in those tables. So, for instance, a user can enter a command to describe a table which will provide the names of the columns in a table and the type of data contained in those columns (see Figure 2.1). Although the table is made visible, a user cannot interact with it directly. Instead, if a user wants to fetch data stored in a table, then the appropriate command must be entered (see Figure 2.2).

Command line interfaces are difficult to use because they require users to learn a command language in order to interact with the system. It will be impossible for users that do not know the command language to interact with the system. A command language such as a Unix shell language or a database query language is not good for casual or novice users. However, command line interfaces are important for specialist users such as software developers, system testers, or system administrators. Such users need flexible ways of interacting with a system. A command line interface can be very powerful, especially when commands can be combined to form command scripts. For instance, a powerful feature of

---

1. SQL: Structured Query Language – a language for manipulating relational databases.

```
SQL>            describe employees
                column          type        null
                ---------       -------     ------
                id              number      not null
                name            char
                manager_id      number
SQL>
```

Figure 2.1

```
SQL>            select name from employees order by name;
                name
                -------------
                Brown
                Jones
                Smith
SQL>
```

Figure 2.2

the Unix operating system is the facility to create shell scripts which can be executed by a user from the command line or periodically by Unix itself.

Direct manipulation user interfaces

Direct manipulation user interfaces are much easier to use than command line interfaces because a user does not have to know a command language in order to interact with the system. Instead, individual user interface objects, such as buttons, scrollbars and windows, are combined to represent entities, such as file systems or database tables, and a user can interact directly with those entities without having to enter commands. A good direct manipulation user interface will allow a user, with no previous knowledge of the interface, to carry out useful and meaningful dialogues with the system.

Direct manipulation user interfaces are easy to use because the state of an entity is made visible to a user and the entity can be manipulated directly by a user. For example, when using an application that controls a file system, a user can see which files are contained in a directory simply by clicking on the directory. Files can be moved from one part of the file system to another by dragging the files to the appropriate directory. In short, users simply perform direct actions *on* objects they can see, rather than enter commands *about* objects they cannot see.

User interface development

A command line interface is relatively easy to develop because established language processing techniques used in compilers can be used. Moreover, a command line interface is much simpler than a direct manipulation interface because a user must complete one dialogue with the system before the next one can be started.

Direct manipulation user interfaces are intrinsically far more complicated than command line interfaces because a user can have several partially completed dialogues that can be suspended and resumed at any time. For instance, a user could enter some text in a field and then start an interaction with another screen object, such as clicking a button or moving a scrollbar. If the user returned to the field in which the text was typed, that text would still be in place and the user would be able to resume the dialogue.

The difficulty faced by developers of direct manipulation user interfaces is to ensure that a user can only ever perform valid operations. For instance, if a user changes the name of a file in a file system, the software must ensure that the user does not leave the name of the file blank. In a command line interface, if a new name was not specified, then the command would be rejected as syntactically incorrect. In a direct manipulation interface, the software must prevent a user leaving a file without giving it a name. The challenge faced by user interface developers is to ensure that all dialogues within a system are co-ordinated so that it is impossible for a user to perform operations that would cause an error in the application. In effect, the developers of direct manipulation user interfaces are responsible for ensuring that the syntax of the interaction is always correct, whereas with a command line user interface, it is the users who are responsible for ensuring the syntax of the interaction is correct.

User interface development tools

Direct manipulation user interfaces (hereafter called 'user interfaces') are extremely large, complicated systems. The applications that are written by developers rely on a large amount of software in the operating system and make use of a large amount of software supplied with the user interface development tools used to construct them. This section provides a brief overview of the main features of development tools that are used to construct user interfaces. It starts with a very brief overview of how a windows-based operating system functions. To describe such a system in detail would take an entire book in itself, but it is useful to have a conceptual understanding of the underlying software system on which applications are built.

A windows-based operating system

A user interface is made up of many objects such as windows, scrollbars and menus. Each user interface object has a unique identifier that is allocated by the operating system. When a user clicks a mouse button or presses a key, that interaction causes an event to be sent to the operating system. When the operating system receives an event, it processes it and then broadcasts it to all the other user interface objects. Each object can then respond to the event in an appropriate way based on its own rules for dealing with that particular event. For instance, an object may repaint itself if it is uncovered by another user interface object, it may hide itself if the parent window is closed, or it may take no action at all.

Operating systems that control graphical user interfaces are large and complicated. To help developers avoid having to understand all the low-level messages in the system, user interface development tools such as Visual Basic and Delphi have been created. These tools handle many of the messages automatically for an application. A relatively small set of messages are made available for developers to use in their applications. With such tools developers can quickly create powerful applications, without having to deal with low-level details.

User interface class libraries

Before the advent of user interface development tools, most user interfaces were created with user interface toolkits. These are essentially libraries of user interface classes which developers can use to create user interface objects such as windows, canvases and buttons. For instance, the code in Figure 2.3 illustrates the sort of library functions that would be used to create a button labelled 'Quit' on a canvas in a window. (A canvas is an area that is used to display screen items and receive user events. A window is the frame that surrounds the canvas – just as a picture frame surrounds a canvas on which a picture is painted.)

```
main ()
{
Window my_window;
Canvas my_canvas;
Button quit_button;

my_window = create(window,500,300);
my_canvas = create(canvas, my_window);
quit_button = create(button, my_canvas,
        label, "Quit",
        on_click_event, when_quit_clicked,
        x_pos, 10,
        y_pos, 280,
        height, 20,
        width, 90);
...
...
}
```

Figure 2.3

Notice the long list of parameters that are passed to the function that creates the Quit button. These parameters specify the properties of the button such as which canvas it appears on, the size and position of the button on the canvas, the label that appears on the button, which procedure is executed when the button is clicked, and so on.

Unfortunately, the parameter list shown in the example is by no means exhaustive – each object can have a large number of properties. One of the main problems with using such libraries is that the precise syntax of the parameter lists must be remembered by developers. There are so many parameters that it is virtually impossible to remember them all and so developers have to refer constantly to programming manuals or spend time copying and pasting existing function calls.

A second significant problem with using such libraries is related to screen design. It is not possible for a developer to see the screen layout without compiling and executing the code.

And then when they can see it, it is not possible to modify the layout directly. They must adjust the appropriate parameters, such as the x,y co-ordinates of an object or the height of an object, and then re-compile the code before executing it again. When fine-tuning the layout of a design, this process may have to be repeated several times before a satisfactory screen layout is achieved.

Elements of a user interface development tool

A user interface development tool provides a development environment with its own graphical user interface. Such tools have revolutionized the way applications are developed because they have made it possible to create user interfaces extremely quickly. There are many tools available and they are widely used throughout the software industry. The basic elements of a typical user development tool are given below.

A screen designer

A screen designer window allows a developer to see the layout of each screen without having to execute the application. The developer can see the objects that make up the screen and it is possible to change some of the properties of the objects. For instance, the size and position of an object can be modified by manipulating it with the mouse pointer or arrow keys.

An object navigator

An object navigator window provides a list of all the objects in the application and all the code associated with each of those objects. Since the code in a user interface application is distributed among the objects, the object navigator provides an effective way of navigating through the code in an application.

A property sheet

Each object has a set of properties, or attributes, associated with it. When a user selects an object either in the screen designer or in the object navigator, the properties of that object will appear in tabular form in the property sheet window. A property sheet for an object simply lists the property names in one column and the values of those properties in another. A user can edit the properties of an item without having to remember any syntax. Significantly, the effect of modifying an object's properties can be seen immediately in the screen designer without having to compile and execute any code.

A toolbox of user interface classes

This is a window that contains a set of user interface classes. A developer can select a class and create an instance of that class (that is, an object) in their application by dragging the required class onto the appropriate canvas. The object will be automatically assigned a set of default attribute values which can be modified by the developer if necessary. For instance, a button will have a particular colour, text label, height, width and so on. The default values can easily be changed in the property sheet window.

Each object will also have certain default behaviours that are defined in the classes from which they are created. For instance, a button will 'know' how to respond when a user clicks it so that some visual feedback is given to the user to indicate that the button click has been registered. This feedback is achieved by changing the bevel on the button to lowered when the mouse button goes down and then raised when the mouse button is released. This behaviour is defined by the button class and cannot be changed by an application developer because it is the behaviour that all buttons must exhibit.

A code editor

A code editor window allows a developer to enter code for an application. Some code editors are interactive in that the code is interpreted as it is entered and so most syntax errors can be captured and highlighted as the code is written. The editors can also change the format of the code as it is entered to force a more consistent coding style.

Notice that the five elements of a user interface development tool are closely integrated. For instance, a developer can select an object such as a button in the object navigator and the properties of that object will be displayed in the property sheet window. If a property (or attribute) of the object is changed, such as the colour being changed from red to blue, then that change will be seen in the screen designer. If an object is double-clicked in the object navigator, then the code editor will appear automatically with the code corresponding to that item displayed in it.

Event-driven software

Large software systems are typically composed of a number of sub-systems which, in turn, are composed of a number of modules. The way in which a system is decomposed into sub-systems and modules is captured in a structural design of the system. However, for modules to work together as a system, they must be controlled so that the procedures and functions they provide are executed at the right time and in the right order. In many systems, a main program is started when the software is installed and this controls the system by calling procedures and functions in other modules. The control of the system is passed from one subroutine to another. The currently executing subroutine relinquishes control either by calling other subroutines or by returning control to its parent.

For instance, in Figure 2.4, control starts in the main program and is passed to subroutine A, then subroutine B and then subroutine C. During the execution of subroutine A, control passes to subroutines D and E. With this type of control, the developers of the system determine the order in which the lines of code are executed. Clearly, parameters to the program may cause the flow of control to vary from one execution to the next, but the execution path is still defined by the developers. This type of control is embedded in many programming languages such as C or Pascal.

User interface software is event driven. Each user interface object can respond to external events such as those supplied by a user, the operating system, or the application itself. For instance, when a user clicks a button on a screen, an event is supplied to the application and the application can be programmed to respond to this event by executing a sequence of code. When the sequence of code completes execution, the application stops and waits for the next event to be supplied. The sequence of external events supplied to the application determines the flow of control.

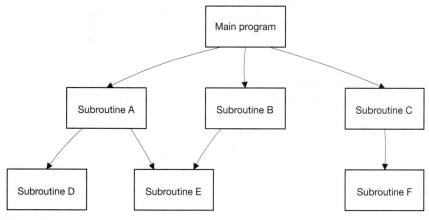

Figure 2.4

User interface objects are programmed to respond to events by using event handlers. Event handlers are procedures that are associated with individual user interface objects and specific events. The code in an event handler is executed in response to a specific event being supplied to a specific object. For example, if a user clicks a particular button in a user interface then the when_mouse_clicked event handler[2] associated with that button is executed. Each object in a user interface has a large set of events that it will recognize. A developer decides which event handlers should contain code in order to achieve a particular effect when the user interacts with the application. Event handlers are only used to augment the default behaviour of user interface objects and it is quite likely that only a small subset of the event handlers will contain code.

The developer of a user interface cannot anticipate the order in which events will occur. Indeed, it is likely that the path through the code will differ every time the application is run. In order to avoid errors occurring in an application, the application code must be written to prevent a user supplying events that could cause an error in the application. For instance, the user interface of a word processor must ensure that a user opens a document before any of the controls for formatting a document are made available. In other words, in order to avoid errors occurring in an application, a user interface must not allow a user to rampage through the interface supplying events in any order. A user can determine the flow of control in an application by supplying events to the software, but the developer of an application is responsible for determining which set of events a user can supply at any given moment.

Summary

Direct manipulation user interfaces are complex systems and powerful development tools are required to help make creating them easier. Such tools have made the production of user interfaces much quicker than would be possible with conventional languages such as C,

---

2. Note that the names of event handlers are not consistent between development tools. The names used throughout this book are not from any particular tool. Instead they have been chosen to clearly identify the event that will cause the event handler to be executed.

because developers do not have to concern themselves with low-level details such as how a button recognizes when a user clicks it with a mouse pointer. Instead, developers just have to define the visual appearance of the button and the code that is executed in response to a user clicking it.

Despite the obvious power of such tools, producing a good user interface with them is expensive. It is common for more than half the budget of a client–server project to be spent on the development and maintenance of the user interface. The reason for this is the complexity of the code that is written in the event handlers of user interface objects. Serious problems can easily be created in the event handler code and the next chapter is concerned with identifying the root cause of those problems.

Chapter 3
A bottom-up approach to user interface construction

User interface development tools are very powerful. They can be used to construct large and complex user interfaces, with only a relatively small amount of code written by an application developer. And yet, despite the power of such tools and the relatively small amount of code that is written, user interface software often has the following characteristics:

- the code can be difficult to understand and review thoroughly;

- the code can be difficult to test in a systematic and thorough way;

- the code can contain bugs even after extensive testing and bug fixing;

- the code can be difficult to enhance without introducing unwanted side-effects;

- the quality of the code tends to deteriorate as enhancements are made to it.

Despite the obvious problems associated with user interface development, little effort has been made to improve the situation. Any practitioner who has worked on large user interface projects will be familiar with many of the above characteristics, which are symptomatic of the way in which the software is constructed. This chapter is concerned with understanding the typical approach to user interface development and why it is not a particularly good approach to take. The remainder of the book will then be concerned with recommending a more rigorous and more scalable technique.

The event–action paradigm

We have already seen that user interface software is event driven. A user supplies an event to an object and a sequence of actions is executed in response to that event. The software then stops and waits for the next event to be supplied. In short, an event supplied by a user determines the sequence of actions that is executed by the software. This is the event–action paradigm and most developers think in terms of it when they are constructing user interface software.

Before we accept this paradigm as a basis for constructing software, let's consider three simple examples of user interface behaviour.

Example 1

Consider the user interface of a typical word processor. Before a user opens a file containing a document, the range of functions available for the user to perform is very limited. For instance, any functions related to formatting the text in a document are either disabled or not visible. When a user opens a document, a much wider set of functions is made available. That is, the event of opening a file makes user interface objects visible that were previously not visible. When a file is closed, the range of objects for a user to interact with is again reduced. In other words, a user's interactions with one object are changing the attributes of other objects.

Key point: A user event supplied to one object can affect the state of another.

Example 2

The word processor described in the previous example was very simplistic. When a user makes changes to a document in the word processor, the underlying file in the operating system needs to be updated to reflect the changes. A user can save changes made to the document by selecting an appropriate menu option. However, if changes are made to a document and a user attempts to close the document without saving, then the following alert message could be displayed in a modal window: 'Do you want to save the changes to doc1?' with three buttons labelled 'Yes', 'No' and 'Cancel'.

The event handler for the close event must also be aware of whether a document has been opened or whether a new document has been created. Because if changes have not been saved when a user supplies the close event, code in the event handler must know whether an existing file should be updated, or whether the user should be asked to name a new file and location in the directory structure.

It is clear that the actions executed in response to the close event are determined by the previous events supplied by the user. The event handler for the close event must determine which event occurred most recently: the document being opened, the document being created, the document being changed, or the document being saved. This information cannot be determined retrospectively; the information must be stored when these events occur, so that the event handler for the close event can determine which actions should be executed. Thus, the user interface object that contains the text of a document and the objects used to open, create, close and save such documents are all linked and they must work together in a co-ordinated way.

Key point: When an event is supplied to a user interface object, the actions executed in response to that event can vary, depending on the previous interactions the user has had with *other* user interface objects.

Example 3

The behaviour of a screen can be influenced by factors other than how a user interacts with it. For instance, the data that is displayed on a screen can affect the behaviour of a user interface. To illustrate the point, consider a business application that is used to display information about customers. Suppose there is a status for each customer which indicates whether they have paid their latest bill on time. The status can have a value of 'Bill Paid' or 'Bill Not Paid'. Suppose there is a button on the screen which, when clicked, will cause a reminder bill to be sent to the customer. To avoid a user sending a reminder bill erroneously, the button should only be enabled if the customer has a status of 'Bill Not Paid' and the date of the bill is earlier than 30 days prior to the current date.[1]

Key point: The data displayed in a user interface object can affect the state and behaviour of other user interface objects.

From these three examples, it is clear that an event alone does not determine the actions that are executed in response to that event. Other factors are taken into account such as the values contained in other user interface objects, the events that have been previously supplied by the user and so on. User interface objects do not behave independently of each other. And, more significantly, the actions that are executed when a user interface object receives an event, are not determined by the event alone.

Thus, despite the wide acceptance of the event–action paradigm, it does not reflect the reality of user interface construction. The paradigm is too simple. It is based on the assumption that user interface objects act independently of each other. And yet quite clearly, the behaviour of individual objects must be co-ordinated with the behaviour of other objects if they are to work together as an application. If the objects did not work together then the user would be able to supply events that would cause errors in the application.

The bottom-up approach to user interface development

The majority of user interface developers think in terms of the event–action paradigm. As a consequence of this, most user interface software is constructed in a bottom-up fashion. That is, individual event handlers are not written in their entirety at one time in the way that conventional subroutines would be written. Instead, the code in event handlers are usually built up gradually until a co-ordinated group of event handlers is achieved. Typically, each event handler starts with a basic sequence of actions that will be executed in response to an event. And because an item may respond to an event in different ways, depending on the context in which it is used, conditional statements are added to determine the context in which the event has occurred and therefore which actions to execute.

In order to determine the context in which an event has occurred, an event handler must make use of information shared between user interface objects. Such information is available for any event handler to use. The information may not necessarily be an explicit global variable; it may, for example, be the value contained in a user interface object or any other attribute of an object.

To illustrate the bottom-up approach to user interface construction, we will consider a calculator application that is distributed with Visual Basic version 5. The user interface of the application is shown in Figure 3.1 and the code that controls the user interface objects is given in Figure 3.2. The intention is not to criticize this particular application, but rather the technique used to construct the software. The application has been chosen because it is small and yet it possesses many of the characteristics of much larger applications.

---

1.   That is, the customer is given 30 days to pay the bill before a reminder bill is sent.

Figure 3.1

```
' ---------------------------------------------------------------------
' Copyright (C) 1994 Microsoft Corporation
'
' You have a royalty-free right to use, modify, reproduce and distribute
' the Sample Application Files (and/or any modified version) in any way
' you find useful, provided that you agree that Microsoft has no warranty,
' obligations or liability for any Sample Application Files.
' ---------------------------------------------------------------------
Option Explicit
Dim Op1, Op2                    ' Previously input operand.
Dim DecimalFlag As Integer      ' Decimal point present yet?
Dim NumOps As Integer           ' Number of operands.
Dim LastInput                   ' Indicate type of last keypress event.
Dim OpFlag                      ' Indicate pending operation.
Dim TempReadout

' ---------------------------------------------------------------------
' Click event procedure for C (cancel) key.
' Reset the display and initializes variables.
Private Sub Cancel_Click()
    Readout = Format(0, "0.")
    Op1 = 0
    Op2 = 0
    Form_Load
End Sub
' ---------------------------------------------------------------------
' Click event procedure for CE (cancel entry) key.
Private Sub CancelEntry_Click()
    Readout = Format(0, "0.")
```

Figure 3.2

```
        DecimalFlag = False
        LastInput = "CE"
End Sub
' -----------------------------------------------------------------------
' Click event procedure for decimal point (.) key.
' If last keypress was an operator, initialize
' readout to "0." Otherwise, append a decimal
' point to the display.
Private Sub Decimal_Click()
        If LastInput = "NEG" Then
                Readout = Format(0, "-0.")
        ElseIf LastInput <> "NUMS" Then
                Readout = Format(0, "0.")
        End If
        DecimalFlag = True
        LastInput = "NUMS"
End Sub
' -----------------------------------------------------------------------
' Initialization routine for the form.
' Set all variables to initial values.
Private Sub Form_Load()
        DecimalFlag = False
        NumOps = 0
        LastInput = "NONE"
        OpFlag = " "
        Readout = Format(0, "0.")
        'Decimal.Caption = Format(0, ".")
End Sub
' -----------------------------------------------------------------------
'Click event procedure for number keys (0-9).
'Append new number to the number in the display.
Private Sub Number_click(Index As Integer)
        If LastInput <> "NUMS" Then
                Readout = Format(0, ".")
                DecimalFlag = False
        End If
        If DecimalFlag Then
                Readout = Readout + Number(Index).Caption
        Else
                Readout = Left(Readout, InStr(Readout, Format(0, ".")) - 1) +
                Number(Index).Caption+
```

Figure 3.2 (Cont'd)

```
Format(0,".")
    End If
    If LastInput = "NEG" Then Readout = "–" & Readout
    LastInput = "NUMS"
End Sub
' ----------------------------------------------------------------------------
'Click event procedure for operator keys (+, –, x, /, =)
'If the immediately preceeding keypress was part of a
'number, increments NumOps. If one operand is present,
'set Op1. If two are present, set Op1 equal to the
'result of the operation on Op1 and the current
'input string, and display the result.
Private Sub Operator_Click(Index As Integer)
    TempReadout = Readout
    If LastInput = "NUMS" Then
        NumOps = NumOps + 1
    End If
    Select Case NumOps
    Case 0
    If Operator(Index).Caption = "–" And LastInput <> "NEG" Then
        Readout = "–" & Readout
        LastInput = "NEG"
    End If
    Case 1
    Op1 = Readout
    If Operator(Index).Caption = "–" And LastInput <> "NUMS" And OpFlag
    <> "=" Then
    Readout = "="
    LastInput = "NEG"
        End If
        Case 2
        Op2 = TempReadout
        Select Case OpFlag
            Case "+"
                Op1 = CDbl(Op1) + CDbl(Op2)
            Case "–"
                Op1 = CDbl(Op1) – CDbl(Op2)
            Case "X"
                Op1 = CDbl(Op1) * CDbl(Op2)
            Case "/"
                If Op2 = 0 Then
```

```
                              MsgBox "Can't divide by zero", 48, "Calculator"
                    Else
                              Op1 = CDbl(Op1) / CDbl(Op2)
                    End If
              Case "="
                    Op1 = CDbl(Op2)
              Case "%"
                    Op1 = CDbl(Op1) * CDbl(Op2)
              End Select
          Readout = Op1
          NumOps =
      End Select
      If LastInput <> "NEG" Then
            LastInput = "OPS"
            OpFlag = Operator(Index).Caption
      End If
End Sub
' -------------------------------------------------------------------------
' Click event procedure for percent key (%).
' Compute and display a percentage of the first operand.
Private Sub Percent_Click()
      Readout = Readout / 100
      LastInput = "Ops"
      OpFlag = "%"
      NumOps = NumOps + 1
      DecimalFlag = True
End Sub
```

Figure 3.2 (Cont'd)

The code is divided into eight parts. It starts with a list of global variable declarations and then there are seven event handlers. The event handlers are for the following events: when the cancel button (C) is clicked; when the cancel entry button (CE) is clicked; when the decimal point button is clicked; when the application is first started; when a number button (0–9) is clicked; when an operator button (+, –, ×, /, =) is clicked; and when the percent button is clicked.

Although some readers may not be familiar with the syntax of the programming language, it should be possible to understand what each line of code means if the following points are born in mind:

* 'Readout' is the name of the display field where the numbers appear after the number buttons are clicked.

* The operator buttons (+, –, ×, /, =) are grouped so that when a user clicks one of them, the same event handler is executed. Each button in the group has an index number and so, for example, the following conditional statement will check whether the minus button has been clicked:

If Operator(Index).Caption = "–" then ...

- In a similar way, the 10 number buttons (0 to 9) are also grouped so that when any one of them is clicked, the same event handler is executed.

- In the event handler for the number buttons, the following statement appears:

Left(Readout, InStr(Readout, Format(0, ".")) – I)

This simply returns the characters to the left of the decimal point in the Readout field.

The following observations can be made about the approach used to construct the application:

- **There is no abstract view of the software** Attempting to understand the overall behaviour of the software is difficult because there is no abstract view of it. Instead, we are left attempting to understand the software line-by-line and gradually build up a picture of how it all fits together.

- **Event handlers are co-ordinated through the use of global variables** A global variable is known throughout the entire application and may be used by any event handler. Using global variables in an event handler makes the event handler impossible to understand in isolation from the rest of the code. Having several distinct units of code accessing the same shared information can easily result in unwanted side-effects when the software is modified. The application makes extensive use of global variables. The global variables are used to pass messages between event handlers so that the user interface objects behave in a co-ordinated way. For instance, the number_click event handler makes use of the LastInput and DecimalFlag global variables. Thus, to understand the number_click event handler, its is necessary to identify and understand the other parts of the application that use these global variables. In short, although the application code is divided into separate event handlers, they are actually bound together by global information.

- **The software is not object oriented** An important characteristic of an object oriented system is that no information is shared between objects. Instead, the state of the system is distributed throughout the objects and each object is responsible for managing its own state information. For instance, when a user interacts with a scrollbar, a message is sent to the scrollbar object to update the position of the sliding button. The position of the sliding button is a visual representation of the object's internal state. The event handler code in the calculator example is not object oriented because the event handlers share information in the form of global variables.

- **The contexts are not explicit** Many of the event handlers contain conditional statements to determine the context in which an event occurs. A combination of the event and the context determines which lines of code are executed. Unfortunately, the contexts are not explicitly named in the code. Instead, conditions are tested in the code but it is not always clear why those conditions are being tested and why certain lines of code are executed if those conditions are true. In short, the different contexts in which an event can occur were not explicitly identified before the code was written.

- **It is difficult to get the software to work correctly** The bottom-up approach to user interface development relies on the skill of the developer to identify all the possible ways in which a user can supply events to the application. This is not an easy task and it must be approached in a systematic way. To illustrate the point, I tested the calculator application for about an hour and found 10 errors, three of which caused the application to crash with runtime errors. (The full details of the errors are given in Appendix A.) Certainly, the application adds, subtracts, multiplies and divides numbers successfully, but it is the peripheral functions such as the cancel entry button, the percent button and operations on negative numbers that caused the errors.

For instance, the cancel entry (CE) button is used for cancelling the last operand entered and yet it can be used at any point during the execution of the application. Ideally the button should be disabled when it is not valid to use it, such as before an operand has been entered. As the application is written currently, a user is forced to learn the syntax of the user interface if the button is to be used correctly.

The percent button is intended to divide the first operand by 100. However, the button can be clicked at any point. Again, the user is being forced to learn the syntax of the user interface if errors in the application are to be avoided. Ideally, the button should only be enabled when the first operand is being entered, or when a result from an operation is achieved.

The application is about 100 lines long and yet it contains a number of serious errors. Business applications are much larger and more complicated than this and yet they are often constructed in a similar bottom-up way.

- **It is difficult to enhance such software** Software constructed in a bottom-up way is difficult to make significant enhancements to. The relationships between user interface objects are usually very simple. And when user interface software is written it is obvious why event handlers check certain conditions and why they execute different actions depending on those conditions. However, many events can affect or make use of the same information and if the behaviour of a user interface needs to be changed, then it is necessary to understand the dependences that exist between objects. It can be difficult to understand the impact of modifying one part of the code without making the change and then testing the software to ensure no side-effects have been introduced. Developing software by trial and error is not good.

Summary

The proliferation of user interface development tools has not been matched by a growth in effective ways of developing code with such tools. In general, user interface code is largely constructed in an ad hoc, informal way without an explicit design. A bottom-up approach to constructing user interface software is not a scalable approach – even simple applications can be difficult to get right.

Most people find it easier to understand a diagram than written text. A diagram is generally more concise and more memorable than words alone. When reading user interface code, trying to understand, visualize and remember the dependences between fragments of code can be difficult. To make user interface software easier to understand, a design notation is required that provides a clear view of how the software works together as a whole. The next few chapters will describe a technique for designing user interface software in a top-down fashion. The calculator application will then be revisited and designed so that it contains significantly fewer errors and is easier to understand.

Chapter 4
The user interface-control-model architecture

The objects that make up a user interface must be co-ordinated to work together as a whole. Thus, when a user supplies an event to a user interface object, the corresponding event handler must determine the context in which the event has occurred in order to determine which actions should be executed. Event handlers determine the context in which the event occurred by accessing information that a number of other event handlers can access and modify (see Figure 4.1). Constructing user interface software based on event handlers communicating via global variables is not a good long-term strategy. It is like constructing a building without solid foundations. The purpose of this chapter is to introduce a software architecture that will provide a user interface with solid foundations on which the code can be written, tested and maintained.

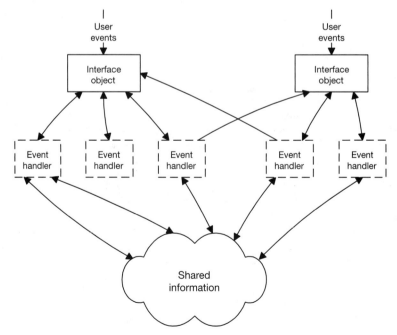

Figure 4.1 The structure of user interface code constructed using the bottom-up approach.

The user interface-control-model (UCM) architecture

Event handlers allow application developers to add code that will be executed when a particular event occurs. An event handler may access or update global information that is available for other event handlers to make use of. The information shared between event handlers is related to the state of the user interface as a whole and not the state of individual user interface objects. For instance, in the calculator example in the previous chapter, there was a global variable called DecimalFlag which was used to record whether a user had entered a decimal point. This variable was used by six out of the seven event handlers.[1]

The information shared between event handlers is used to control the user interface as a whole. In other words, the event handler code is used to make individual objects work together as an entity that means something to a user. When a user interacts with an application, the interaction is with the group of objects that make up the user interface and not with individual objects. The code that makes the objects work together is distributed throughout the event handlers.

A better approach would be to centralize the control of the user interface in a small number of control objects (see Figure 4.2). Each control object would be responsible for co-ordinating the behaviour of a group of related user interface objects, such as all the objects that appear on a canvas. The user interface objects are not just simple objects such as data entry fields, menu items, buttons and so on. They can also be larger and more complex objects such as a hierarchical tree object (the left part of the Windows 95 Windows Explorer).

The event handlers associated with user interface objects are simply used to forward events supplied by the user to the appropriate control object. In other words, when a user supplies an event, the event handler simply calls the appropriate method belonging to the control object. The control object maintains the state of the user interface as a whole. When a control object receives a message from a user interface object, the message and the current state of the control object are used to determine the actions that will be executed and possibly update the state information maintained by the control object. The control objects are responsible for sending messages to the user interface objects when a user event occurs. For instance, a control object may cause a user interface object to change colour or become disabled and so on.

The control object can also send messages to model objects. A model object maintains the long-term information held by the system which survives executions of the application. Typically this layer in the architecture is a database that can be accessed by several users simultaneously. The model objects are not concerned with how the information is presented to the user. Control objects are responsible for moving information between the user interface and the model layers. User interface objects do not access model objects directly and model objects do not send messages to user interface objects.

Although the model layer of the UCM architecture has been described in terms of objects, the layer can be a relational database: in which case, the control objects would perform

---

1. I consider it to be used by the Cancel_Click event handler, because this calls the Form_Load event handler which does make use of it.

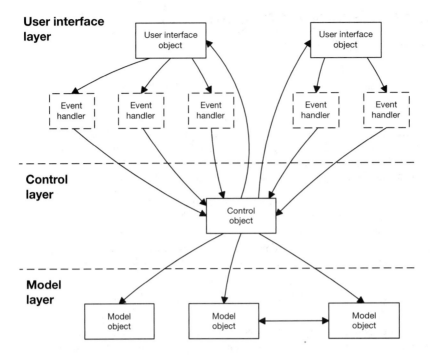

Figure 4.2 The UCM architecture for user interface software.

database operations such as inserts, updates, deletes and retrievals. The control layer would still be responsible for controlling the information that is passed between the user interface and model layers.

Implicit in the above discussion is the fact that control objects are only concerned with application-specific code. The behaviour of individual user interface objects, or even groups of user interface objects, is not specified in the control layer unless that behaviour would normally be coded in an event handler. For instance, in most development tools it is possible to specify the order in which a user can tab between fields in a screen. When a user clicks the tab key, the cursor moves from one field to the next in an order specified by the developer (see Figure 4.3). However, this behaviour is not specified in the control layer because it would not normally be coded in an event handler. Instead, such behaviour is a defined as a property of the objects and it is specified in the object property sheets.

The control layer provides a user interface with an explicit state that can be used to determine the different contexts in which events occur. The state of the control objects relate to the state of the application as a whole and not individual user interface objects. The role of the control objects is to centralize the control of the user interface objects with the intention of increasing the stability of the application by making it easier to understand. The concept of having three types of objects which are related to the user interface, the control of the software and the long-term information of the system, is consistent with Jacobson's experience of stable systems being created from objects that are biased towards presentation, behaviour or information (Jacobson et al., 1993).

The UCM architecture may sound good in principle, but creating control objects that are easy to understand requires a powerful design notation. The danger is that each control

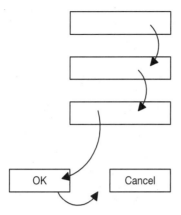

Figure 4.3 A user can tab between user interface objects.

object will be constructed from a set of global variables that can be accessed and updated by a set of procedures: in which case, understanding the code will be no easier than understanding the code written using the bottom-up approach.

The event–state–action paradigm

In the case of a command line user interface, a user can enter any command at any time and the user interface will respond accordingly. If there is an error in the syntax of the command or the commands are entered in the wrong order then an error message will be displayed to the user.

With a direct manipulation user interface, the developer is responsible for ensuring that a user can only supply valid events at any given time. Thus if an application requires a user to perform event A before event B, the application developer must ensure that event B is not possible until event A has been performed. Preventing an event occurring can be achieved by making certain objects disappear or become disabled. Effectively, as a user interacts with a user interface, the user interface moves from one set of possible events to another (see Figure 4.4). The events that a user supplies will cause the software to move from one finite set of possible events to another. In other words, the user interface moves from one state to another and the state defines the set of possible events that a user can supply. The states define the context in which an event occurs.

This is the event–state–action paradigm. This is not a theory of how user interface software could be constructed. It is the nature of all direct manipulation user interfaces. In most cases, the states are not made explicit in the user interface code. However, if these states were to be drawn in a diagram and used as the basis for constructing the control layer objects, then user interface software would be considerably easier to construct.

A state-based approach to user interface construction is not a new idea, but the approach is not generally regarded as being viable because of the large number of states and event arrows that result when designing anything other than trivial user interfaces. However, these problems are a result of using state transition diagrams as the design notation and the

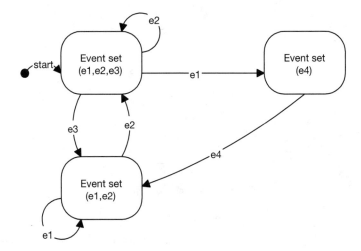

Figure 4.4 A user interface moves from one set of possible events to another.

problems can be overcome by using the statechart notation (Harel, 1987) which is a much more powerful and expressive state-based language. The next chapter presents a direct comparison between the two notations with the intention of showing that statecharts can be used as the basis of the control layer objects.

Chapter 5
A design notation for control layer objects

The event–action paradigm is based on the idea that each event supplied by a user determines which actions are executed in response to that event. In Chapter 3 it was demonstrated, by way of simple examples, that the event–action paradigm did not accurately describe the structure of user interface code. The actions that execute in response to user events are affected by the context in which they occur. In other words, the user interface objects that appear in an application must be co-ordinated to work together as a whole. It was argued that the majority of user interface software is constructed by developers who think in terms of the event–action paradigm and as a result the code that is written in event handlers makes use of global information.

In Chapter 4, the notion of an event–state–action paradigm was introduced. It was argued that all user interface software is based on the event–state–action paradigm – the only difference being whether the state information is explicit or implicit. The user interface-control-model (UCM) architecture was described as a way of explicitly centralizing the state of an application in a layer of control objects, rather than have it implicitly distributed throughout the event handlers of individual user interface objects. In the UCM architecture, the events supplied by a user are used by event handlers to call methods in the appropriate control objects. The control objects are responsible for invoking the appropriate actions in response to an event, maintaining the current state of the application and ensuring the user interface objects work together as a whole. Control objects are not concerned with specifying the attributes and behaviour of individual user interface objects, unless those attributes or behaviours vary as the user supplies events to the software.

The UCM architecture provides a vision of how user interface software should be structured, but it does not offer any practical information on how to actually achieve this vision. This chapter, and indeed the remainder of this book, is concerned with designing control layer objects.

The basic philosophy of the control layer is that a user interface as a whole moves from one state to another. The current state determines the set of events that can be supplied by a user. Describing the control layer in terms of states and events naturally leads to the idea of using state transition diagrams to model the control layer. Unfortunately, state transition diagrams have a number of very serious problems associated with them. In short, they do not provide a scalable solution. They cannot be used to model very large, complex systems – the very type of system a user interface is. The design notation used in the control layer objects must be applicable to very large, complex user interfaces because there is little point in using a notation that breaks down under the weight of increased size and complexity – simple user interfaces are easy to construct, it is the complex ones that need to be designed.

The statechart notation solves the serious problems associated with state transition diagrams. Rather than simply presenting statecharts as a solution, it is a worthwhile exercise to demonstrate just how limited state transition diagrams are. Merely describing the problems associated with them is not nearly as effective as having first-hand experience of the problems. This chapter will provide both a state transition diagram and a statechart that will control a CD player application. The intention is not to say: 'statecharts are a better notation than state transition diagrams, therefore go ahead and use them'. State transition diagrams are hopelessly inadequate for the purposes of specifying a user interface and so any alternative notation must be significantly better. My intention is to demonstrate the extent to which statecharts are superior to state transition diagrams.

A natural language specification of a CD player user interface

Although the behaviour of a CD player application may be intuitive, to describe the behaviour of such an application in natural language can be surprisingly difficult. There are many rules related to when the buttons are enabled and disabled, what is displayed in the text fields of the window and what happens when the user supplies events to the application. A simple illustration of the CD player is given in Figure 5.1 and a natural language spec of the player is given in Figure 5.2.

Figure 5.1 The CD player. The buttons are (from left to right): Play, Pause, Stop, Previous, Reverse, Forward, Next and Eject.

Most specifications written for real projects are not as detailed as this. They usually leave many aspects of a system unspecified and open to interpretation by developers. Even if a serious attempt is made to specify a system in detail, it is almost impossible to write one without ambiguity, inconsistency, incompleteness and redundancy. This spec is no exception and some of the problems will be identified later in this chapter.

For most real projects, the above specification is far too detailed. This is a very small application and yet the specification of the behaviour is quite long and quite difficult to describe.

1   There shall be eight buttons named: Play, Pause, Stop, Previous, Next, Forward, Reverse, and Eject.

2   There shall be two text fields for displaying data. They shall be named Time and Track.

3   When there is no disc in the CD player or when the CD player drawer is open, the system shall be in a state named <No CD Loaded>.

4   When the CD player drawer is closed and a CD is in the CD player, the system shall be in one of three possible states: <CD Stopped>, <CD Playing>, or <CD Paused>.

5   When in the <No CD Loaded> state, with the drawer open and a CD in the drawer, pressing the Eject button shall cause the drawer of the CD player to close and the system shall enter the <CD Stopped> state.

6   When in the <No CD Loaded> state, with the drawer open and no CD in the drawer, pressing the Eject button shall cause the drawer of the CD player to close and the system shall remain in the <No CD Loaded> state.

7   When in the <No CD Loaded> state, pressing the Play, Pause, Stop, Previous, Next, Forward and Reverse buttons shall have no effect.

8   The <CD Playing> state is entered from the <CD Stopped> state by a user clicking the Play button.

9   The <CD Stopped> state is entered from the <CD Playing> state by a user clicking the Stop button.

10 The <CD Paused> state is entered from the <CD Playing> state by a user clicking the Pause button.

11 The <CD Playing> state is entered from the <CD Paused> state by a user clicking the Pause button or the Play button.

12 When in the <CD Stopped> state, the <Time> field shall display 00:00 and the <Track> field shall display [1].

13 When in the <CD Stopped> state, the Pause and Stop buttons shall be disabled.

14 When in the <CD Playing> state, the Play button shall be disabled.

15 When in the <CD Stopped>, <CD Playing> or <CD Paused> states, clicking the Next button when the current track is not the last track on the CD, will cause the CD player to move to the next track, the <Time> field will display 00:00 and the <Track> field shall display the track number.

16 When in the <CD Stopped>, <CD Playing>, or <CD Paused> states, clicking the Next button when the current track is the last track on the CD, will cause the CD player to move to the first track, the <Time> field will display 00:00, the <Track> field shall display [1] and the <CD Stopped> state will be entered.

17 When in the <CD Stopped>, <CD Playing> or <CD Paused> states, clicking the Previous button when the current track is not the first track on the CD, will cause the CD player to move to the previous track, the <Time> field will display 00:00 and the <Track> field shall display the track number.

18 When in the <CD Stopped>, <CD Playing> or <CD Paused> states, clicking the Previous button when the current track is the first track on the CD, will cause the CD player to move to the start of the first track, the <Time> field will display 00:00 and the <Track> field shall display [1].

cont'd

Figure 5.2 A natural language specification of a CD player application.

19   When in the <CD Stopped>, <CD Playing> or <CD Paused> states, clicking the Forward button down will cause the CD to stop playing and the CD to step forwards through the CD in one-second intervals; each step will take no more than 0.1 seconds. For each step, the <Time> field will display the current track time and the <Track> field will display the current track number. The application will stop stepping through the CD when the user stops holding down the Forward button with the mouse pointer, or the end of the CD is reached. If the end of the CD is reached, the <CD Stopped> state will be entered and the <Time> field will display 00:00 and the <Track> field shall display [1].

20   When in the <CD Stopped>, <CD Playing> or <CD Paused> states, clicking the Reverse button down will cause the CD to stop playing and the CD to step backwards through the CD in one-second intervals; each step will take no more than 0.1 seconds. For each step, the <Time> field will display the current track time and the <Track> field will display the current track number. The application will stop stepping through the CD when the user stops holding down the Reverse button with the mouse pointer, or the start of the CD is reached.

21   When in the <CD Playing> state, the <Time> field shall be updated every second with the elapsed playing time of the current track and the <Track> field shall display the current track number.

22   When in the <CD Paused> state, the values in the Time and Track fields will be displayed initially and then after one second they will be hidden. After a further second they will be displayed again. This displaying and hiding cycle will continue while the system is in the <CD Paused> state.

23   When in the <No CD Loaded>, <CD Stopped>, <CD Playing> or <CD Paused> states, the balloon help for the buttons shall be as follows: Stop button = Stop, Previous button = Previous Track, Next button = Next Track, Forwards button = Step Forward, Reverse button = Step Backwards.

24   When in the <No CD Loaded> state and the CD player door is open, the   balloon help for the buttons shall be as follows: Play button = Play, Pause button = Pause, and Eject button = Close.

25   When in the <No CD Loaded> state and the CD player door is closed, the   balloon help for the buttons shall be as follows: Play button = Play, Pause button = Pause, and Eject button = Eject.

26   When in the <CD Stopped> or <CD Playing> state, the balloon help for the buttons shall be as follows: Play button = Play, Pause button = Pause, and Eject button = Eject.

27   When in the <CD Paused> state, the balloon help for the buttons shall be as follows: Play button = Resume, Pause button = Resume, and Eject button = Eject.

Figure 5.2 (Cont'd) A natural language specification of a CD player application.

Typically, detailed descriptions of user interfaces are not produced because maintaining them becomes more difficult than maintaining the software itself. It is very difficult to modify repeatedly a large natural language specification without introducing inconsistencies. The challenging delivery deadlines of most real projects would almost certainly result in a spec of such detail being quickly abandoned.

Unfortunately, when a less detailed spec is written, many aspects of the user interface's behaviour are left for the developer of the application to decide. For a small application, this may not be a significant problem if the developer is sensitive to the needs of the users and understands the tasks that they will perform with the application. However, in a large system with many developers working on different parts of the system, maintaining consistency between user interface modules is a very significant problem. It is easy for a user interface to be produced that works in different ways because different developers make different decisions. Of course, good testing will resolve many of the inconsistencies, but this is an expensive way to tackle the problem. A further problem with large user interfaces is that few of the developers will have met users and understood the tasks they will be performing with the system. Without such knowledge it will be difficult for developers to make good decisions about the user interface design.

In short, writing a brief natural language spec forces developers to make assumptions about many aspects of a user interface's behaviour. And writing a detailed natural language spec, which attempts to specify every aspect of a user interface, will almost certainly result in the spec being abandoned completely because it is too time consuming and difficult to keep up to date.

Many in the industry claim that specs should not be written and instead user interface prototypes should be developed which should act as the specification of the user interface. Unfortunately, this line of reasoning does not hold water because, if the prototype is sufficiently detailed to capture the behaviour of the user interface, then it is no longer a prototype – it *is* the user interface. In effect this is coding without a spec and the main problem with this approach is related to testing the software. Without a spec, testing is reduced to a subjective inspection of the user interface, because there is nothing that defines what the application is supposed to be doing. Furthermore, storing all the detailed knowledge of an application in the heads of the current development team is a very short-term approach and one that is doomed to failure in the longer term. The long-term maintenance of such a system will be extremely difficult if the original team members no longer work on the project.

The solution to this conundrum is not to write a spec at all! Let me make my position clear. I am not against specifications of user interfaces, I am just against specifications written in natural languages. One of the main problems with using natural languages for specifications is their inherent ambiguity. The semantics of each word is not well defined and when words are combined into sentences and paragraphs, the ambiguity can be magnified further. Even when precise and accurate descriptions are produced, they are often very long and difficult to understand.

I believe the best way to capture the precise behaviour of a user interface is to produce a model of the user interface behaviour in a graphical language that has well-defined semantics. The advantage of this approach is that many of the problems with natural language specifications are avoided and the specification itself can be converted directly into control layer objects, without the usual problems associated with translating requirements into a design and then a design into code.

A specification language for the control layer

Finite state machines

A finite state machine is a model of a system which can only be in one of a given number of possible states at any moment in time. A finite state machine accepts input events (or stimuli) that cause an output (or actions) and possibly a change in state. Both the output actions and the next state of the machine are pure functions of the input event and the current state. Thus

Next state = F (Current state, event)
Actions   = G (Current state, event)

There are many notations commonly used to represent finite state machines. Two such representations are: state transition diagrams (STDs) and state transition matrices (STMs).

State transition diagrams

In STDs, a circle is used to denote states and an arrow connecting two states is used to denote a potential transition from one state to another (see Figure 5.3). Each event arrow is given a label made up of two parts. The first part is the event that will cause the transition to occur between two states. The second part of the label is separated from the event by a slash (/) and lists the actions that occur in response to the event.

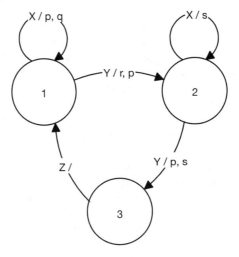

Figure 5.3

Often it is not practical to include the actions associated with a state transition on the event arrow because there may be several actions with long descriptions. In such cases, the diagram can be drawn without the action labels and a table can be used to supplement the diagram to provide the complete details[1] (see Table 5.1).

Table 5.1

Current state	Event	Action	Next state
1	X	p, q	1
1	Y	r, p	2

---

1. Clearly in this instance the actions are brief, but it is not unreasonable to assume actions could be calls to subroutines with lengthy names which would be difficult to fit in a diagram.

Table 5.1 (Cont'd)

Current state	Event	Action	Next state
2	X	s	2
2	Y	p, s	3
3	Z	–	1

State transition matrices

An STM is a table in which each row is labelled with a state and each column is labelled with an input event (see Table 5.2). Every possible system state is assigned a row and every possible input event is assigned a column. A combination of a state and an event define the next state and the required system actions and these therefore appear at the intersection of a column and row.

Table 5.2

	Events					
	X		Y		Z	
Present state	Next state	Actions	Next state	Actions	Next state	Actions
1	1	p, q	2	r, p	–	–
2	2	s	3	p, s	–	–
3	–	–	–	–	1	–

Mearly and Moore models of finite state machines

In the preceding sections, Mearly models of a finite state machines have been discussed. In this type of model, the actions are associated with the transition from one state to another. An alternative model of a finite state machine is a Moore model in which the actions are associated with the state rather than the transition between states. In a Moore model, a transition is labelled only with an event and the state is labelled with the state name and the actions associated with that state. Mearly and Moore models are identical with respect to their expressive power and simple algorithms exist to convert one to another.

A finite state machine for the CD player

The CD player application introduced earlier in the chapter has the following UCM architecture (see Figure 5.4).

The user interface layer contains eight buttons, two fields and three timers. The buttons and text fields correspond to the user interface objects shown in Figure 5.1. The timers are used for updating the Track and Time fields in different scenarios. The Play timer is used to update the two fields every second when a CD is being played. The Step timer is used to update the two fields every 0.1 seconds when a user is stepping through a CD using the Forward or Reverse buttons. The Pause timer is used to make the values in the two fields disappear for one second and reappear for one second repeatedly when a CD has been paused.

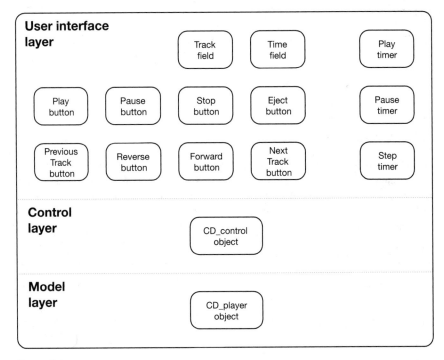

Figure 5.4

The control layer contains one object and this will co-ordinate the behaviour of the user interface objects so that they behave as the CD player specified earlier.

The model layer contains an object that controls the actual CD player. The object provides a set of methods which can be called by the control object. These methods allow the CD player to be controlled and allow information about the CD player to be retrieved. A description of the public methods of the CD_player object is given below:

> **CD_player public methods:**
> **Open_drawer;**
> Causes the CD player drawer to open.
> **Close_drawer() return boolean;**
> Causes the CD player drawer to close. When the drawer has been closed, the function will return the value true.
> **Stop;**
> Causes the CD player to stop and the current track and time to be lost.
> **Play(Track_no, Time);**
> Starts playing the CD at the specified track number and time (in seconds) within that track.
> If the track number and time are not valid for the CD then the CD will not start to play.
> When the end of the CD is reached, the CD player will stop playing the CD.
> If the CD player has been paused, calling the play procedure will cause the CD to resume playing at the point it was paused at.
> **Pause;**

Causes the CD currently playing to be paused. The track number and time at which the CD is paused will be remembered.

cd_loaded () return boolean;

Returns True if a CD is in the machine, returns false otherwise.

current_track () return number;

Returns the current track number. Returns 0 if the CD is not playing or there is no CD in the machine.

current_time () return number;

Returns the current elapsed time of the current track. Returns 0 if the CD is not playing or there is no CD in the machine.

previous_track;

Causes the CD player to step backwards one track from the current track.

If the current track is the first track then calling this procedure will cause the CD player to move to the last track. The current time will be set to 0 when this procedure is called.

If the CD is playing when this function is called, then it will continue to play after the step has occurred.

next_track;

Causes the CD player to step forwards one track from the current track.

If the current track is the last track on the CD then calling this procedure will cause the CD player to move to the first track. The current time will be set to 0 when this procedure is called.

If the CD is playing when this function is called, then it will continue to play after the step has occurred.

last_track () return boolean;

Returns True if the current track is the last track.

Forward_one_sec;

Causes the CD player to move forwards one second from the current track and time.

If the end of the CD is reached then the CD player will move to the start of the first track.

If the CD is playing when this function is called, then it will continue to play after the step has occurred.

Back_one_sec;

Causes the CD player to move backwards one second from the current track and time.

If the start of the first track is reached then calling this procedure will cause the CD player to move to the end of the last track.

If the CD is playing when this function is called, then it will continue to play after the step has occurred.

The purpose of this section is to investigate the possibility of using a finite state machine for controlling the behaviour of the user interface objects that constitute a CD player. Given that the application is controlling an electrical device, and that the use of state machines is widespread in the electronics industry, I emphasize that the state machine is being used to control the user interface objects and not the CD player itself. The control of the CD player will be hidden in the cd_player object and is not in the scope of this book. Here we will identify the advantages and disadvantages of using a finite state machine for controlling user interface objects.

As discussed earlier, a finite state machine can be represented in many different ways. The choice of representation is an entirely personal one because all the representations are equivalent and do not offer any difference in expressive power. I prefer to use state transition diagrams supplemented with event-action tables. The requirements specified in Figure 5.2 will be used as the basis for constructing the state transition diagram.

Requirements 1 and 2 identify the user interface objects that are visible to users. They do not specify any behaviour that needs to be modelled in a state transition diagram.

The basic STD shown in Figure 5.5 can be drawn based on requirements 3 to 14. When the application is started, the starting arrow indicates the application starts with the drawer of the CD player closed. (Note: the CD drawer could be open when the application is started, therefore an action associated with the start event should cause the drawer to close.) A user can open the CD drawer by clicking the Eject button and then, after placing a CD in the CD drawer, close the drawer by clicking the Eject button. This will cause the application to enter the CD Stopped state. A user can start to play the CD in the machine by clicking the Play button and this will cause the application to enter the CD Playing state. The CD can be paused by a user clicking the Pause button (causing a transition to the CD Paused state) and resumed by clicking either the Pause button or the Play button (causing a transition from the CD Paused state to the CD Playing state). Finally the CD can be stopped by clicking the Stop button causing a transition to the CD Stopped state.

This model of the CD player application assumes a user puts a CD into the machine before clicking the Eject button to close the CD drawer. This limitation of the model immediately demonstrates a significant limitation of finite state machines. In order to determine the next state after a user clicks the Eject button, the application needs to check whether a CD is in the machine. Thus, for the CD player to be modelled accurately, the next state is not simply a function of the current state and the event supplied by the user. Instead, the next state must be a function of the current state, the event supplied by the user and some condition that must be evaluated to true in order for the transition to occur. That is, a simple extension is required to the basic state transition diagram notation which allows conditions to be associated with events.[2] When an event occurs, if the associated condition evaluates to true, then the

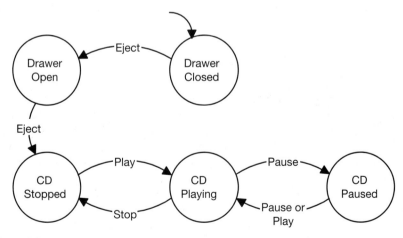

Figure 5.5

---

2. Conditions, or guards, are part of the statechart notation. I have introduced them into the state transition diagram notation in order to continue with the design.

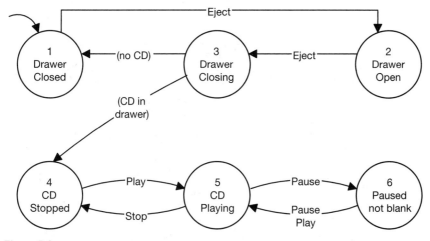

Figure 5.6

transition and the corresponding actions will be executed. By using conditions in state transition diagrams, a more accurate model of the CD player application can be constructed (see Figure 5.6). Note that conditions are parenthesized in order to distinguish them from events.

The diagram now contains an additional state called Drawer Closing. When the CD drawer is open, the application is in state 2 (Drawer Open). The CD drawer can then be closed by clicking the Eject button and the application enters state 3 while this action is occurring. After the CD drawer has closed, the application will then move from state 3 to state 1 if there is no CD in the drawer or from state 3 to state 4 if there is a CD in the drawer. The Drawer Closing state is required because the next state cannot be determined until the CD drawer is closed and the application has detected the presence or absence of a CD. In this instance, the transitions from 3 to 1 and from 3 to 4 are determined solely by conditions. However, it is more typical for a transition to be dependent on both an event and a condition.

The state diagram shown in Figure 5.6 highlights some problems in the natural language specification of the application. Firstly, there is nothing that specifies the behaviour of the application when the Eject button is clicked after a CD is loaded. I will assume the Eject button can be clicked when the CD is stopped, playing or paused and, in all three cases, the event will cause the drawer to open. Secondly, there is nothing that specifies what happens when a CD has been paused and a user clicks the Stop button. Does the application remain in the paused state (state 6) or does it enter the stopped state (state 4)? I will assume the stopped state will be entered. The state diagram capturing these extra requirements is given in Figure 5.7.

Table 5.3 defines the attributes of the user interface objects in the six states of the diagram in Figure 5.7. Note that in Table 5.3 'd' stands for disabled which means the object is greyed out and not available for use by a user; 'e' stands for enabled which means the object is available for a user to interact with.

Table 5.4 defines the actions and state transitions that are executed in response to the various events and conditions that can occur.

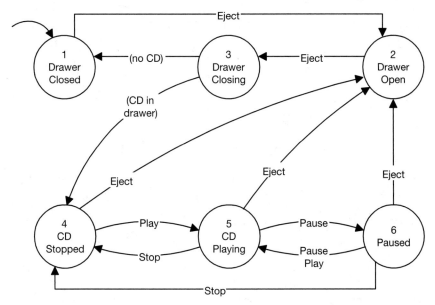

Figure 5.7

Table 5.3

User interface object	1	2	3	4	5	6
Play	d	d	–	e	d	e
Pause	d	d	–	d	e	e
Stop	d	d	–	d	e	e
Previous_Track	d	d	–	e	e	e
Reverse	d	d	–	e	e	e
Forward	d	d	–	e	e	e
Next_Track	d	d	–	e	e	e
Eject	e	e	–	e	e	e

Table 5.4

Current state	Event and conditions	Actions	Next state
start	Application started	cd_player.close_drawer;	1
1	Eject button clicked	cd_player.open_drawer;	2
2	Eject button clicked	cd_player.close_drawer;	3
3	(cd_player.cd_loaded = false)	none	1
3	(cd._player.cd_loaded = true)	none	4

Table 5.4 (Cont'd)

Current state	Event and conditions	Actions	Next state
4	Eject button clicked	cd_player.open_drawer;	2
4	Play button clicked	cd_player.play;	5
5	Eject button clicked	cd_player.stop; cd_player.open_drawer;	2
5	Stop button clicked	cd_player.stop;	4
5	Pause button clicked	cd_player.pause;	6
6	Eject button clicked	cd_player.open_drawer;	2
6	Stop button clicked	cd_player.stop;	4
6	Pause button clicked	cd_player.play;	5
6	Play button clicked	cd_player.play;	5

Requirements 15 to 18 specify the behaviour of the Next Track and Previous Track buttons. These buttons allow a user to step through a CD, either backwards or forwards, one track at a time. The behaviour of the buttons changes when the beginning or end of the CD is reached. Specifically, if the CD is at the last track when the Next Track button is clicked then the CD will stop playing. And if the CD is at first track when the Previous Track button is clicked then the CD will move to the start of the first track.

The state diagram can be extended to capture this behaviour (see Figure 5.8). Eleven extra events have been added to this diagram and the details of the extra transitions are given in Table 5.5. Notice the duplication of events. The 'previous & (not first)' event and the

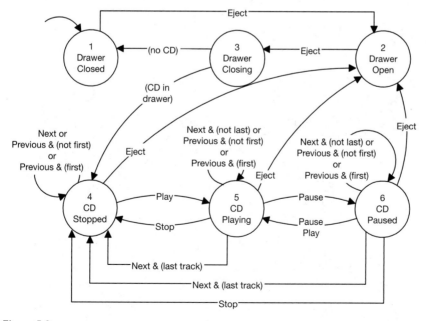

Figure 5.8

'previous & (first)' event are attached to states 4, 5 and 6. Furthermore, the 'next & (not last)' event and the 'next & (last)' event are attached to states 5 and 6. There are in fact only five distinct events that have been added, but they have been duplicated because they can occur in different contexts. This is not good. The state transition diagram is beginning to look too complicated and unstructured and the CD player has not been fully specified yet.

Table 5.5

Current state	Event	Actions	Next state
4	Next Track button clicked	cd_player.next_track; track_no := cd_player.current_track; current_track_time := cd_player.current_track_time;	2
4	Previous Track button clicked AND (cd_player.current_track = 1)	cd_player.go_track(1); track_no := cd_player.current_track; current_track_time := cd_player.current_track_time	4
4	Previous Track button clicked AND (cd_player.current_track > 1)	cd_player.previous_track; track_no := cd_player.current_track; current_track_time := cd_player.current_track_time;	4
5	Next Track button clicked AND (cd_player.last_track = true)	cd_player.go_track(1); track_no := cd_player.current_track; current_track_time := cd_player.current_track_time;	4
5	Next Track button clicked AND (cd_player.last_track = false)	cd_player.next_track; track_no := cd_player.current_track; current_track_time := cd_player.current_track_time;	5
5	Previous Track button clicked AND (cd_player.current_track = 1)	cd_player.go_track(1); track_no := cd_player.current_track; current_track_time := cd_player.current_track_time;	5
5	Previous Track button clicked AND (cd_player.current_track > 1)	cd_player.previous_track; track_no := cd_player.current_track; current_track_time := cd_player.current_track_time;	5
6	Next Track button clicked AND (cd_player.last_track = true)	cd_player.go_track(1); track_no := cd_player.current_track; current_track_time := cd_player.current_track_time;	4

Table 5.5 (Cont'd)

Current state	Event	Actions	Next state
6	Next Track button clicked AND (cd_player.last_track = false)	cd_player.next_track; track_no := cd_player.current_track; current_track_time := cd_player.current_track_time;	6
6	Previous Track button clicked AND (cd_player.current_track = 1)	cd_player.go_track(1); track_no := cd_player.current_track; current_track_time := cd_player.current_track_time;	6
6	Previous Track button clicked AND (cd_player.current_track >1)	cd_player.previous_track; track_no := cd_player.current_track; current_track_time := cd_player.current_track_time	6

Requirements 21 and 22 are concerned with the behaviour of the Time field and the Track field when a CD is playing and when it is paused. When a CD is playing, the Track field displays the current Track number and the Time field displays the length of time the current track has been playing. Note that the spec does not define what happens when a CD is playing and it reaches the end of the last track. I have assumed it will stop and have added the transition from state 5 to state 4. Note that it could have been designed to resume playing at track 1.

When a CD is paused, the Track field displays the Track number and the Time field displays the length of time the current track has been played for when the CD was paused. When a CD has been paused for one second, the values in the Track and Time fields are hidden for one second before reappearing again one second later. Whilst a CD is paused this behaviour is continually repeated. To model this behaviour in the state transition diagram, a second CD Paused state is required (see Figure 5.9).

Through the addition of state 7, the number of event arrows has increased by 12 and the structure of the state diagram has become chaotic and difficult to read. States 6 and 7 are almost identical – the only difference lies in whether or not the values in the time and the track fields are visible (see Table 5.6). However, because of this difference, all the events arrows attached to state 6 must be duplicated for state 7.

The diagram in Figure 5.9 has become difficult to understand and will be difficult to make changes to. It should be apparent to most readers that the state transition approach is not feasible. However, it is worth pressing on and completing the final part of the design just to emphasize how bad it can get.

Requirements 19 and 20 require yet more states and event arrows. These requirements are concerned with the behaviour of the Forward and Reverse buttons. When a user holds the Forward button down, the CD player will step forward one second at a time, but instead of taking one second it will take just 0.1 seconds. The CD player will continue stepping forward through the CD until either the user stops holding down the mouse button on the Forward button, or the end of the CD is reached. If the end of the CD is reached then the CD Stopped state will be entered. When the user releases the Forward button then,

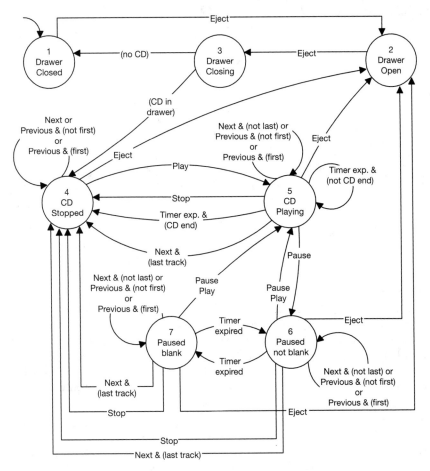

Figure 5.9

Table 5.6

User interface object	1	2	3	4	5	6	7
Play	d	d	-	e	d	e	e
Pause	d	d	-	d	e	e	e
Stop	d	d	-	d	e	e	e
Previous_Track	d	d	-	e	e	e	e
Reverse	d	d	-	e	e	e	e
Forward	d	d	-	e	e	e	e
Next_Track	d	d	-	e	e	e	e
Eject	e	e	-	e	e	e	e
Time field	v	v	-	v	v	v	i
Track field	v	v	-	v	v	v	i

Note : 'v' stands for visible and means that the values in the field are visible. 'i' stands for invisible and means the values in the field are not visible.

depending on whether the CD was previously playing, paused or stopped, the CD will either resume playing at that point, be paused at that point, or be stopped at that point.

When a user holds the Reverse button down, the CD player will step backwards through the CD at one second intervals, but again only taking 0.1 seconds for each interval. The CD will be stepped through until the beginning of the first track is reached or the user releases the Reverse button. If the beginning of the first track is reached then the stepping will stop. When the user releases the Reverse button then, depending on whether the CD was previously playing, paused or stopped, the CD will either resume playing at that point, be paused at that point, or be stopped at that point.

To model these requirements, two extra states are required for each of states 4, 5, 6 and 7. Figure 5.10 shows the basic state diagram, where state X should be substituted with 4, 5, 6 or 7. Holding down the Forward or Reverse buttons causes the application to enter states in which the Track and Time fields are updated every 0.1 seconds. This is achieved by creating a timer on entry to the state. When the timer expires, another timer is created, the CD player is made to step in the appropriate direction, and the fields are updated with values from the CD_player object. This process continues until the state is exited.

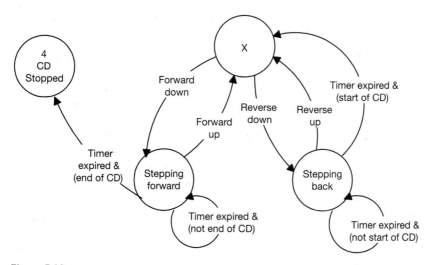

Figure 5.10

As we have already seen, the diagram in Figure 5.9 is already far too complicated. I will not attempt to expand it with an additional eight states.

Finally, requirements 23 to 27 are concerned with the balloon help of the user interface objects. Balloon help is simply an attribute of the user interface icon buttons. If the attribute has a value then when the mouse pointer is placed over the button, the help will appear. The state diagram should only be concerned with behaviour that changes and therefore only the balloon help for the Play, Pause and Eject buttons will be modelled. The variation in help can be achieved by changing the necessary attribute in the different states (see Table 5.7).

Table 5.7

	1	2	3	4	5	6	7
Play help	Play	Play	-	Play	Play	Resume	Resume
Pause help	Pause	Pause	-	Pause	Pause	Resume	Resume
Eject help	Eject	Open	-	Eject	Eject	Eject	Eject

Finite state machines and the control of user interface objects

The use of finite state machines for the system specification has been suggested many times. However, our attempt to model the behaviour of a CD player application with a state transition diagram has highlighted a number of significant problems with the approach:

1   **Finite state machines cannot model user interfaces without being extended** The user interface could not be modelled using a pure finite state machine. The next state and actions could not be determined by the current state and an event. The notation had to be extended with conditional statements on some of the event arrows. Also, some of the transitions contained conditions without events.

2   **The number of states increased rapidly with only a modest rise in the complexity of the system being modelled** The start of a very rapid growth in the number of states was evident: first the Paused state was split into two states and then two states were added to each of the Stopped, Playing and Paused states. The number of states grew from 6 to 7 to 15.

3   **There were many duplicated states and events** For instance, there were four stepping forwards states and four stepping backwards states. Such duplication causes a duplication of event arrows and can cause duplication of new states.

4   **The state transition diagram was large and difficult to read** The state diagram became increasingly difficult to understand as the number of events and states increased. Eventually, the attempt to add yet more states and events was abandoned.

5   **State transition diagrams are not scalable** The CD player is a small application and yet the state diagram that modelled its behaviour could not be made to fit onto a page of this book. Many user interface applications are significantly more complicated than this.

The problems associated with state transition diagrams have long been known. For example, Martin and McClure (1985) say that state transition diagrams are difficult to read, difficult to draw and change, non-user-friendly, not good for stepwise refinement and not good for large, complex specifications.

The only benefit that was gained through attempting to model the user interface with a state transition diagram was that it highlighted a number of problems in the natural language specification of the CD player. This indicates that there is some merit in a state-based approach, but it is clear that STDs are not a suitable specification language for a user interface application. With a significantly better notation, such an approach has got the potential to improve the specification of a user interface and ultimately improve the quality of the software itself.

Statecharts

The remaining part of this chapter is intended to give a flavour of the statechart specification of the CD player. Chapter 7 provides a complete introduction to the statechart notation and, without reading that chapter, some of the material presented here may not be readily understandable. However, it is not necessary to understand the precise details of the statechart at this stage. The intention is to give an appreciation of how much more concise and structured the statechart version is in comparison to the natural language spec and the state transition diagram. When you are more familiar with the statechart notation, return to the CD player statechart if you wish to understand it in detail. The full details of the statechart are given in Appendix C.

Introduction to statecharts

For a long time, people have understood the appropriateness of the event–state approach to specify complex reactive systems. Despite the appropriateness of the approach, they have lacked a notation that avoids large numbers of states and event arrows and one that is rich enough to allow modularity and abstraction. The lack of these basic properties has hindered the serious use of an event–state approach in the specification of large user interfaces.

Recognizing the limitations of state transition diagrams, David Harel (1987) proposed an extension to the STDs called statecharts. Statecharts are important because they provide a very rich and expressive notation that allows complex systems to be specified concisely and at different levels of abstraction. The statechart notation was developed by Harel whilst he was consulting for the Israeli aircraft industry on the development of a complex avionics system. Statecharts were used as the main method for the behavioural specification of the system. Since then, the notation has been adopted in a wide range of application domains such as telecommunications and aerospace. Statecharts are also part of some object oriented methodologies such as Object Modelling Technique (OMT) (Rumbaugh et al., 1991) and Unified Modelling Language (for example, Fowler and Scott, 1997).

A full description of the statechart notation will be given in Chapter 7, but for now a brief introduction to statecharts will be given by demonstrating how the behaviour of the CD player can be modelled using them.

CD player example

There are essentially two high-level states the CD player can be in. The first is when there is no CD in the machine and the second is when there is a CD in the machine. The application could move from the 'No CD Loaded' state to the 'CD Loaded' state after the CD drawer has been closed and a CD has been detected in the drawer. To move in the reverse direction, a user would have to click the Eject button in the CD Loaded state. This simple behaviour is captured by the statechart in Figure 5.11.

The basic notation is very much like a state transition diagram with a few obvious differences. The states are represented by rounded rectangles instead of circles. A default starting state is marked with an arrow terminated with a solid circle. The default starting state is the state that the statechart starts in when the application is started. As before arrows are labelled with events and/or conditions.[3] To readily distinguish conditions from events,

---

3.   Earlier in the chapter, conditions on event arrows were used to extend the basic STD notation. This concept was taken from the statechart notation.

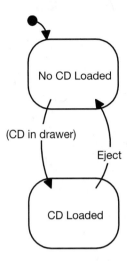

Figure 5.11

conditions are shown in parentheses. The only significant difference between the statechart and a conventional STD is that the event arrows can start and finish inside a state, rather than at the edge of a state. The reason for this is that a state can be an abstract state with lower-level states contained within it. For instance, consider the 'No CD Loaded' state in Figure 5.11: we can zoom into this state and see that it actually contains a group of substates (see Figure 5.12 and Table 5.8). The 'CD Drawer Closed' and 'CD Drawer Open' states are self-explanatory. There is a third substate which the application enters when the CD drawer is in the process of closing. The reason for this is that at the point when the Eject button is clicked in state 2, the CD player has no way of detecting whether a CD is loaded. Therefore, the next state cannot be determined until the CD drawer has closed and the application can attempt to detect the presence of a CD (there is an assumption here that the application will wait until the CD drawer is closed before it continues to execute the next line of code). If there is no CD in the drawer then the application stays in the No CD Loaded state, but moves to the CD Drawer Closed substate. If there is a CD in the drawer then the application moves to the CD Loaded state.

As in the state transition diagram, the CD Loaded state has three basic substates: CD Playing, CD Stopped and CD Paused (see Figure 5.13). When a CD is loaded, the application enters the CD Stopped state which is indicated by the default starting arrow within

Table 5.8

Current state	Event	Actions	Next state
start	Application started	cd_player.close_drawer;	1
1	Eject button clicked	cd_player.open_drawer;	2
2	Eject button clicked	cd_player.close_drawer;	3
3	(cd_player.cd_loaded = false)	none	1
3	(cd_player.cd_loaded = true)	none	CD loaded

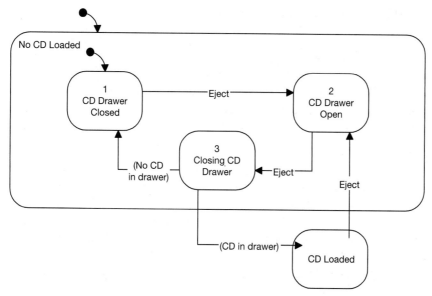

Figure 5.12

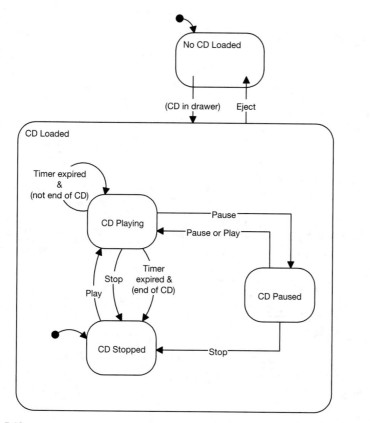

Figure 5.13

the CD Loaded state. From this state, a user can choose to start the CD playing by clicking the Play button which will cause a transition to the CD Playing state. From this state a user can choose to leave the CD playing until the end of the CD (in which case it will return to the CD Stopped state when the CD ends), or the CD can be stopped or paused.

As we know from the state transition diagram of this application, the Pause state must cause the values in the Time and Track fields to oscillate repeatedly between visible and invisible. In the STD, this was achieved by using two Paused states but this resulted in an extensive duplication of the transitions and states attached to the Paused state. In the statechart version of the application, we will again use two states, but this time they will be internal to the Paused state (see Figure 5.14). The advantage of this approach is that, as far as other states are concerned, there is only one Paused state – not two. And therefore the number of event arrows and states attached to the Paused state do not have to be duplicated as they did in the state transition diagram.

The semantics of the Paused state are as follows. When the state is first entered from the CD Playing state, state 6 (Time and Track fields not blank) is entered by default. The transition to the Paused state has an action that causes a one second timer to be created. When this timer expires the resulting event will cause a transition to state 7 (Time and

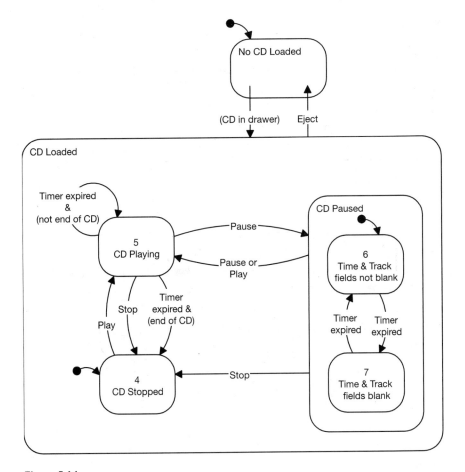

Figure 5.14

Track fields blank) and an action associated with that transition will cause another one second timer to be created. When this timer expires, state 6 will be entered again and another timer will be created. Thus the process continues until the CD Paused state is exited by any one of the following events: the Stop button is pressed, the Play button is pressed, or the Pause button is pressed. Notice that the event arrows for all three of these events start at the edge of the CD Paused state. This means that whether the application is in state 6 or state 7, the Play or Pause buttons being clicked will cause a transition to state 5 and the Stop button being clicked will cause a transition to state 4.

We will now extend the statechart to model the behaviour of the Next Track and Previous Track buttons. Recall that, in the state transition diagram, we were forced to add event arrows to each of the four main states (CD Playing, CD Stopped and the two CD Paused states). This is not a desirable solution because such arrows cluttered the diagram. Statecharts provide an elegant solution to this problem with what is called the history mechanism. The history mechanism is used to remember the last state that the statechart was in within a particular set of states. Thus on returning to the set of states, the most recently visited of the states in the set will be entered. The use of the history mechanism in the CD application is shown in Figure 5.15. There are three new event arrows which are related to either the Next Track or the Previous Track buttons being clicked. In all three cases, the start of the event arrow is attached to the edge of the CD Loaded state and terminates on an H enclosed in a circle (which represents the history mechanism). For example, consider the 'Next Track & (track <> last)' event and condition. If the statechart is in any of the sub states contained within the CD Loaded state and the user clicks the Next Track button and the current track is not the last track on the CD, then the corresponding actions will be executed (moving the CD player to the start of the next track and updating the Track and Time fields) and then the statechart will return to the last substate it was in. Thus, if the CD application was in the CD Stopped state, then the CD Stopped state will be entered again. If the application was in the CD Playing state, then this state will be re-entered. This use of the history mechanism is possible because the actions associated with the event are the same for each of the four states within the CD Loaded state.

It is worth pausing at this moment to compare the statechart in Figure 5.15 with the equivalent state transition diagram in Figure 5.9. The statechart is less chaotic and is much easier to read and, importantly, it does not contain duplicate states or events. Bear in mind that at this point in the design of the state transition diagram, an extra eight states and associated transitions were required in order for the CD player to step forwards and backwards one second at a time using the Forward and Reverse buttons. It was not possible to fit these into a diagram that would fit onto a page of this book. However, the statechart version requires just two extra states to model this behaviour (see Figure 5.16).

The compete statechart for the CD player, showing the details of both the No CD Loaded and the CD Loaded states, along with the event–action table is given in Appendix C.

This chapter has only given an overview of the statechart notation and a complete description will be presented in Chapter 7. Significantly, something that is not best illustrated by the CD player example, is how scalable the approach is. A user interface can be decomposed into modules and each module can be specified independently of each other. This is a very important point and will be addressed later in the book.

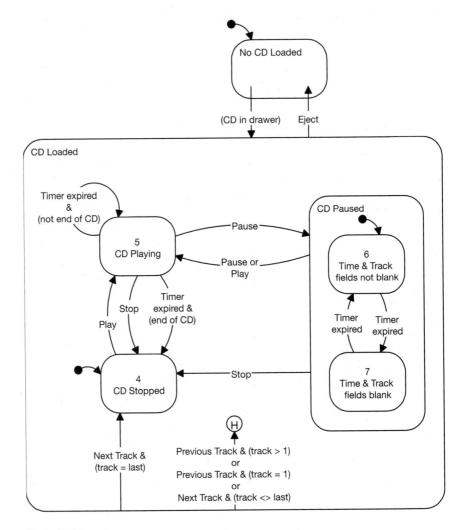

Figure 5.15

Conclusion

Statecharts and natural language specifications

The natural language specification of the CD player is composed of many basic fragments of information of the general form 'when event E occurs in state S, if condition C is true, then perform the following actions A'. For example (requirement number 5): 'When in the <No CD Loaded> state, with the drawer open and a CD in the drawer, pressing the Eject button shall cause the drawer of the CD player to close and the system shall enter the <CD Stopped> state'.

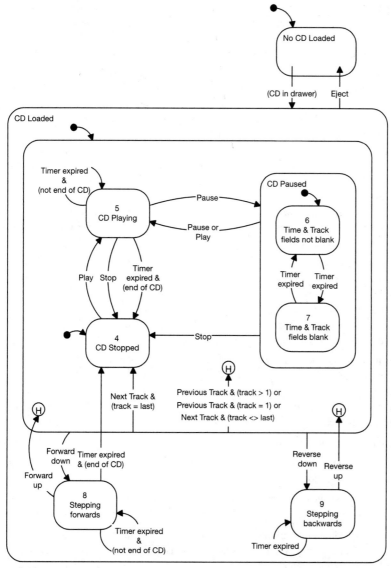

Figure 5.16

The difficulty with describing a user interface, or any complex reactive system, using a natural language is rooted in the lack of formal semantics. A specification of a system must be unambiguous and at the same time concise and amenable to modification throughout the lifetime of the system. There must also be an effective way of translating the specification into code. I do not believe that natural language specifications are a viable way of working for most real-world projects. Throughout this chapter many gaps in the specification of the CD player application were identified. It is not acceptable to work with a specification language that, in all practical senses, can only specify part of a system.

A popular line of argument in defence of natural language specifications is that non-technical people, such as customers and users, can read and review the specification of the system. This may sound like a convincing argument against specifying a user interface with a statechart, or any other technical language. Indeed Davis (1990), in a survey of techniques for specifying the dynamic behaviour of a system, ranked statecharts seventh out of 10 techniques in terms of understandability by computer-naïve people. [4, 5]

However, although natural language is easy to read, it is not easy to review a large natural language specification. Any software practitioner, who has experienced reviewing real natural language specifications with non-technical people, knows that a large amount of verbal explanation is required at review meetings. Quite simply, the specs are too large and too difficult for the majority of people to read and understand. They have real difficulty assimilating all the information in the spec and then visualizing how the user interface will behave when implemented. If you don't believe me ask yourself whether you actually read the specification of the CD player. I would guess that less than half the readers of this book will have read every line of the specification. And even fewer will have studied it in detail attempting to spot problems in it. Did you spot any of the problems that were highlighted later in the chapter? I suspect not. Now imagine what it would be like when faced with a spec for an application that is 200 pages long.

It is far more effective for engineers to capture accurately the behavioural aspects of a user interface in a set of statecharts and then to describe the behaviour of the interface to non-technical people in review meetings. Non-technical people do not have to understand statecharts. Any questions asked by reviewers can be answered by translating the statechart into plain, spoken language. This is how the majority of specification reviews proceed anyway, regardless of the specification language.

Even if a user interface is accurately specified in natural language, there is no guarantee that the specification will be accurately translated into code. With a statechart, the translation is much easier to achieve and, in fact, it can be automated. Furthermore, it is much easier and quicker to test a user interface specified using a statechart than it is when specified in natural language.

To summarize, a statechart is far superior to a written specification for the following reasons:

1   The statechart notation has precise semantics and therefore results in unambiguous specifications.

2   The statechart notation is a rich notation that is expressive enough to specify a user interface.

3   The diagrams are concise and can be defined as a hierarchy and thus they are easy to understand even for very large systems.

4   A statechart is faster to create and easier to understand than the words for the same information.

5   It is easy to achieve a complete specification of a user interface using a statechart because it is easy to spot all the scenarios that need to be specified.

---

4.   The other techniques are: natural language, finite state machines, decision tables, program design language, statecharts, requirements engineering validation system, requirements language processor, specification and description language, PAISLey, and Petri nets.

5.   I should make it clear that Davis was also firmly against the use of natural languages for specifying the dynamic behaviour of a system. Furthermore, statecharts were ranked highest, or equal highest, in all the other categories.

6   Statecharts allow inconsistencies in the behaviour of different parts of the user interface to be identified easily.

7   A statechart can be converted to code very easily, or even automatically.

8   A statechart can be tested easily and thoroughly.

9   It is easier to keep a statechart in step with the code of a user interface than it is to keep a natural language spec in step with the code.

10   Statecharts are simple and intuitive to learn and use.

Statecharts and state transition diagrams

From the very nature of user interfaces, it is apparent that states and events are a natural medium for describing their behaviour. Finite state machines are a formal mechanism for collecting and co-ordinating such fragments to form a whole. However, it is generally agreed that, because of the large number of states and events organized in an unstructured way, finite state machines are not appropriate for describing complex systems. The feasibility of a state-based approach for specifying a user interface relies on a specification language that results in diagrams that are concise, well structured, modular and hierarchical.

There are many different notations used to represent finite state machines, such as state transition diagrams and state transition matrices. However, such notations do not address the fundamental problems associated with finite state machines. The statechart notation is not just another notation for a finite state machine; statecharts are a major step forward for state-based notations. They provide a much richer and much more powerful specification language than any finite state machine notation. All the serious problems associated with finite state machines are solved by statecharts:

1   The number of states in a statechart rises in proportion to the complexity of the system being specified. In finite state machines, the number of states tends to increase rapidly with only a modest increase in the complexity of the system being specified.

2   Statecharts avoid duplicate states and duplicate event arrows. This avoids large, chaotic diagrams that are difficult to understand and difficult to modify.

3   The states in a statechart have a hierarchical structure, which means the system being modelled can be considered at different levels of abstraction. The modular nature of the states ensures that it is not necessary to understand an entire state-chart in order to understand just one part of it. In a nutshell, statecharts are to state transition diagrams what modular decomposition and abstraction are to monolithic code.

Statecharts: the behavioural language for user interfaces

The UCM architecture presented in the previous chapter is underpinned by the statechart notation. The control layer objects in the architecture are responsible for co-ordinating the user interface objects so that they work together as an application. Statecharts enable the control layer objects to be realized. In other words, statecharts are used to co-ordinate the behaviour of user interface objects.

The approach is successful for two reasons:

1   It uses a very powerful state-based notation for specifying the control layer objects.

2   It does not attempt to specify every minor detail of a user interface. The approach is built on solid object oriented principles. The objects in the user interface layer of the UCM architecture have default behaviour that is defined by the classes of those objects. The control layer is only concerned with co-ordinating the behaviour of the user interface objects as a whole.

It should be apparent that the control objects are not just design and code entities; they are also used in the requirements and user interaction design phases of a project. Using state-charts throughout the life-cycle of a project avoids many of the problems commonly associated with translating requirements into designs and then designs into code.

Part 2
User interface software design

The following four chapters are concerned with the design of statecharts to control user interfaces. I emphasize that they are about the design of statecharts and not user interaction design. The concerns of this book are not about understanding a user's tasks and designing a user interface to support those tasks. Instead, this book is concerned with capturing the behaviour of a user interface in a semantically precise notation *after* the user interaction design has been completed. Specifying the control of a user interface with a statechart will not impose any limitations on the design of the user interface from a user's perspective. A statechart does not cause a bad user interface – weak user interaction design skills cause bad user interface.

Design is not a sequential process and therefore little value would be derived from defining a sequence of steps to follow when designing a statechart for a user interface. Instead, a designer needs the following four things from a method:

1 A **design notation** with precise semantics to capture designs and communicate them to others.

2 **Practical advice** on what needs to be recorded in a design and what is superfluous.

3 A set of **design techniques** to help apply the notation to design problems. Such techniques should be well defined and applicable to common design problems. Designers should be ready to spot opportunities to use such techniques.

4 A set of **design heuristics** to help move the design process towards a successful conclusion. Design heuristics are less tangible than design techniques and relate more to the way in which a designer should be thinking.

The following chapters will address each of the four aspects of a method that are listed above.

The statechart notation used in this book is the original notation first introduced by David Harel in his paper: 'Statecharts: A visual formalism for complex systems' (Harel, 1987). In the years since this paper was written, there seem to have been many suggestions for changing the notation and extending it in particular ways. The statechart notation is an extremely expressive and intuitive language. I have no desire to add complexity to a notation, especially when the power of that notation lies in the simplicity of the design entities which can be combined to model complex systems. However, I have made some very minor extensions to the notation and where I have done so I will explain why those extensions are useful.

The practical techniques, standard techniques and design heuristics are derived from my own experience of using statecharts to construct user interfaces for real business systems. Surprisingly, although there is a considerable amount of literature describing statecharts, I have found very little practical advice on how to actually design them. Most works seem to focus on either repeating what Harel has already written or extending the notation with unnecessary complexity.

Chapter 6
The statechart notation

The aim of this chapter is to provide a comprehensive description of the syntax and semantics of the statechart notation developed by David Harel. Unless otherwise stated, the syntax and semantics are those defined by Harel.

Simple transitions

A statechart is simply a network of states and events. Figure 6.1 shows a simple transition from one state to another. This should be read as follows: 'if event 1 occurs in state A and condition C is true at the time, then make the transition to state B'.

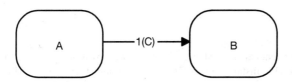

Figure 6.1

Events, conditions and states should be given brief but meaningful labels. When choosing labels, a balance needs to be found between lengthy descriptions that will clutter the diagram and brief identifiers that will convey little if any information about the entity.[1]

It is possible for there to be a number of actions associated with each transition. For example, an action may cause data to be copied from one variable to another, or data to be inserted into a database table and so on. It is not usually possible to fit actions into the diagrams and so associated with each statechart is an event–action table that provides the precise details of every state transition in the diagram. Table 6.1 shows a typical entry in an event–action table. In this particular example, if the Create button is clicked when the system is in state 10 and the status field contains the value X, then the associated actions will be executed and state 6 will be entered.

---

1. Many of the diagrams in this chapter do not represent systems at all. They have been drawn to explain the statechart notation and therefore the labels that have been used are brief identifiers. However, for the statecharts that do correspond to a system, meaningful labels have been used.

Table 6.1

Current state	Event and conditions	Actions	Next state
10	Create button clicked and (status field = 'X')	Insert data P into the database table Q; Commit the database transaction;	6

States with depth: refinement and clustering

In a state transition diagram all the states appear at the same level in the diagram. In a state-chart, however, the states are usually arranged in a hierarchy. In other words, states have depth. A state hierarchy is represented by drawing states within states. For instance, Figure 6.2 shows two states A and B. Both these states have a lower level of detail. Although this lower level of detail is not shown in the diagram, it is apparent that they exist because event 2 starts inside state A and event 4 terminates inside state A.

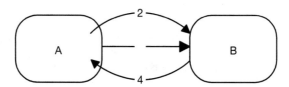

Figure 6.2

States A and B provide a high-level abstract representation of the system. Thus, someone would be able to gain an understanding of the system by looking at the states at this level in the hierarchy. For instance, in the CD player example, there were two high-level states: 'CD Loaded' and 'No CD Loaded'. These two states provided a good abstract view of the application. A lower level of detail could be understood by looking inside either of the two states.

Returning to the example in Figure 6.2, to understand precisely how it will behave when it is in state A, it is necessary to look at the lower level of detail contained within that state (see Figure 6.3). When the system is in state A, it is also either in state C or state D at the next level in the hierarchy. There can be any number of levels in a state hierarchy and events can originate and terminate at different levels. For instance, event 2 starts at state C and terminates at state B even though C is at a lower level in the hierarchy than state B.

Depth allows a state diagram to be viewed at different levels of abstraction. It provides an effective way of managing the design of a complex system. The high-level states can be identified first and the lower-level details can be deferred. Systems designed as a hierarchy are generally easier to understand because the structure of the system is not obscured by irrelevant details.

Depth in statecharts is not restricted to refining states into lower-level states. States can also be used to cluster groups of states in order to reduce the number of event arrows in a state-chart. For instance, in the statechart in Figure 6.4, event 2 will cause a transition to state C when the system is in state A or state B. The two states can be clustered using another state .

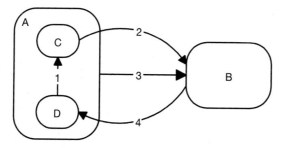

Figure 6.3

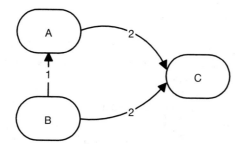

Figure 6.4

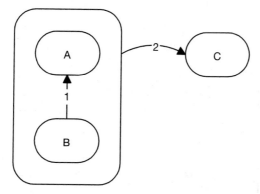

Figure 6.5

and the two event arrows can be replaced by just one that is attached to the clustering state (see Figure 6.5). Clearly, in this example the number of event arrows has only been reduced by one. However, if a large group of states is clustered by a state, then a very significant reduction in the number of arrows can be achieved.

Thus depth serves two purposes: clustering and refinement. Clustering is concerned with grouping states together in order to reduce the number of event arrows in the diagram and is therefore is a bottom-up approach. Refinement is concerned with identifying high-level states and, importantly, allowing the lower-level details of those states to be delayed until a later time. Refinement is therefore a top-down approach.

Depth offers several advantages:

1   The low-level details of high-level states can be produced simultaneously by different people.

2   The system is easier to understand because it can be viewed at different levels of abstraction and the details of one part can be understood without having to understand the entire system in detail.

3   The design can be divided into small parts that can fit onto pages of a design document.

4   The number of event arrows in a system can be significantly reduced.

Default start states

In a finite state machine there is a start state which determines which state the system starts in by default. Similarly, statecharts have a concept of a default start state but, unlike a finite state machine, there can be several start states because a statechart is a hierarchy of states and each level in the hierarchy must start somewhere. Also, statecharts allow concurrency (which will be introduced later in the chapter) and thus a start state is required for each concurrent state diagram.

A start state is identified by a short arrow terminated with a solid circle. For example, in Figure 6.6, the default start state at the highest level in the statechart is state A (rather than state B). Within state A, the default starting state is D. Thus, when the system is started the initial state will be state D within state A.

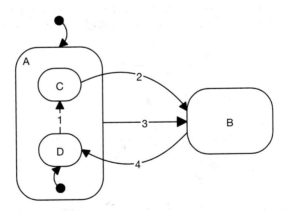

Figure 6.6

End states

Curiously, Harel does not define an end state in his notation. Most (if not all) systems are designed to shut down at some point in their execution. The Unified Modelling Language (see, for example, Fowler and Scott, 1997) includes statecharts and the symbol used for the end state in that notation is a solid circle surrounded by an empty circle (see Figure 6.7). This symbol will be used for end states in the statecharts throughout this book. An action typically associated with an event that terminates at an end state is one that will cause the application to close down.

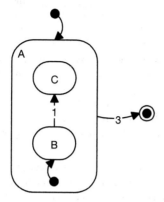

Figure 6.7

The history mechanism

The history mechanism provides a way of entering a group of states based on the systems history in that group. That is, the state entered is the most recently visited state in the group. For instance in Figure 6.8 when event 5 occurs and state A is entered the history mechanism is used to determine the next state within A. This is read as 'enter the most recently visited

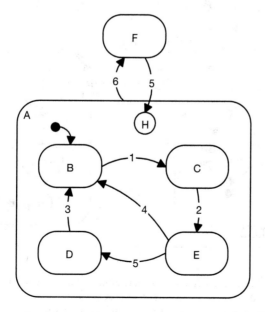

Figure 6.8

state in the group (B, C, D, E) or enter state B if this is the first visit to the group'. Note that the history of a system in a group overrides the default start state. Note also a default start state must be specified for a group that uses the history mechanism for when the group is entered for the first time

The history of a system is only applied to the level in the hierarchy in which it appears. To apply the history mechanism at a lower level in the state hierarchy, it is necessary to use a history symbol in the lower levels. For example, in the statechart in Figure 6.9, on entering state C the history symbol indicates that either state B or state C is entered depending on which was visited last. If state C had been the last state visited and the last state visited within A had been state F, then when event 1 occurs the history symbol at the level of B and C will cause the system to enter state C. Within state C, the default start arrow is attached to a history symbol and therefore the system will enter state F (the last state visited). Within state C, notice how the default start arrow is attached to the history symbol which in turn is attached to state G. This indicates that if state C has not been visited before, then state G is entered by default.

An asterisk can be attached to the history symbol to indicate that the history of the system should be applied all the way down to the lowest level in the state hierarchy. For instance, in Figure 6.10 suppose state D was the most recently entered state in state A. When event 1 occurs, the asterisked history symbol indicates that the history of the system should be applied to all the lower-level states. In this case, state B will be entered in preference to state C and then state D will be entered in preference to state E. This process will continue right down to the lowest level in the hierarchy. Thus, if D contained lower-level states then the history of the system would be used to determine the last state within D.

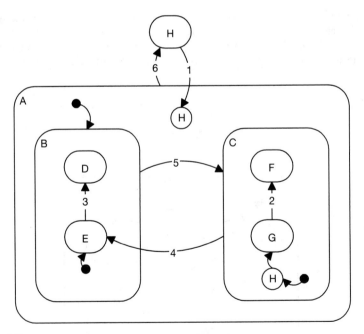

Figure 6.9

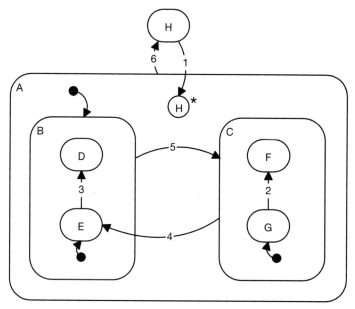

Figure 6.10

Concurrency

As we have seen, one of the most serious problems with state transition diagrams is that the number of states can grow rapidly with only moderate increases in the complexity of the system being modelled. To demonstrate the rapid growth in the number of states, a simple user interface example will be used. The example will then show how concurrency can be used to control the number of states very effectively.

In the toolbar of many applications such as word processors and drawing tools it is common to find buttons that change the format of the text selected by the user. For example, three such buttons labelled B, I and U could be used to specify whether the currently highlighted text should be displayed in **bold**, in *italics* or underlined. The user can choose to display the highlighted text in any combination of the three formats.

In terms of a state diagram for controlling these buttons, the format of the text selected in the application will determine the initial state of the system. For example, Bold off, Italics off and Underline off represents a different state to Bold on, Italics off, Underline off. The eight possible state combinations are shown in Figure 6.11.

When a user clicks the B, I and U buttons, the system will change states and cause the format of the highlighted text to change. These events have not been shown because the diagram would be too chaotic even at this stage. (There are three possible exits from each state, because the user could click any one of the three buttons, and there are eight states, so there are 24 state transitions.)

As the design stands it is just about manageable, but if the complexity of the user interface is increased by adding more functionality then the number of states is set to rise dramatically.

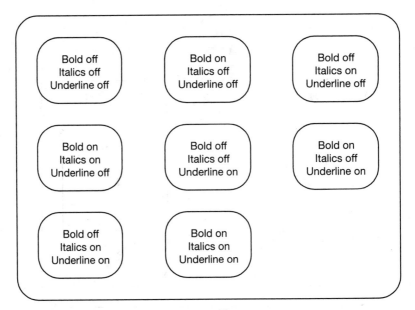

Figure 6.11

For instance, it is common to be able to align text to the left and right, to centre it, or to justify it. It may also be possible to format the text in other ways, such as automatically numbering paragraphs, or starting paragraphs with bullet points.

Now this is quite a simple extension to the application, but the number of states in the STD will increase disproportionately to the increase in complexity of the system. First consider the four alignment buttons. At any given moment, the text can either be left aligned, right aligned, centred or justified. This means the alignment buttons can be in one of four possible states. There are eight existing states, so each of those states will have to be duplicated four times for the four new states. That is, the state diagram will grow to 32 (4 × 8) states.

Now consider the numbering and bullet points. A user can choose to precede each paragraph with a number, a bullet point or with nothing. Thus, for each of the existing 32 states, the software could be in one of three states. In other words, there must be 96 (32 × 3) states to model these buttons in this way. This is a prohibitively large number of states and transitions for such a simple part of a user interface. This clearly demonstrates why state transition diagrams are not a viable option for designing user interfaces.

Let's take a step back and take a look at the problem again. The reason for the rapid increase in the number of states is because every combination of the states is represented explicitly. However, many of the screen items are not dependent on the behaviour of other screen items. And so representing every possible state combination introduces artificial relationships between states. If the behaviours of two user interface objects are independent of each other, then there is no reason for their behaviour to be specified in a single state transition diagram. If a state diagram only models the behaviour of user interface objects that are related to each other, then the number of states can be significantly reduced.

For instance, a user can click the Bold button, the Italics button and the Underline button independently of each other. These screen objects are not directly related to each other so there is no reason to control them with the same STD. Figure 6.11 can be redrawn with

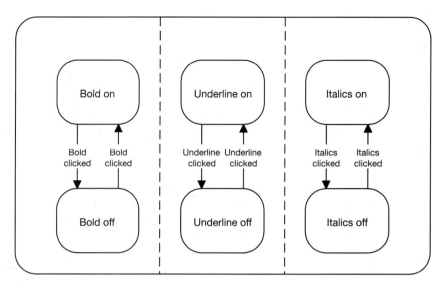

Figure 6.12

three state diagrams that run concurrently. The notation used in statecharts to represent concurrency is to separate concurrent components with dashed lines (Figure 6.12)

The statechart shown in Figure 6.12 has three concurrent components and therefore the current state of the statechart is made up of three values – one for each concurrent component. For example, the statechart could be in the state (Bold on, Underline off, Italics on). When a user clicks the Bold button there will be a transition to the Bold off state but there will be no change in the other two state diagrams and so the new state will be (Bold off, Underline off, Italics on).

The Left align, Right align, Centre and Justify buttons do not operate independently of each other. They are, in fact, a group of radio buttons because, at any given moment, just one of the four buttons can be pushed down. If a user pushes down a different button, the previously pushed-down button is forced to pop up. The statechart in Figure 6.13 models the behaviour of the buttons.

The current state is defined by the last button the user clicked. The diagram has got quite a lot of event arrows but these can be reduced because the statechart has two particular characteristics:

1   every state is connected to every other state;

2   every state terminating at any given state has the same event label.

Because the statechart possesses these characteristics, it can be simplified by replacing the arrows with those shown in Figure 6.14. This has a reduced number of event arrows, but it is equivalent to the statechart in Figure 6.13. For instance, whichever of the four states (Left, Right, Centre or Justify) the statechart is in, when the Centre button is clicked there will be a transition to the Centre state.

Finally, the numbering and bullet points buttons are related to each other in that, at any given time, only one of the buttons can be pushed down. However, they do not behave as a true radio button group because it is possible for neither of the buttons to be pushed down. Clicking a button that is pushed down will release it from the pushed-down state. Figure 6.15 is a statechart that models the behaviour of the two buttons.

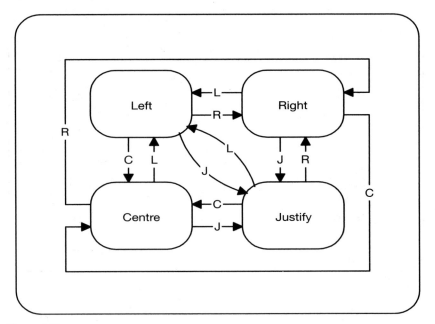

Figure 6.13

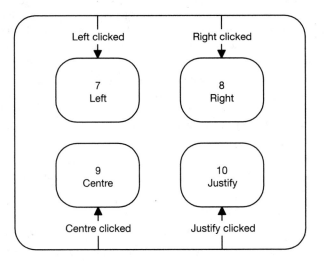

Figure 6.14

It should be apparent that we now have five statecharts that are independent of each other and can therefore run concurrently and Figure 6.16 shows them combined in a single statechart. The current state of this statechart has five parts – one for each concurrent part. For instance, the statechart could be in the following state: [Bold on, Underline on, Italics off, Left, None].

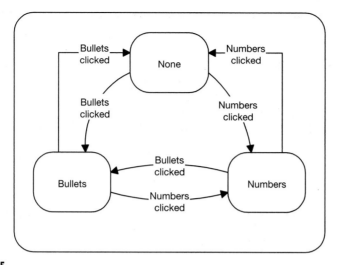

Figure 6.15

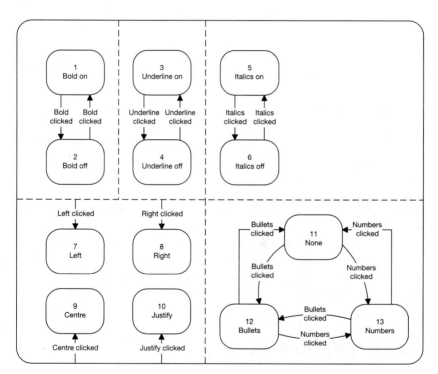

Figure 6.16

Notice how there are only 13 states compared to the 96 states in the equivalent state transition diagram. Furthermore, there are only 16 event arrows in the statechart. Using concurrency within a statechart avoids rapid increases in the number of states and events. For instance, if there was a statechart with five concurrent components each containing six states, then the total number of states in the equivalent STD would be 7776 ($6 \times 6 \times 6 \times 6 \times 6$) compared to just 30 states in the statechart.

I will conclude this section on concurrency with a more general description of concurrent parts.

State H is split into two components A and B (see Figure 6.17). Entering state H causes state (D,F) to be entered. Event 1 will cause the transitions D to C and F to E to occur simultaneously[2] and so the new state will become (C,E).

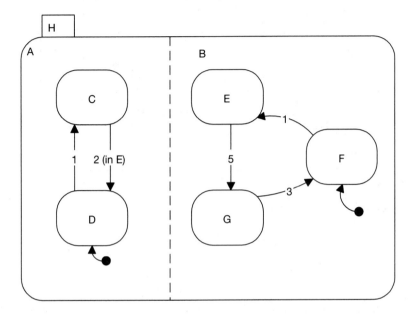

Figure 6.17

Notice that transition 2 from state C to state D has the condition 'in E', which indicates that the transition will only occur if component B is in state E. For example, if the system is in state (C,E) then event 2 will cause the state to move to (D,E). This means that states A and B are not completely independent of each other; state A must know something about the inner state of B.

Transitions across the divide between A and B are not allowed. If such transitions were permitted then the whole idea of independent concurrent state diagrams would be abandoned.

There are several different ways of entering and exiting concurrent states. Figures 6.18 to 6.25 illustrate some of them.

Delays and time-outs

A delay mechanism can be imposed on any state within a statechart. A delay on a state will prevent a user being able to perform events in that state for a specific period of time after entering that state. For instance, in Figure 6.26, on entry to state A clicking the 'OK' button will

---

2.   In reality, the transitions are not simultaneous – one will occur before the other. However, developers should not rely on them occurring in a particular order.

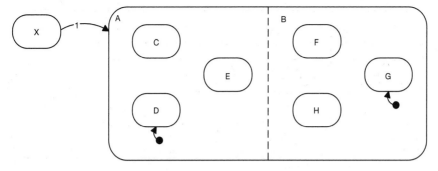

Figure 6.18 Event 1 causes entrance to the default states (D, G).

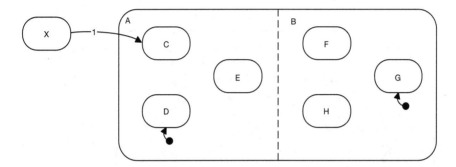

Figure 6.19 Event 1 causes entrance to state C and the default state G.

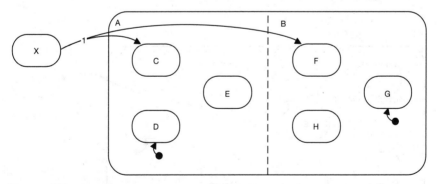

Figure 6.20 Event 1 causes entrance to the states (C, F).

have no effect until 10 seconds have elapsed. After the statechart has been in state A for 10 seconds, if the user clicks the OK button then this will cause a transition to state B.

A time-out mechanism can also be imposed on any state. For instance, in Figure 6.27, if the software remains in state C for 20 minutes and no events have been supplied, then the software will time-out and there will be a transition to state D. Note that if a user clicks button A at any point in the 20 minutes then the timer will be reset and a further 20 minutes will have to elapse without the user supplying an event before the time-out can occur.

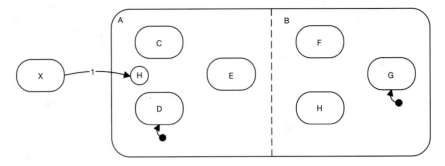

Figure 6.21 Event I causes entrance to the most recently visited state in A (or D if it is in A for the first time) and the default state G.

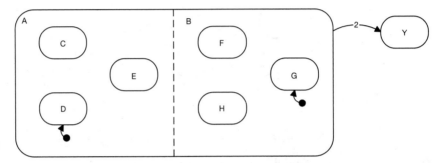

Figure 6.22 When event 2 occurs, state Y will be entered. Event 2 is an unconditional exit from the concurrent state and is therefore the most general form of exit.

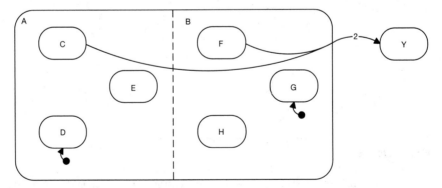

Figure 6.23 State Y will be entered when the concurrent state is in (C, F) and event 2 occurs.

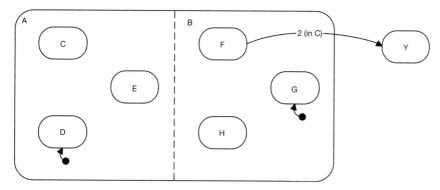

Figure 6.24 State Y will be entered when the concurrent state is in (C, F) and event 2 occurs.

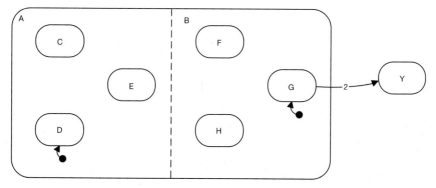

Figure 6.25 State Y will be entered when the B component of the concurrent state is in state G and the A component is any state.

Figure 6.26

Time-outs can be useful when specifying the behaviour of a user interface. For instance, suppose a user forgets to close down an application at the end of a day. To guard against this, the software can be designed to shut itself down automatically if it is not used for 20 minutes (Figure 6.28).

The action associated with the time-out event is the one that will close down the application. Any user event that occurs within state A will reset the timer and prevent a time-out occurring for a further 20 minutes.

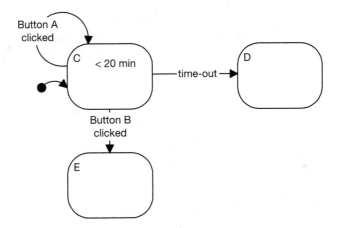

Figure 6.27

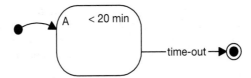

Figure 6.28

Transient states

Transient states are different from normal states because none of the transitions leaving such a state is triggered by events. Instead, the transitions are simply conditions without an associated event. Since there are no events associated with transitions leaving the state, on entry to the state, the conditions on the event arrows are evaluated and the next state is entered immediately; hence the transient nature of the state. In effect a transient state delays the entry to the next state until the actions associated with an event have been executed.

Transient states are not part of the original statechart notation, but they are needed when designing user interfaces that retrieve data from a database. They can also be used to simplify designs. Examples of how transient states can be used will be given in subsequent chapters and they will be used extensively in the case studies.

Event priorities

When event arrows contain conditions, there is a possibility that more than one condition could evaluate to true. To avoid introducing non-deterministic behaviour in the statechart, relative priorities can be assigned to the events leaving a state. Event priorities are not part of Harel's notation.

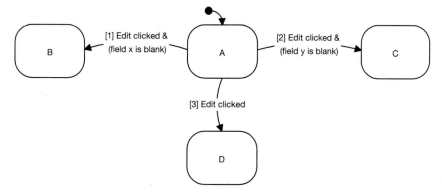

Figure 6.29

The convention used in this book is to precede the label on an arrow with a number in square brackets to indicate the relative priority of the transitions if more than one of the conditions could evaluate to true. For example, in the statechart in Figure 6.29, if field x and y are both blank, then when the Edit button is clicked in state A, then state B, C or D can be entered. However, because the transitions have been prioritized, the transition to state B will occur because this has a higher priority than the other two transitions.

Clearly, it is possible to write the conditions on the event arrows such that only one condition can be true at any given moment. However, this can result in very large and convoluted conditions that are prone to error when the software is modified. Assigning priorities to events is an effective way of keeping conditions on event arrows simple.

Parameterized states

In Harel's paper, he introduced a number of advanced ideas that were not considered mature enough to be included in the statechart notation. One such idea was concerned with replacing several very similar states within a statechart with just one state that accepts parameters. This idea of parameterized states does not seem to have been taken further and there is no standard notation for such states. However, I have found the concept to be quite useful when controlling modal alert messages in a user interface. This is only a very limited application, but nonetheless a useful one. Details of how to use parameterized states will be given in Chapter 9.

Summary

Statecharts extend conventional state transition diagrams with the notions of depth and concurrency. The state diagrams that result are highly structured and compact. Thus small diagrams can express complex behaviour. Statecharts counter many of the objections raised against conventional state diagrams and make the possibility of a state-based approach to controlling user interface objects a plausible one.

Chapter 7
The pragmatics of the statechart notation

This chapter contains practical information related to constructing statecharts. The advice is not concerned with how to design a statechart, but instead is concerned with the nuts and bolts of what needs to be captured in the design process.

Assigning names to states

Every state in a statechart should be given a name to identify its purpose. In most cases, the name should be a meaningful one that concisely conveys what that the state represents. Selecting good names is an important task because without them, it can be very difficult to understand the semantics of the design. Without meaningful names, the people who may have to maintain your designs will be left asking questions such as: 'I know when I click the Edit button I go to state 38, but what does being in state 38 actually mean? What does it represent?'

Alert states are parameterized states. To indicate this, all alert states should be labelled: 'Alert (message)'. The '(message)' part of the label indicates that the state requires a parameter. The parameter is set by one of the actions associated with any event arrow entering the state.

Transient states are often difficult to name in that they do not necessarily represent anything meaningful from a user interface perspective. They are used when the current state and an event cannot determine the next state without evaluating the result of an action first. In other words, they are a device for delaying the exit from a state until the actions associated with such an event have been executed. Thus they rarely represent anything meaningful and it usually makes most sense just to label them with the word 'Transient'.

States that have been introduced into a statechart for the purpose of clustering other states do not necessarily represent anything meaningful. It is common to leave such states unnamed since they are primarily a technique for reducing the number of arrows in a statechart. Note that high-level states that are introduced as part of a hierarchical decomposition should be given a meaningful name because they are an abstract representation of part of the system and therefore clearly mean something.

Assigning identifiers to states

Every state in a statechart should have a numerical identifier which is unique within that statechart. Numerical identifiers are required because they are concise and therefore more convenient to use in event–action tables than state names.

An exception to this rule is states that have been used to cluster other states. A statechart is only ever in a cluster state by implication of being in a state within that cluster. For instance, the two event arrows in Figure 7.1 are represented by the event–action table shown in Table 7.1. Notice that the state used to cluster states 1 and 2 is not explicitly used in the event–action table. Instead all the transitions are expressed in terms of states 1, 2 and 3 – the states at the lowest level in the hierarchy. Note that this is not the case for states that are part of the hierarchical decomposition. Such states do have identifiers and are discussed in the next section.

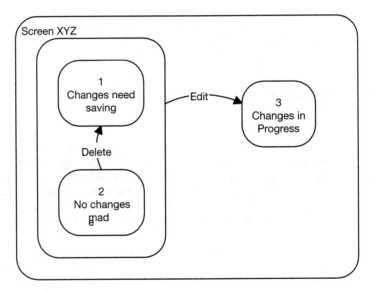

Figure 7.1

Table 7.1

Current state	Event	Actions	Next state
1, 2	Edit	Action A	3
2	Delete	Action B	1

State variables: state hierarchies and concurrent parts

State transition diagrams have one advantage over statecharts in that only one variable is required to keep track of the current state of the state diagram. Statecharts are a much richer notation and therefore require more variables to keep track of the current state. In this section we will consider what state variables are required and why.

Statecharts are not flat structures. In effect they have three dimensions because they have a hierarchy of states. In other words, states can be refined to show a lower level of detail. When the details of the statechart are specified in an event–action table, both the level in the state hierarchy and the current state within that level must be identified. For example, the statechart in Figure 7.2 has a three-level hierarchy of states. At level 1 (the highest level) the statechart is controlled by state variable A and can be in either state 1 or state 2. Notice the convention for labelling a state:

<State ID> <State Name> <[State variable]>

The state variable component of a state label is not required for all states. It is only required for states that have a lower level of detail. For example, in Figure 7.2, state 4 does not have a lower level of detail (this is indicated by the fact that it has no state variable). However, state 9 has got a lower level of detail and the state variable I is used to record the current state in this lower level of detail.

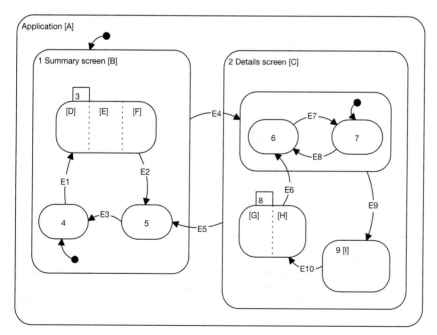

Figure 7.2

The statechart in Figure 7.2 is in either state 1 or state 2 at the highest level in the state hierarchy. If it is in state 1, then it can also be in state 3, 4 or 5 at level 2 in the state hierarchy. If it is in state 3, there is yet another level of detail. The states within state 3 are not specified in this diagram, but it is clear that a lower level of detail exists because state 3 has three concurrent parts and each one is controlled by a separate state variable (D, E and F). Thus, when in state 3, the following state variables will define the current state of the statechart: A, B, D, E and F. When in state 4, only variables A and B are used to define the current state.

Notice that in state 2, states 6 and 7 have been clustered. Since such states are introduced as a device for reducing the number of arrows in a diagram, they are not really part of the state hierarchy and therefore they are not controlled by a state variable.

Some readers may think that defining which state variables control which part of the statechart is part of the coding process. However, state variables are required during the design process so that each transition can be identified accurately in event–action tables. By having precise event–action tables, translating the design into code is made easy.

Event–action tables

It is possible to define a statechart with one large event–action table. However, this is not practical for two reasons. First, the number of state variables could be very large. For instance, the statechart in Figure 7.2 has nine state variables. To define all the events in an event–action table would require all nine state variables in both the current state and next state columns. For each transition, all nine variables will not be used. For example, Table 7.2 shows the state transitions for four event arrows from the statechart in Figure 7.2. As can be seen, very little space is left for the columns labelled Event and Actions.

Table 7.2

Current state									Event	Actions	Next state								
a	b	c	d	e	f	g	h	i			a	b	c	d	e	f	g	h	i
|	5								E3		|	4								
|	3, 4, 5,								E4		2	0	7							
2	6								E7		2		7							
2	6, 7, 8, 9,								E5		|	5	0							

A second reason for not using such an approach is that it does not allow several people to design different parts of the same user interface. In large development projects, a user interface is split between developers in a team, each developer being responsible for designing and coding a set of screens. Having a single event–action table does not support this way of working and is therefore not useful for real projects.

To avoid such problems, a number of event–action tables should be produced which capture the events associated with parts of the statechart. In order to make these statechart modules work together, it is necessary to define event–action tables for the transitions that move from one module to another.

For example, for the statechart in Figure 7.2, it would make good sense to define two event–action tables: one for the Summary screen (partly shown in Table 7.3) and one for the Details screen (partly shown in Table 7.4). In addition to these tables, two event–action tables are required to define the transitions from one screen to the other. Notice that two tables are required – one for transitions from the summary screen to the details screen (Table 7.5) and another for transitions from the Details screen back to the Summary screen (Table 7.6). Notice that event–action tables for interfaces can be readily identified because the state variables in the current state column are different from the state variables in the next state column.

Table 7.3 Part of the event–action table for state 1.

Current state					Event	Actions	Next state				
a	b	d	e	f			a	b	d	e	f
1	5				E3		1	4			

Table 7.4 Part of the event–action table for state 2.

Current state					Event	Actions	Next state				
a	c	g	h	i			a	c	g	h	i
2	6				E7		2	7			

Table 7.5 The event–action table for the interface between state 1 and state 2

Current state		Event	Actions	Next state	
a	b			a	c
1	3, 4, 5	E4		2	7

Table 7.6 The event–action table for the interface between state 2 and 1.

Current state		Event	Actions	Next state	
a	c			a	b
2	6, 7, 8, 9	E5		1	5

There are no hard and fast rules for breaking up an event–action table. The aim should be to have tables with no more than about 5 or 6 state variables. Generally, each screen will have its own event–action table. If there are a particularly large number of state variables controlling a screen, then states with lower-level statecharts could be moved into separate tables. The parts of a statechart that are specified in a separate event–action table should have simple interfaces with the other parts of the statechart.

Level of detail in the event–action table

How much detail should be recorded in an event–action table? It is possible to describe the user interface in high-level terms that are not specific to any development tool. Such statecharts provide an abstract specification of the software without defining the precise details of how the user interface is coded. However, it is possible to supplement an event–action table at implementation time with lower-level details such as the names of specific procedures or functions. The main benefit of this approach is that it has the potential to make the code very easy to understand. However, if there is too much detail in the table then inevitably more effort will be required to keep the design and the code consistent during the maintenance phase of the system.

Therefore it is recommended that the event–action table should be written as an abstract specification rather than one that is syntactically consistent with the code. The table should show what the software does rather than how it is actually done. By maintaining this level of detail, minor changes to how the software is coded should not require corresponding changes to the specification. Having said that, I can see no benefit in being dogmatic on this issue. Terms used in the specification are often translated into procedure names in the code. This is a natural process and the specification should not necessarily be considered weak for being too similar to the code.

State–item tables

The state–item tables that appear in this book are generally very simple. In most cases they simply define whether an item is enabled, disabled or unaffected by the statechart being in a particular state. Of course, a state may control user interface items in more complex ways than this and it could change *any* property of an item. For example, a state could affect an item's *x, y* co-ordinates, height, width, colour, font and whether it is visible or invisible; it could set a format mask on a field; it could affect the label associated with an item, the icon associated with an item, the items that appear in a pull-down option list, whether a user is required to enter a value in a field, and so on. If the characteristics of an item change during the execution of the application then these changes should be captured in states. The state–item tables used in the case studies later in this book may well be too simple for some applications. It may be required to define a list of properties for each item in each state. For example:

Item: Field Z	
Property	*Value*
Height	20
Width	100
Colour	Red

A state can also define that an alert should be displayed. Nothing needs to be recorded in the state-item table about the details of an alert. The message is a parameter to the state and is set by an action on every event arrow entering the state. The buttons that appear in the alert message (such as OK and Cancel, or Yes, No and Cancel, and so on) are defined by the event arrows in the statechart itself.

Chapter 8
Standard design techniques

The intention of this chapter is to establish a set of basic techniques that can be used when designing statecharts for controlling user interfaces. These techniques are the building blocks of the statechart approach to constructing such interfaces. The techniques will not solve every design problem developers will encounter, but they should go some way to helping solve a substantial number of them.

Controlling the number of states in a statechart

Most user interfaces are large complex systems. Typically there will be dozens of states that the software can be in and it is usually impossible to show all these states in a single diagram. The objectives of the design process should be:

- to divide the design up into independent parts, each with different levels of detail;
- to avoid duplicate states;
- to avoid unnecessary states.

There are two primary techniques for reducing the number of states in a statechart: concurrency and depth. Each will be considered in turn.

Concurrency

The primary technique available in the statechart notation for avoiding a large number of states is through the use of independent concurrent parts. The primary objective of the design process is to identify groups of closely related user interface objects. Objects in one group should not be closely related to objects in another group. For example, in the word processor example in Chapter 7, it was clear that the buttons for controlling the format of text could be used independently of each other. In other cases, for example the CD player application, all the user interface objects have to work together closely. In that example, there was no opportunity to use concurrent parts.

Depth

Depth can be used to reduce significantly the number of states in a statechart. For example, consider the statechart in Figure 8.1. Suppose states D1 and D2 are identical. Having duplicate states in a statechart is something to be avoided at all costs. It is easy to think that having an extra state will not cause too many problems. However, a duplicate state can lead to a rapid increase in the number of states. For example, D1 and D2 could interact with two other states (see Figure 8.2). In other words, a single duplicate state could easily be the root of many duplicate states. The way to avoid such problems is to use depth in a statechart. For example, the statechart in Figure 8.2 could be designed with states D1 and D2 consolidated in a single state D (see Figure 8.3). Notice the use of the history mechanism to determine which state should be entered when event 2 occurs in state D.

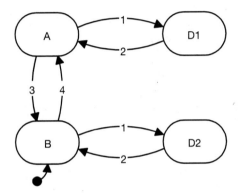

Figure 8.1

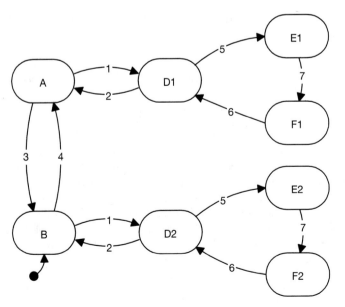

Figure 8.2

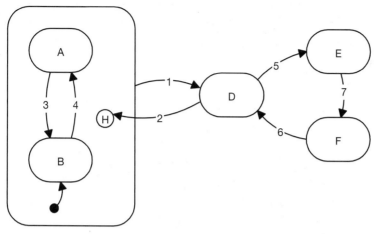

Figure 8.3

Controlling the number of event arrows in a statechart

Some of the techniques for reducing the number of event arrows in a statechart are described below.

Clustering

If there is a set of states and the same event causes a transition from each of them, then the states can be clustered with a superstate and each of the individual events can be replaced by just one arrow attached to the superstate. For instance, the number of event arrows in Figure 8.4 can be reduced through the use of clustering (see Figure 8.5).

History

In Harel's original paper on the statechart notation (Harel, 1987), he demonstrated a useful technique for reducing the number of events in a statechart. If a set of states have the same event attached to them (see Figure 8.6) then all these event arrows can be replaced with a single event arrow used in conjunction with the history mechanism (see Figure 8.7).

Transient states

In many cases, the combination of an event and a condition determines the next state. However, in some instances, the event plays no part in determining the next state. The event triggers the transition but it is the condition associated with the event that determines the next state. In such circumstances, using a central transient state can reduce the number of event arrows. For instance, in Figure 8.8, state 5 is a transient state. The conditions c_1, c_2, c_3 and c_4 determine the next state regardless of the event that caused the transition to the transient state.

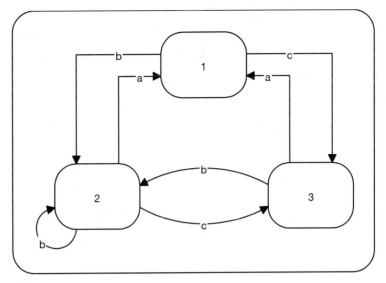

Figure 8.4

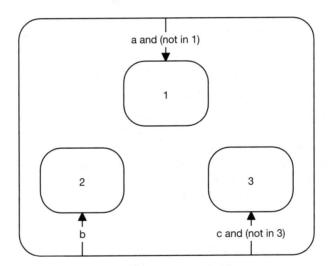

Figure 8.5

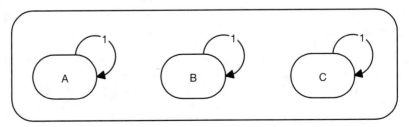

Figure 8.6

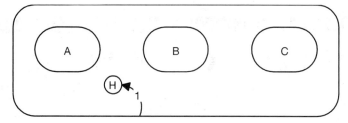

Figure 8.7

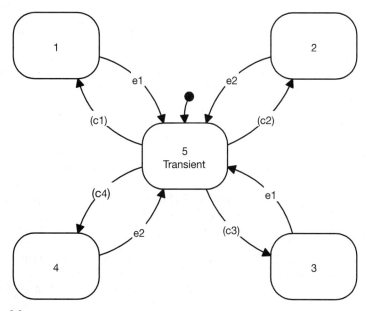

Figure 8.8

Attaching several events to one arrow

Many of the statecharts in this book contain arrows with more than one event attached to them. Having a separate arrow for each event is not an efficient use of space. If more than one event is attached to an arrow then they are separated with the word 'or'. For example, 'Edit clicked or Add clicked' is an arrow label that represents two separate events with separate entries in an event–action table. Obviously, it would not be a good idea to put more than one condition on an arrow leaving a transient state, because it would look like one condition.

Displaying modal alerts

When a modal alert message is displayed, the user cannot use any other function within the application until the alert window is closed. All the other user interface objects in the application are unavailable for use while the alert window is displayed. Modal alert messages

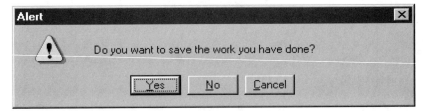

Figure 8.9

are used to force the user to react to the application before continuing to use it. For instance, if a user decides to close an application by selecting a menu option, then the alert message in Figure 8.9 could be displayed if the user has not saved the work done in the application.

In terms of software design, when a modal alert message is displayed, the application enters a state in which the user must respond to the alert by clicking one of the buttons in the window before any other event can be performed. Thus, for each alert message, there could be a corresponding state in the statechart design.

For instance, consider the statechart in Figure 8.10. The normal processing of the application is controlled by states 2 and 3. The application is in state 3 when the user has not made any changes to the data presented in the user interface. If the user does modify any data, then a transition to state 2 occurs. If the user clicks the Save menu option, then the application returns to state 3. When the user clicks the Close menu option, the actions caused by this event will differ depending on which of the two states the application is in. If it is in state 3, then the data in the screen matches the data stored in the database and so the application can be closed without any further dialogue with the user. However, if the application is in state 2, then the data in the screen does not match the data in the database and so the user interface is designed to display the alert message shown in Figure 8.9. The application enters state 1 which causes the alert message to be displayed. The user must respond to the alert message by clicking one of the buttons: Yes, No or Cancel. If Yes is

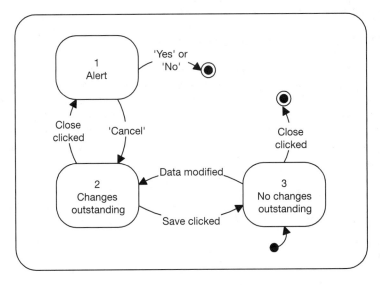

Figure 8.10

clicked then the data is saved to the database and the application is closed. If No is clicked, then the data in the screen is discarded, the database is not updated and the application is closed. If Cancel is clicked then the application returns to its previous state and no other action is taken.

This simple example demonstrates how the dialogue within an application can be suspended by using a state that corresponds to a modal alert message. However, some readers may have reservations about this approach. In certain circumstances, for instance when validating data, it may be necessary to display many different alert messages. Adopting the strategy of one state per message could result in a huge statechart that is more complicated to code than the bottom-up approach.

For instance, consider the statechart in Figure 8.11 which is part of a personnel database application. The default starting state is a high-level state that corresponds to the main screen of the application. Clicking the New button in the main screen causes a transition to state 2 which corresponds to a subwindow for entering details about a new employee. A user can return to the main screen by clicking either an OK button or a Cancel button that are contained in the subwindow. If the Cancel button is clicked then a new employee is not created in the database. If the OK button is clicked then, before an employee is created, all the mandatory fields in the subwindow are checked to ensure they contain valid values. For instance, if the surname field is blank then state 3 is entered, if the forename field is blank then state 4 is entered and so on. (Notice the used of prioritized events to indicate which event will occur if more than one condition is true.) The problem with using this approach is related to the number of alert states that could result. If there are a large number of fields, each with a number of validation checks, then the statechart could be massive and yet offer little benefit. In this instance, the code that results from the bottom-up approach would be easier to understand (see Figure 8.12).

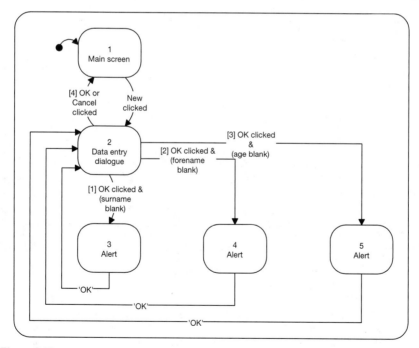

Figure 8.11

In such circumstances, it is necessary to control the number of alert states. This can be achieved by using just one alert state that has parameters which are set when an event arrow enters the state. Common parameters to pass to an alert state are the message to be displayed and the *x, y* co-ordinates of the alert dialogue box.[1] Note that the number of buttons and the labels on the buttons are normally static because the event arrows are attached to specific states. By using parameterized states, the statechart in Figure 8.11 can be simplified to that shown in Figure 8.13. The three prioritized event arrows entering the alert state will have actions associated with them that will pass the appropriate alert messages as parameters to the alert state.

Some readers may still be sceptical of this approach. After all, the validation of the fields can easily be achieved without using a statechart (see Figure 8.12). For this particular behaviour, I concede that a statechart approach offers little benefit over a bottom-up approach. However, I believe a statechart should be used to define the validation for two reasons:

When_button_pressed : OK button
```
if (surname is null) then
        display_alert('A surname must be entered for the employee', 'OK');
elsif (forename is null) then
        display_alert('A forename must be entered for the employee', 'OK');
elsif (age is null) then
        display_alert('The age of the employee must be entered','OK');
else
        display_canvas('main');
end if;
```

Figure 8.12

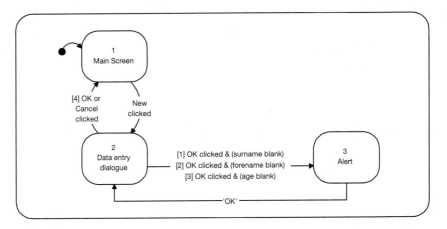

Figure 8.13

---

1. The *x, y* co-ordinates may be included to ensure an alert dialogue window does not obscure the user interface object to which it refers when it is first displayed. Of course, a good user interaction design would also ensure that the modal window is movable (a property of the dialogue window).

1   It describes the behaviour of the user interface in a way that is consistent with the rest of the system. Thus, the statechart will give a complete view of the syntax of the user interface. It is bad practice to define only part of the syntax, on the grounds that the rest of it is easy to code directly.

2   It provides an abstract view of the software which is useful for both reviewing the design and testing the code.

Backtracking through an application

Moving forwards through an application is usually easier than backtracking. For instance, when an OK button is clicked in a window the next state is easy to determine. When a Cancel button in a window is clicked, the application must remember which state it was in last and move back to that state. This is achieved using the history mechanism.

For instance, a subwindow can be called from more than one window. If the Cancel button is clicked in the subwindow then the history mechanism can be used to determine which window called the subwindow (see Figure 8.14).

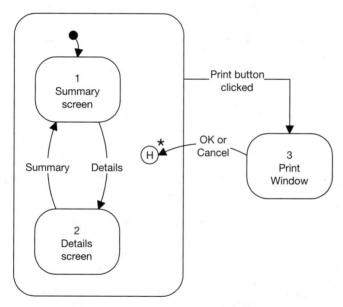

Figure 8.14

Designing database applications

In certain circumstances, a user event in itself may not determine what the next state is. For instance, suppose a user event triggers the following actions:

1   Retrieve a set of data from a database.

2   Put the retrieved data into a scrolling list in a particular screen.

3   Highlight the first row in the list.

Suppose the data retrieved from the database contains some kind of status value. When a user selects a row in the scrolling list, the status value of that row will determine how the user will be able to interact with the other screen items.

The difficulty with modelling this screen behaviour lies with the event that first retrieves the data from the database. Under normal circumstances, the current state and the user event would determine the next state. However, in this case, the next state will be determined by the status of the first row in the list item *after* the data is retrieved. In other words, at the point when the user performs the event that causes the above three actions, the next state cannot be determined until the first two actions have been performed.

To solve this problem it is necessary to introduce a transient state in the state diagram. In Figure 8.15, the event that causes the data to be retrieved from the database is labelled 'Update button clicked'. This event causes a transition from state G to state E and the three actions listed earlier to be executed. State E is a transient state because none of the event arrows leaving it have user events – they only have conditions. After the actions associated with the transition G → E have been executed, one of the three conditions will be satisfied and the appropriate state will be entered (that is, state B, C or D). In other words, while the data is being retrieved from the database, the statechart will wait in state E. When the database query is complete and the status of the first row is known, the transition can be made to the appropriate state.

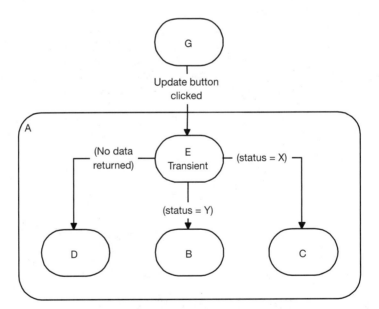

Figure 8.15

Chapter 9
Design heuristics and design tests

Design is an iterative process. Designers rarely arrive at a complete design immediately. As a design process proceeds, errors and omissions in earlier drafts are found and better ways of expressing the same ideas are discovered. A necessary part of any design process is the need to inspect the design for problems or omissions. It is usually impossible to understand the required behaviour of a user interface and then immediately produce a statechart design for that interface. Designs must start somewhere and gradually evolve to a finished product. This chapter is concerned with heuristics that will help facilitate the design process.

I make no apologies for any apparent informality in the heuristics. Software design is generally an informal and creative process that applies a formal notation to express a solution to a problem. Be under no illusion: software design is not easy. The skills required to produce good software designs can only be acquired through experience.

The heuristics in this chapter will not guarantee that a good design will be produced. Instead, they are intended to help you think in a way that will help solve the design problems you will face. The heuristics are not intended to be a set of steps that must be followed rigidly. They are really intended as a way of getting novice statechart designers started. There is nothing worse than reading a design book that covers a notation in incredible detail, but offers little or no advice on how to apply the notation to design problems.

Of course, the heuristics and design tests do not have to be applied in any particular order. For instance, the design tests can, and should, be applied throughout the design process. The overall design strategy is gradually to identify the states of a statechart from the top level downwards. However, it is necessary to understand the behaviour of individual items in order to identify the states and it is impossible to use a purely top-down approach.

Design heuristics

Identify the high-level statechart

The first step in most statechart designs is to identify the high-level states in the design. These states usually correspond to screens (canvases) that a user can navigate between. It is good to have a firm understanding of which user events will cause the user interface to move between different cavases early in the design process. This allows the user interface to be divided into parts that can be constructed by different developers. By establishing the interfaces between screens early in the design process, problems related to integrating screens can be avoided.

Hint: Design one screen at a time, but start to understand how two screens interact reasonably early in the process.

An application may be composed of, say, five main screens that a user can navigate between. Therefore there will be five high-level states. Within each screen, certain events may cause subwindows to appear. For instance, when a user selects a Print option in a menu, a Print subwindow appears. Such subwindows have a corresponding state. That state may appear at the highest level in the statechart or within a high-level state. Determining where a state appears in the hierarchy is largely determined by the number of screens that can cause the subwindow to appear. If a subwindow can only be called from a particular screen, then the state for the subwindow is likely to appear within the state that corresponds to the calling window. However, if a subwindow can be called from more than one screen, then the state that corresponds to the subwindow would appear at the highest level in the hierarchy.

Hint: The high-level states in a statechart correspond to the windows and subwindows in a user interface.

Screen rules

After the high-level states have been identified, the next step is to consider each of the states in more detail. The best starting point is to write down all the items in or associated with a screen. In other words, buttons, menu items, text items, radio buttons, scrolling lists and so on. Also consider keyboard shortcuts (such as 'Ctrl' and 'c' which usually allows a user to copy an entity).

The next stage is to identify whether the behaviour or appearance of an item is constant or whether it varies. For example, 'Ctrl' and 'c' will only copy an item if that item is selected. 'Ctrl' and 'v' will only paste an item if that item has been copied. When a button is clicked, will it always perform the same actions, or will those actions vary depending on the context in which it is used? Is an item always enabled, or does it become disabled at times? Does an item change colour – if so when? Do items appear and disappear?

The point of screen rules is to identify the behaviour of items, not so much in terms of what they will do (that is, the actions), but rather when they are available to a user and what the differences in their behaviour are. Screen rules are fragments of a user interface's behaviour that must be combined together in a statechart. They are an important first step in clarifying the behaviour to be modelled and, more importantly, what the common behavioural contexts are.

For example, suppose there is a scrolling list displayed in a screen and there are two buttons associated with that list. One of the buttons can be used to delete an element in the list and the other button can cause a subwindow to be displayed containing further details of the selected element in the list. At this stage in the design process, don't think too strongly in terms of the actions (such as deleting elements from a list or opening up subwindows), but instead think in terms of the states of the user interface objects. In the scrolling list example, think in terms of the states of the buttons. What if there are no elements in the list? In this case, it would make sense to disable both buttons because there will be no element in the list to delete or view the details of. If there are items in the list, then both buttons should be enabled. There are clearly two potential states for controlling the two buttons. The transitions between the states can be identified, by identifying the events and conditions that cause items to appear in the list.

The screen rules that need to be identified are summarized below.

Entry and exit rules

What user events cause a screen to be entered or exited? What events cause an application to be closed? Are there different conditions that can affect the behaviour? For example, when data is changed in a canvas but has not been saved to a file or database, will exiting from the screen or closing the application cause different behaviour in these circumstances than if the data had been saved? Are there permissions that restrict access to certain screens based on some privilege granted to a user? Do some users have read-only access to certain screens and others have read-write access? Can a screen be entered if there is no data available to display in that particular screen?

Identify any modes

A mode is a state that the software can enter and where the effect of a user event changes depending on the mode. Modes are not necessarily bad. For example, in a drawing package it may be possible for a user to select a pencil, a spray can or a paint brush. The mode that the drawing tool is in is visible to the user because the cursor icon can be made to change to a pencil, spray can or paint brush. The events that the user performs will have different effects depending on the mode that the user interface is in. This is a good use of modes because a user only has to remember one set of commands for the different drawing tools. If a user interface contains modes such as this, then these are obvious candidates for states.

A screen may have to operate in read-only mode and in read-write mode. A screen may have very different behaviour with different data displayed in it. For example, in a personnel database application, a screen may behave in considerably different ways depending on whether a person is a full-time employee, a part-time employee or a freelance contractor. Identify what characterizes these modes and at what point the mode may change. For instance, can a mode change within a screen, or just on entry to it?

Identify the screen items that have varying behaviour

Identify all the screen items whose behaviour changes as a user interacts with the screen. There are many ways in which a user interface item can change: for instance, enabled to disabled, visible to invisible, position a to position b, colour x to colour y and so on. Also, identify items whose attributes may never change, but whose actions may differ under different circumstances. Identify not just the change in behaviour, but what events and conditions cause the change in behaviour.

Identify the screen items that have constant behaviour

There are surprisingly few screen items that always behave in exactly the same way regardless of the context in which they are used. It is worthwhile considering each item in turn and confirming that the behaviour really is constant.

Note that screen rules are a means to an end. They are only temporary design entities and so do not have to be written in the precise tones of a requirements document. The designer of the statechart will be the only person who uses the screen rules. They should not be kept after the statechart has been designed, because all the information stated in them will be translated into the statechart. Attempting to keep a set of screen rules and a statechart in step with each other is an unnecessary overhead that few projects will be able to afford. Statecharts should be the definitive specification of a user interface's behaviour.

Identifying states: converting screen rules to a statechart

Having identified the screen rules, the next task is to draw a statechart that defines the required behaviour of each screen item as specified in the screen rules and ensure the screen items work together as a whole.

You may need to change the way you think about a user interface in order to be successful in converting screen rules to a statechart. Many people find state modelling a natural, intuitive process, but some find it unnatural and a little awkward. To be successful, you need to think in terms of the abstract states that the user interface can be in, rather than the actions that result from the events supplied by a user. For those that usually develop user interfaces using a bottom-up approach, this is a key shift in the way a user interface is developed. With a bottom-up approach, developers think in terms of the actions that must be executed in response to an event and then determine the different contexts in which the events can occur in a largely ad hoc way. When designing statecharts the process is reversed. The designer first identifies the contexts (states) in which the events can occur and then the actions are identified for the events. Identifying the states first builds a solid framework on which events and actions can easily be added.

Any type of user interface can be specified in terms of events, conditions, states and actions. If the user interface does something clever from a user's perspective, then it is the actions that will cause this to happen. A statechart only controls when actions occur. It is *not* the case that statecharts are only suitable for designing certain types of user interfaces.

Clearly, some user interfaces are more complicated than others. For instance, a drawing package that allows a user to design and move three-dimensional objects is clearly more difficult to design, code and test than an interface that allows a user to fill in an electronic form. However, the difference in such applications lies in the user events that the software must recognize and the actions that must be performed in response to those events. The statechart is only concerned with the complexity of a user interface's states and not the complexity of actions. If the development tool can recognize the required events and allow all the required actions to be implemented, then a statechart can be designed to control the application.

For example, there is nothing special about dragging and dropping screen entities. In terms of statechart modelling, this behaviour is no different from any other behaviour such as clicking a button or selecting a menu item. Don't think in terms of how it looks from a user's point of view, because, from an internal viewpoint, this behaviour can be described in terms of events, conditions, states and actions.

For instance, the statechart in Figure 9.1 models a drag and drop function in an application. The application contains data which can be selected and dragged to certain locations. States 1 and 2 are used to determine whether or not data is selected. If data is selected, the statechart moves to state 2. Holding the left mouse button down in that state causes the drag action to be initiated and, for each mouse movement, the mouse move event causes the display to be updated with the new position of the mouse pointer and the selected data. When the user releases the mouse button, if the location of the mouse pointer is a valid place to drop the data then the data is transferred to that location and the statechart enters state 1. If the data is dragged to an invalid place, then the statechart remains in state 2 without any actions being executed. In short, the actions associated with dragging and dropping data (such as updating the screen or updating data in a database) may be complicated, but the statechart that controls when these actions are performed is quite simple.

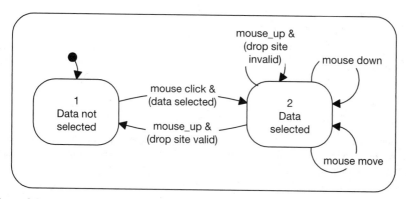

Figure 9.1

Identifying the states from the screen rules is inevitably an experimental process. There may be several ways of modelling a particular behaviour. The route to a good design is to keep ideas fairly fluid in the early stages. Don't opt for a particular solution without first experimenting with other approaches. It may require a considerable amount of lateral thought to come up with significantly different designs.

The top-level states correspond to the main screen and subscreens. The more difficult task is associated with identifying the states at the next level down. A good starting point is to consider the screen modes. If screens seem to operate in different modes then the statechart may be designed to switch between modes at this level. Some examples of modes are as follows:

- changes in the status of data, for example when a full-time employee is displayed and when a contractor is displayed;

- when a user has a particular privilege;

- when a file is open or closed. For example, in a word processor, without a document open, the functions available are very limited.

In this way, the behaviour of the screen is completely separated at a fairly high level. This is useful if the mode affects the behaviour of a screen in a very significant way such as the majority of screen items behaving in different ways. If the mode changes have only a small impact, then modelling a screen switching between high-level states may not be the best solution.

Consolidate related behaviour

Next you need to look for common events and conditions that will cause a number of screen items to change state. What do these states represent? Can related screen items be brought together into the same states?

An objective should be to identify objects from the screen rules that clearly work together to provide a service to a user. If the screen items work together and affect each other's behaviour then they are likely to be controlled by the same part of the statechart. (For example, if cut, copy and paste can be performed by menu items, icon buttons, and key presses then these related functions can be controlled by the same part of the statechart.)

Hint: Search for groups of user interface items that work together as an entity. Each group is likely to be controlled by a concurrent part of a statechart.

If there are two concurrent components of a statechart, then those components should be controlling different screen items. In general, a design will be difficult to understand if states in concurrent parts of a statechart are determining the appearance of the same user interface object.

Hint: A screen item should be controlled by precisely one part of a statechart.

This does not preclude the same user event appearing in more than one part of a statechart. However, the actions would normally be associated with one event and the other event(s) are used to synchronize behaviour in another part of the statechart.

Separate unrelated behaviour

When designing a statechart, a primary objective is to cluster related behaviour within states. Independent behaviour should be modelled in different states. Separating independent behaviour in the statechart allows parts of the design to be understood and modified in isolation from the other parts of the statechart.

When working on a screen, try to identify the aspects of its behaviour that are completely independent of each other. If such behaviour can be identified, and it usually can, then use independent concurrent parts to model the behaviour.

If a design seems to be becoming large and unwieldy, then stop and ask yourself whether there is a more structured approach. Ensure depth is being used effectively to divide the statechart up into manageable chunks.

Hint: Use depth extensively to structure a statechart.

Keep statecharts looking tidy

As your statechart design evolves, keep the diagram looking tidy. Few, if any, event arrows should overlap and the diagrams should avoid looking cramped. This may not sound important, but a well-presented statechart is always easier to understand and maintain than a untidy one.

Keep dependencies out of independent concurrent parts

Figure 9.2 contains a dependency which is a condition attached to an event arrow of the form '(in state X)'. Such a condition makes the behaviour of one part of a statechart dependent on the behaviour of another concurrent part. In other words, when event c occurs in state 4, the transition to state 3 will only occur if the other 'independent' concurrent part is in state 2. This is not good software design because it weakens the independence of the concurrent parts. The use of dependencies weakens a design and should therefore only be used as a last resort.

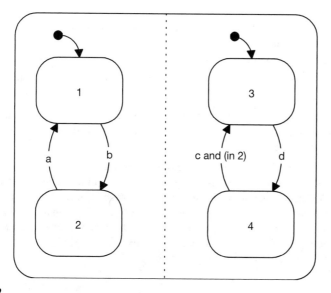

Figure 9.2

Dependencies make testing more difficult. It is considerably easier to understand and test a statechart with concurrent parts that run independently of each other because each one can be tested in isolation from the rest. If dependencies are used then a sharp increase in the number of test cases is required.

Dependencies also make the long-term maintainability of the software more difficult because changing one concurrent part may cause an unwanted side-effect in another part. To illustrate the point, suppose a particular state was composed of 12 concurrent parts and each one of these parts was drawn on a separate page in a design document. If there were dependencies between the 12 parts, then it would make the task of understanding the statechart difficult simply because of the size of the design. Furthermore, it would not necessarily be obvious why the parts were dependent on each other. However, if the 12 parts were completely independent of each other, then any one of them could be modified in isolation from the rest.

Hint: Keep concurrent parts independent by not using dependencies of the form '(in state X)'.

If a design contains unavoidable dependencies between concurrent parts, then consider merging the two parts into one on the grounds that they probably shouldn't have been separate in the first place. Merging concurrent parts may increase the number of states and event arrows, but the benefit may be increased clarity of the design.

Hint: If concurrent parts have unavoidable dependencies then consider merging them.

For instance, suppose we wanted to design a statechart that models the copy and paste functions available in Microsoft Word. There are three ways to copy text: the Copy menu item, the Copy icon button, and the key combination 'Ctrl' and 'c'. Similarly, there are three ways to paste copied text: the Paste menu item, the Paste icon button and the key combination 'Ctrl' and 'v'. The behaviour of the six user interface objects is as follows:

- If no text is highlighted, then the Copy menu item will be disabled and clicking either the Copy icon button or pressing <Ctrl> c will cause the computer to make a short beep noise.

- If no text is in the copy buffer, then the Paste menu item will be disabled and clicking either the Paste icon button or pressing <Ctrl> v will cause the computer to make a short beep noise.

- If text is highlighted and any of the three copy objects are used, then the text is stored in the copy buffer.

- If text is stored in the copy buffer, then using any of the three paste objects will cause the text to be pasted at the current cursor position and the selected text to be deselected.

The statechart in Figure 9.3 could be used to model this behaviour. The Copy menu is disabled in state 1 and enabled in state 2. The Paste menu is disabled in state 3 and enabled in state 4. Without going into the detail of how the statechart behaves, it is clear that there are a lot of dependencies between the two concurrent parts. This immediately suggests a problem with the design. The two parts are very closely related to each other and therefore the design will probably be easier to understand if they are merged.

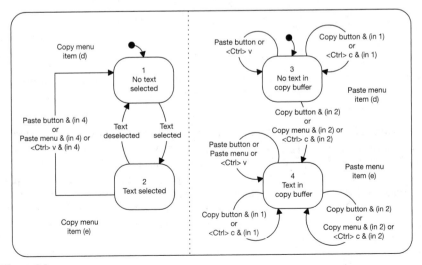

Figure 9.3

Figure 9.4 shows an alternative statechart controlling the copy and paste objects. In state 5 the Copy and Paste menus are disabled. In state 6, the Copy menu is disabled and the Paste menu is enabled. In state 7 the Copy menu is enabled and the Paste menu is disabled. In state 8 both the Copy and Paste menu items are enabled. This statechart is considerably easier to understand because there are no concurrent parts with dependencies.

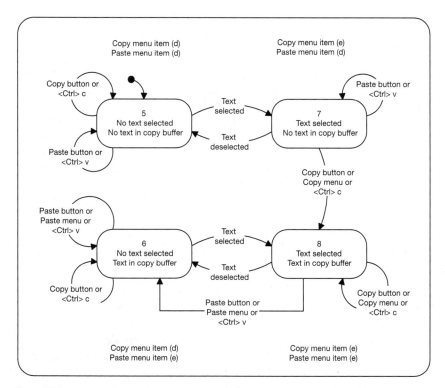

Figure 9.4

In this example, the number of states has not increased when the two concurrent parts were merged. However, if there were more than two states in either of the two concurrent parts, then merging them would have to be carefully considered because the resulting statechart could be large and unwieldy.

Synchronize concurrent parts with simultaneous events

It is possible for a single user event to cause simultaneous state transitions in concurrent parts. This is perfectly acceptable and occurs quite frequently in designs. Generally speaking, actions will only be associated with one of the event arrows – the primary event arrow. The other event arrows should really be seen as a way of synchronizing the other concurrent parts with the part containing the primary event arrow. For example, when a user deletes an item from a list by clicking a delete button, this event may cause a transition which results in the action of deleting the item from the list. The same delete event may also cause a simultaneous transition in a concurrent part to a state in which an Undo button is enabled. This second transition would not have an action associated with it, since its purpose is to synchronize the Undo button with the delete event.

Hint: When designing simultaneous events, typically only one event should cause actions to occur. The other events should be used to synchronize the concurrent parts with the primary event arrow.

Be wary of actions on states

It is possible to add actions to a state which are executed on entry to that state. This may seem an economical approach to reducing the amount of code that needs to be written if there are several events arrows entering that state. However, in the long term, actions associated with states can make the software more difficult to maintain. For instance, a new event could be added which terminates at a state with actions. If those actions are not required when the event occurs then a significant change would be required to the state-chart. Furthermore, if the actions associated with a state are changed, it is necessary to ensure that the change is appropriate for all the arrows entering that state. Actions on states are like global variables. They can be very powerful, but they also have the potential to cause many problems.

Hint: Use states to control the attributes of user interface items rather than executing actions. All actions should be associated with events.

Avoid event arrows that transcend many levels in a state hierarchy

It should be possible to understand a statechart without having to understand the details of lower-level states. This can be achieved by avoiding transitions crossing too many levels in the state hierarchy. Try to restrict event arrows so that they only move from one level to the next, rather than jumping several levels. Also avoid having transitions from states deep in one part of the statechart to states deep in another part.

A transition such as the one shown in Figure 9.5 is not a good hierarchical design. When using depth to refine a state, try to design the statechart so that each level in the hierarchy does not contain events from higher levels. For instance, the statechart in Figure 9.6 is better because the event from state A terminates at state B which is at the same level. Default start arrows are used to model the required transition to D.

Clearly, when depth is used to cluster states as a means of reducing the number of event arrows in a statechart, then it is perfectly acceptable for arrows to transcend this cluster state. This is because a cluster state is not being used for hierarchical decomposition, so it is not intended to be viewed at an abstract level.

Naming states

Each state should be given a meaningful name. If you cannot think of a name that conveys what the state represents then this may suggest there is a problem with the design. If the

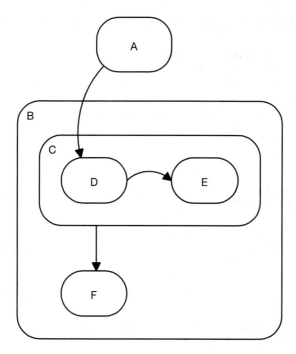

Figure 9.5

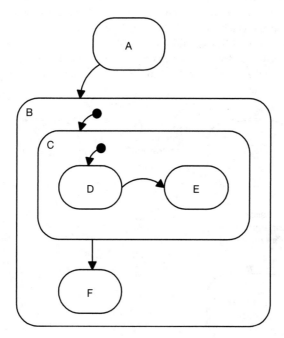

Figure 9.6

meaning of the state cannot be identified in the design process then how will it be understood during the maintenance of the system? Each state must explicitly represent something.

The route to a state should be irrelevant

It should never be assumed that a previous state has defined an attribute of a user interface object and so does not need to be defined again in the current state. For instance, in Figure 9.7, if state 1 enables a particular button, then state 2 should not rely on it having been enabled by state 1. If it is supposed to be enabled in state 2, then state 2 should explicitly enable it again. In short, the current state should define the state of the application.

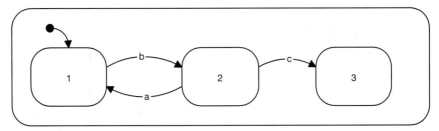

Figure 9.7

Avoid convoluted conditions

The conditions associated with an event can sometimes be simplified by using prioritized events. For instance, the statechart in Figure 9.8 is part of a calculator statechart. When the equals button is clicked in state 1, the conditions on the two event arrows ensure that if the user is attempting to divide by zero then the 'Division by zero' state is entered. Otherwise, the Result state is entered. The conditions associated with the arrow leading to the Result state are not as easy to understand as they could be. The statechart in Figure 9.9 has prioritized the events so that the division by zero condition is evaluated before the transition to the Result state is made.

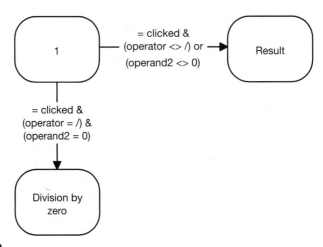

Figure 9.8

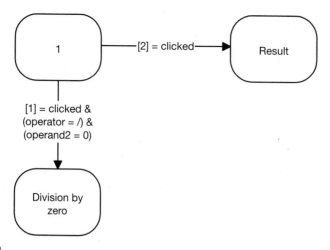

Figure 9.9

Design tests

This section contains a set of tests that designers should consider applying to their designs. Most of the tests are fairly obvious. However, it is worthwhile listing them because they serve as a warning of what can go wrong in a statechart. It is not intended for the tests to be applied to a statechart when it is completed; they should be applied during the design process to avoid introducing problems.

Has all the required behaviour been modelled?

An obvious question, but one that is often overlooked. For a user interface statechart it is a simple task to identify gaps in the required behaviour. Ask yourself the following questions: Have all the screen items been defined in the state–item table? Does each event associated with each screen item appear in the event–action table? Also think in terms of the different types of data, or different types of user the user interface may have to handle.

For example, suppose a screen contains two lists of data items and the user interface allows a user to move items between the two lists. As data is moved between the two lists, one of them may become empty. A statechart may be designed based on the states shown in Figure 9.10. Such a design is based on the assumption that there will always be data in at least one of the lists when the program is started and also that items cannot be removed from the lists. Are these valid assumptions, or should there be a state labelled 'No items in List 1, No items in List 2'?

Also, look for transitions that could be missing. For each state, look at every user interface object related to that state and consider whether the events associated with interacting with those objects have been modelled. If an event in a particular state does not cause a transition then justify whether that event really should be impossible. Also check whether the state needs to do something to prevent a user supplying that particular event. For instance, if a button has no effect in a state then it probably needs to be disabled.

| No items in List 1 | Items in List 1 | Items in List 1 |
| Items in List 2 | Items in List 2 | No items in List 2 |

Figure 9.10

Is it possible to reach all states?

This sounds obvious but it is easy to miss a default start state off a concurrent part, or miss a default start state out of a state that uses the history mechanism (a default start state is needed for the first time the group of states is entered). Also, if a state is unreachable from another set of states then justify why this is so.

Are there any dead states?

In its simplest form, a dead state cannot be exited when events are supplied to it. Such a state will cause the user interface controlled by the statechart to lock up when that state is entered.

More generally, dead states are groups of states from which an end state cannot be reached. In other words, it may be possible to cycle round a set of states, but it is not possible to leave that set of states and reach an end state.

To avoid dead states, it is not simply a case of checking that every state has an arrow leaving it. It is important that the conditions on the event arrows are checked. For instance, the conditions on an event arrow may prevent a state being exited in certain circumstances. Also, check that there are no conflicts between the screen items disabled or hidden by the state and the events that cause the state to be exited. For example, a statechart may have a state in which a Save button being clicked will cause the state to be exited. However, if the Save button is disabled in that state and there are no other events that could cause the state to be exited, then it is a dead state.

Is the behaviour of the statechart deterministic?

The next state in a statechart should be determined by the current state, an event and possibly a condition associated with the event. However, it is possible to introduce non-deterministic behaviour into a statechart. In other words, when an event occurs in a particular state, the next state could be one of several.

There are two common occurrences of such non-determinism which should be avoided. The first is when the same event combined with different conditions, appears on several arrows leaving the same state. For example, in Figure 9.11, when in state B, if the OK button is clicked and both the Printer field and Copies field do not contain values then the next state could be either C or D. This is a flaw in the design which must be corrected. This is a fairly trivial example which can easily be resolved by using prioritized events.

Clearly, some conditions can never be true at the same time. For example, consider the three conditions: $(x > 0)$, $(x < 0)$ and $(x = 0)$. For any given value of x, only one of the three

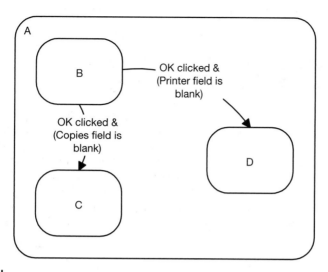

Figure 9.11

conditions can be true. However, if a second variable is used in the conditions then there is a possibility of non-determinism and the use of prioritized events should be considered.

Hint: If the same event with different conditions leaves a state, then only one of those conditions should evaluate to true at any given time. If this cannot be guaranteed, then the events should be prioritized to avoid non-deterministic behaviour.

The second common occurrence of non-determinism in statecharts is when the same event occurs at different levels in the statechart. For example, the statechart in Figure 9.12 possesses non-deterministic behaviour when the current state is state C and event 1 occurs. The next state could be either state B or state F. The statechart needs to be corrected to ensure that only the intended transition can occur.

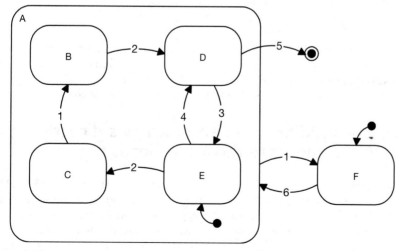

Figure 9.12

Hint: When designing very deep statecharts, try to avoid the same event occurring at very high levels and very low levels in the state hierarchy.

Does the statechart rely on the order of 'simultaneous' events occurring?

Even though 'simultaneous' events in concurrent parts of a statechart must be implemented sequentially, it is bad practice to rely on 'simultaneous' events occurring in a particular order. There is no syntax in the statechart notation for specifying an order and therefore neither the design nor the code should take advantage of the order in which the transitions occur. For example, in the statechart in Figure 9.13, when the statechart is in state B and C and event 1 occurs, it should not matter whether the actions associated with the transition B to D occur before or after the actions associated with transition C to E. Furthermore, it should not matter whether state D is entered before or after state E.

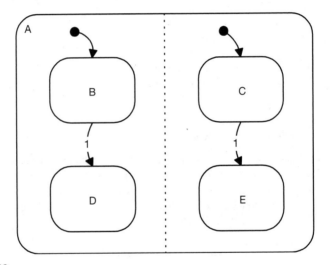

Figure 9.13

The semantics of the statechart notation dictate that such events occur simultaneously. If certain actions are required to be performed before another, or a certain state is required to be entered before another, then the design of the statechart should make this required behaviour explicit rather than being left as an implicit anomaly in the code.

Are the conditions on event arrows directly related to the state the arrow leads to?

The conditions on event arrows are not ad hoc, informal tests. The conditions should be directly related to the state to which the event arrow leads. For instance, let's return to the example of moving items between two lists. Suppose there is an Add button to move items from list 1 to list 2 and a Remove button to move items from list 2 to list 1. Consider the (incomplete) statechart in Figure 9.14. When there are items in list 1 and the Add button is clicked, the statechart uses conditions to determine whether the item about to be moved

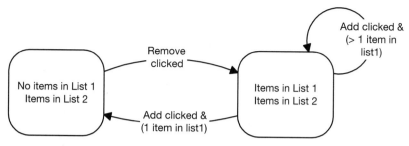

Figure 9.14

from list 1 is the only item in that list. If it is, then there is a transition to the state that models the user interface when there are no items in list 1. In other words, the condition is used to test whether the next state should be entered.

Hint: The conditions used in a statechart should always be directly related to the states they lead to. Conditions should not make use of variables and the status of user interface objects unless those variables and objects are modelled in some way by the destination state.

Ensure the actions are always executed for a transition

The actions executed when a particular event occurs should always be the same. In other words, the actions should not contain conditional statements that will cause different actions to occur. This is especially true when enhancing a statechart during the maintenance phase. If conditional statements are used to determine the actions associated with a transition, then this suggests that more states or more event arrows are needed.

Clearly, an individual action can contain conditional statements. For instance, if an action sets the status of all the items in a list to some value, then there will be a loop and a condition to determine when the last item has been reached (see Figure 9.15). This is not a problem. There would, however, be a problem if the action contained a condition which only allowed the statuses to be updated if the user had a particular privilege. Such a condition should appear in the statechart design and not just in the code.

```
loop
    current_record.Status = 'X';
    if current_record.last_record = true then
        exit loop;
    end if;
    next_record;
end loop;
```

Figure 9.15

Part 3
Case studies

The last few chapters have been concerned with designing statecharts for controlling user interfaces. They have focused on the basic notation and the techniques that can be used. The purpose of the next few chapters is to introduce a number of case studies that will demonstrate how to put the techniques into practice.

The CD player example in Chapter 5 served to illustrate the basic principles of controlling a user interface with a statechart, but the interface did not have many of the characteristics of a business application which most professional developers are required to develop. Statecharts have been used on a number of very large, complex business systems and so there are a number of potential case studies to draw upon. Unfortunately, the requirements of large complex systems can be difficult to understand even when working with them full-time. To include such designs in a book would give little benefit to readers. Instead, I have opted to design two small user interfaces that possess many of the characteristics of real business systems. The case studies have been selected in order to allow readers to quickly understand the requirements of the system and the main tasks the users will perform.

It is important to appreciate that the case studies are for the design of the underlying software and not for the user interaction designs. Any limitations in the interaction designs are a result of weaknesses in my interaction design skills and do not demonstrate some intrinsic flaw in the statechart approach to user interface construction (as was suggested by one reviewer of an early draft of the book). The purpose of this book is to improve the construction of user interfaces and I therefore ask readers to focus their attentions on the statechart designs, rather than on the interaction designs.

The case studies have been implemented and tested and should not contain any serious errors. Of course I cannot guarantee that they are perfect – testing only shows the presence of errors, not their absence.

The case studies have a client–server architecture and are designed to be used by several users accessing a shared relational database. This does not represent a limitation in the type of user interface that can be designed with statecharts; there is no reason why web-based user interfaces, for example, cannot be designed using them.

The case studies will be built up step by step starting with the tasks that the user of the system will have to perform, right through to a complete statechart design for controlling the user interface. For some readers, this may seem a ponderous approach. However, I have adopted this approach because there is little benefit in providing a case study that is either incomplete or does not show readers how it has been derived. The case studies are intended to be helpful to those readers who will go on to use the technique to design their own user interface software. Unfortunately, there are no magic steps that can be followed to produce a good design. All software design is evolutionary in nature. Designs are gradually progressed from simple beginnings to larger and more complex representations. The case studies are presented in a way that is intended to reflect this evolution.

For all the case studies, in addition to the statecharts themselves, a complete set of event–action tables and state–item tables is provided. This is not intended as padding – these tables are essential components of the design. In essence, the event–action tables and state–item tables provide the complete specification of the statechart. The pictures of statecharts can only be an abstract representation of the software because it is usually impossible, through lack of space, to fit all the necessary details into the diagrams. The complete text related to the events, conditions and actions on the event arrows, and the precise definitions of what each state represents, must be contained in support tables. However, such tables would be difficult to understand and modify without a picture of the statechart. Hence, for a complete specification of the behaviour of a user interface, statechart diagrams, event–action tables and state–item tables are necessary.[1]

I would encourage readers to implement one or more of the case studies in order to evaluate the statechart approach. To aid those who choose to implement the case studies, the complete designs are given in the appendices. These do not contain descriptive text and are not built up step by step.

There are two main case studies: a fault reporting application and a student database application. But before looking at these, we will return to the calculator application which was first introduced in Chapter 3 and redesign it with a statechart.

---

1. A statechart design provides the detail of a user interface at a certain level of abstraction. The precise details of individual user interface objects are not contained in a statechart design. Details such as the balloon help that appears when a user places the mouse pointer over an icon button, the position of a user interface object and so on, should be captured directly in the user interface development tool.

Chapter 10
Case study 1: A calculator

In Chapter 3, a calculator application was introduced which characterized the bottom-up approach to user interface development. In this chapter, the same user interface objects will be used but the code that controls those objects will be designed using a statechart. The aim will be to create an application that is easy to understand, easy to enhance and does not contain errors such as those listed in Appendix A. Furthermore, the application will be made easier to use because it will only allow a user to perform valid events at any given time.

The broad operation of the calculator is based on a user entering an operand, then an operator, then another operand and then clicking the equals button to get a result. This behaviour can be modelled by the statechart shown in Figure 10.1. The statechart starts in the state labelled 'Start' and a user can click the number buttons or the decimal point button to begin entering the first operand. The state labelled 'Operand 1' has a lower level of detail (which is indicated by the state variable B) which ensures that a user can only enter valid operands. After an operand has been entered, the user can click an operator button and

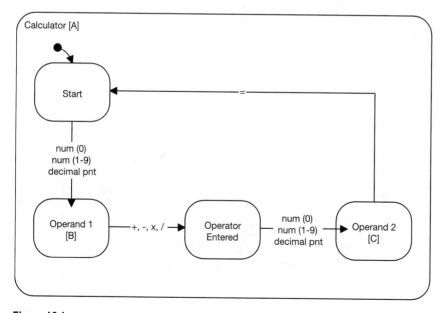

Figure 10.1

cause the 'Operator Entered' state to be entered. The user can then start to enter a second operand and the 'Operand 2' state is entered. The 'Operand 2' state has a lower level of detail which will be similar to the 'Operand 1' state. After entering the second operand, the equals button can be clicked and the result will be calculated and the Start state will be entered again.

This is a simplistic view of the calculator. The statechart needs to be extended to take into account negative numbers, dividing by zero, the Cancel button, the Cancel Entry button and the percent button.

The statechart in Figure 10.1 assumes that the operands are positive numbers. It is possible that a user may enter a negative number before starting to enter either of the operands, by clicking the minus button. When the minus button is clicked before an operand is entered, the Readout field should be made to show a minus sign. After the minus sign is displayed, the user can enter the operand as usual. The statechart can be extended with two additional 'Negative Number' states (see Figure 10.2). Notice that when a user selects an operator and enters state 4, it is possible to select a different operator and remain in state 4. However, if

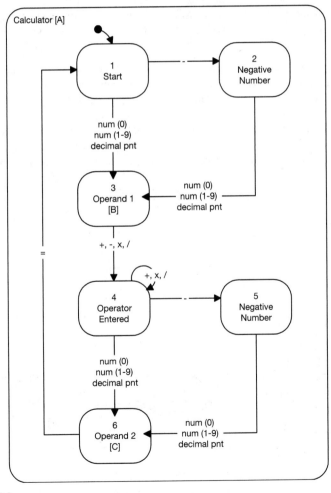

Figure 10.2

the minus button is selected in state 4 then this indicates that a negative number is about to be entered and not that the operator has been changed.

When a user clicks the equals sign in state 6, the statechart enters the Start state again. However, this is not quite the behaviour that is required because the user may wish to use the result of the calculation as the first operand in the next calculation. In which case, after a result is returned, the user will expect to click an operator button and then enter the second operand. The statechart needs to be extended to include a result state. Also, after a user has entered the second operand, it should be possible to enter another operator without clicking the equals button. In other words, it should be possible to enter a sequence such as: 3 + 4 − 2 =. The statechart can be extended to that shown in Figure 10.3.

In the version of the application given in Chapter 3, if a user attempted to divide the first operand by zero then an alert message was displayed informing the user that division by

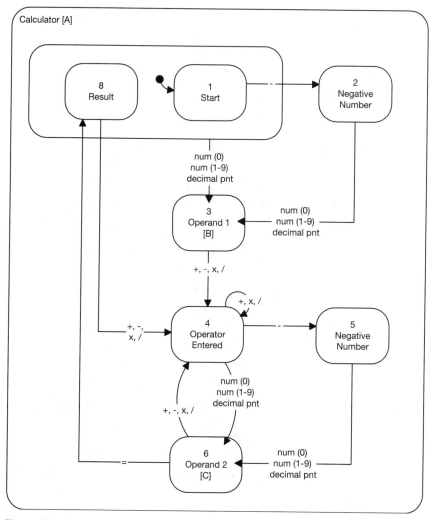

Figure 10.3

zero is not allowed. A similar alert message can be made to appear by attaching an alert state to state 6 (see Figure 10.4). State 7 is entered if the user attempts to divide the first operand by zero. Notice that this event takes priority over the events that lead from state 6 to state 4 or state 8.

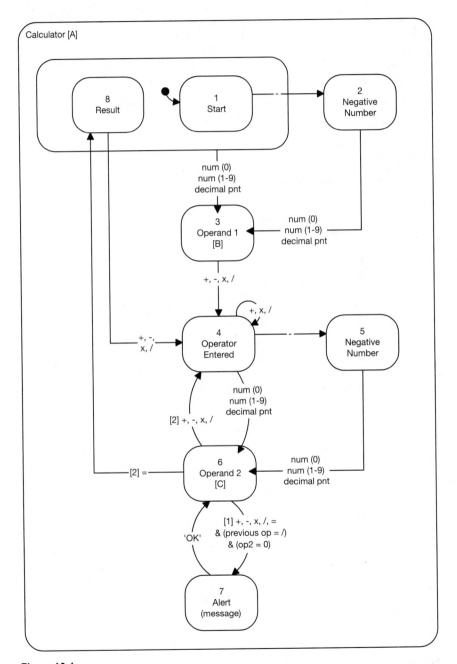

Figure 10.4

The Cancel button can be clicked at any time and this will cause any operation being performed by the user to be abandoned and state 1 to be entered. An arrow attached to the outermost state will model this behaviour (see Figure 10.5).

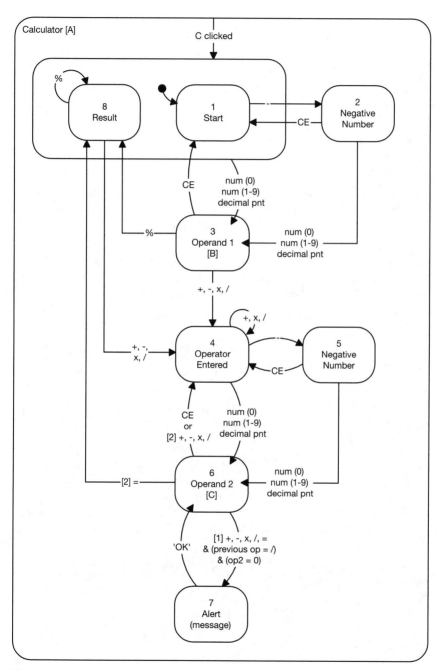

Figure 10.5

Table 10.1

| | A | | | | | | | |
User interface Object	1	2	3	4	5	6	7	8
CE (Cancel Entry)		d	e	e	d	e	e	–	d
% button		d	d	e	d	d	d	–	e

The Cancel Entry button can be used to cancel the last operand entered. It does not cancel the last operator entered. Thus the button should only be enabled and available for use in states 2, 3, 5, and 6 (see Figure 10.5 and Table 10.1).

The percent button divides the first operand by 100. It should only therefore be enabled when the first operand is being entered, or when a result has been reached (since a result can be the first operand of a calculation). Thus, the percent button is only enabled in states 3 and 8. When the button is clicked, state 8 is entered (see Figure 10.5 and Table 10.1).

States 3 and 6 have lower levels of detail that control how a user can use the number buttons and decimal point buttons to ensure that they only enter valid operands. The statecharts for both states are very similar and are shown in Figures 10.6 and 10.7.

If a user clicks the zero button, then state 9 is entered. If the user clicks the zero button again then it has no effect. Thus, only one zero is shown in the Readout field. States 10 and 11 are used to ensure that a user can only enter one decimal point in an operand. The application stays in state 10 until the decimal point is clicked and then state 11 is entered.

The full details of the event–action tables are given in Appendix B.

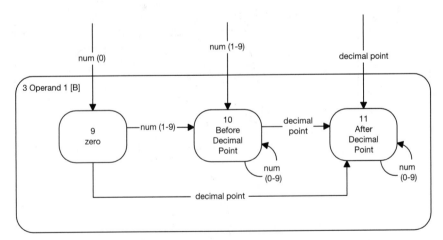

Figure 10.6

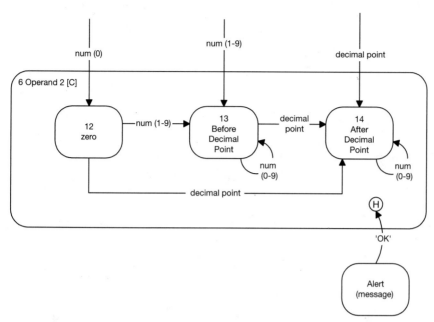

Figure 10.7

Chapter 11
Case study 2: A fault reporting application

Introduction

When software systems are tested, the faults that are found are usually recorded in a database. The case study in this chapter is a fault reporting application that can be used for such a purpose. It allows faults to be recorded and progressed through a simple life-cycle in order to resolve the fault. The application is not intended to have all the features of a sophisticated fault reporting application. Instead, the functionality of the application has been reduced to a basic level so that the design strategy for the software is readily understandable. This case study is useful because it has many of the characteristics of much larger business applications. Many businesses are concerned with progressing data through a life-cycle of some form, with different people acting on the data at different points in the life-cycle. Such software can be complicated to construct and even more difficult to enhance. If significant changes are made to the life-cycle, or the types of users who can act on the data are changed, then the chances of introducing unwanted side-effects are often high.

This chapter provides a very simple and elegant solution to the problem of being able to make significant enhancements to such software. It is important to appreciate that the overall design strategy for the application can be used for considerably more complicated user interfaces.

High-level requirements and main tasks of the users

The fault reporting (FR) application is to be used to raise fault reports and progress them through to a satisfactory resolution. The faults are typically raised during the testing of a software product.

A user of the application can be granted one or more of the following roles: Originator, Analyst or Implementer. The Originator role allows users to raise fault reports and then at a later stage confirm whether or not a fault has been fixed. The Analyst role allows users to decide whether a fault is really a fault and what should be done to fix it. The Implementer role allows users to record when a fault has been fixed and what changes have been made to fix the fault.

The roles granted to a user are set up by an administrator of the application. Users are required to log in to the application and the unique username is used to determine the roles that are granted to the user. For instance, a tester would typically be assigned the Originator role and a development team leader may have all three roles. It is possible for a user to be granted no roles, in which case they would have read-only access to the fault reports.

Each fault has a status associated with it and as a fault is progressed the value of the status changes. Figure 11.1 shows the life-cycle of a fault. Bear in mind that this is a logical model of the life-cycle – it is not a statechart. The labels on the arrows indicate the events that will cause the change in status to occur. Each status change can only be made to happen by users with the appropriate roles granted to them. The necessary roles for each status change are shown in parantheses on each event arrow.

A user granted the Originator role can raise new fault reports. When a fault is in the process of being created, it has a status of New (which is indicated by the default starting arrow in Figure 11.1). When a user has entered the details of the fault, the fault is created and its status is set to Raised.

A fault with a status of Raised can be progressed by a user with the Analyst role. An analyst can reject the fault, if it is not considered to be a fault, and cause the status to be set to Rejected. Alternatively, if the fault report is a genuine fault, then the analyst can progress it, in which case the status is set to Evaluated. In either case, the user will be able to record an analysis of the problem or give a reason why it is not considered to be a fault.

A fault with a status of Evaluated can be implemented by a range of different people such as developers, designers, technical authors and so on. When an implementer fixes a fault with a status of Evaluated, the user will be able to enter text describing what they have done to fix the problem and then progress the fault report by setting the status to Implemented.

When a fault has a status of Implemented, the fault should be tested to ensure it has been fixed successfully. A user with a role of Originator (but not necessarily the same person that created the fault report) can test the software and then record whether the fault has been fixed or not. If it has been fixed successfully, then the fault will be progressed to a status of Fixed, otherwise it will be progressed to a status of Not Fixed.

A fault with a status of Not Fixed is similar to a fault with a status of Raised. An analyst can either request the fault to be implemented and cause the status to be set to Evaluated, or reject the fault and cause the status to be set to Rejected.

Overview of the user interface screen

When a user progresses a fault, the details of the fault and any comments entered by other users must be available for the user to see. The intention is to use the same user interface screen in a variety of different contexts which are determined by the role of the user and the status of the fault displayed in the screen. For instance, if a user is only granted the Origi-

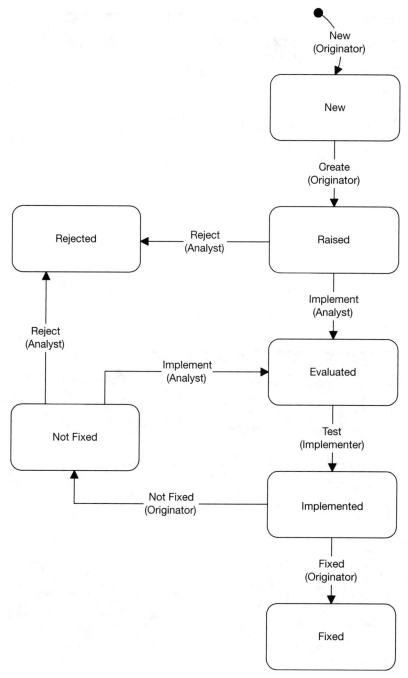

Figure 11.1

nator role and a fault is displayed with a status of Evaluated, then that user will not be able to progress the fault or edit its details. However, if a different user with a role of implementer viewed the same fault, then the screen would allow that user to progress the fault.

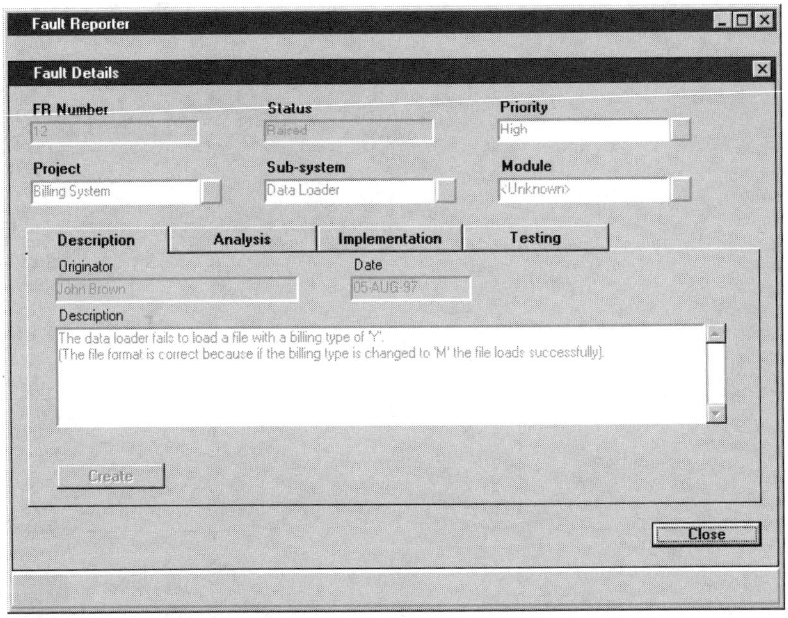

Figure 11.2 The Description tab-card.

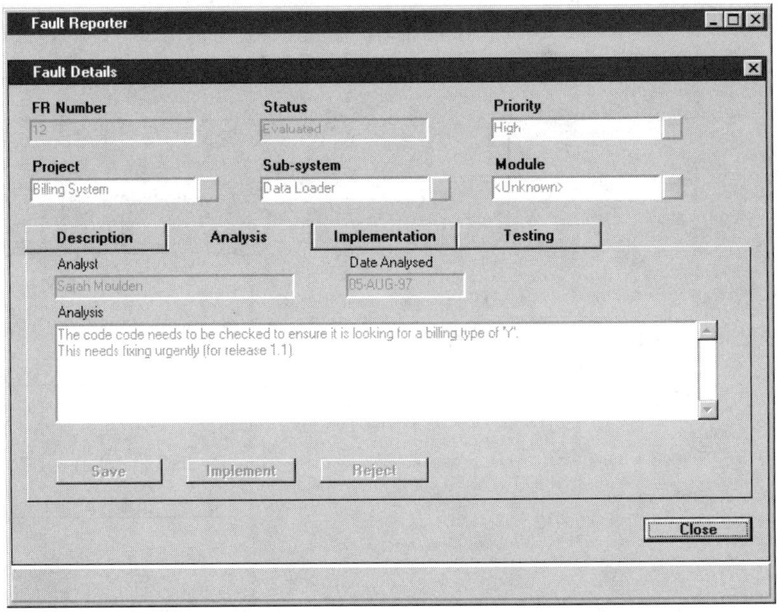

Figure 11.3 The Analysis tab-card.

The faults screen has two main areas: the header fields and a tab-card. The header contains the unique Fault Report Number, the Status of the fault, the Priority of the fault, the Project that the fault is raised against, the sub-system within that project and the Module within the sub-system. There are four tab-cards. The Description tab-card (see Figure 11.2) contains a description of the fault, the name of the person who raised the fault and the date on which the fault was raised. The Analysis tab-card (see Figure 11.3) contains the analysis of the

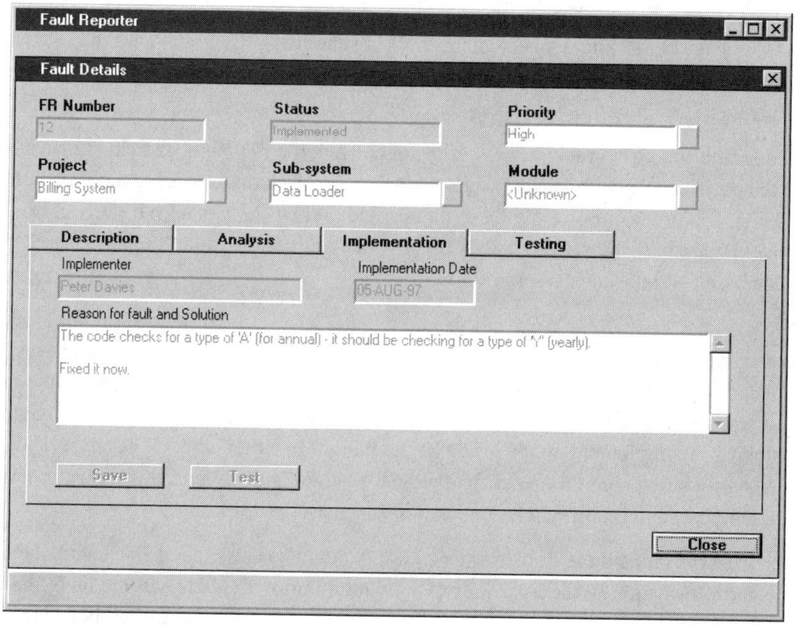

Figure 11.4 The Implementation tab-card.

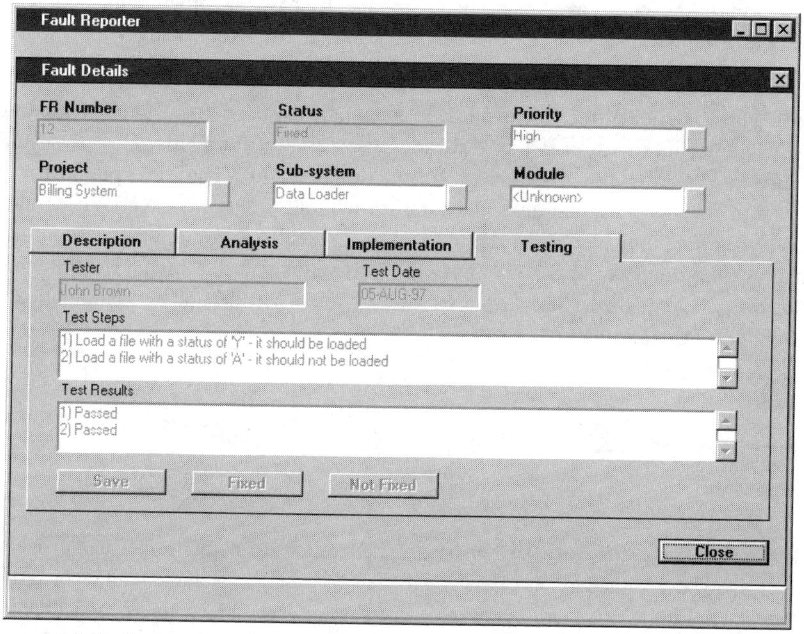

Figure 11.5 The Testing tab-card

fault, the name of the person who analysed the fault and the date the analysis was entered. The Implementation tab-card (see Figure 11.4) contains the details of what was done to fix the fault, the name of the person who fixed the fault and the date on which it was fixed. The Testing tab-card (see Figure 11.5) contains the details of the tests carried out, the results of those tests, the name of the tester and the date the testing was performed.

A user can enter details in the Description tab-card when a fault report is first being created. The Originator field, Date field and Status field are automatically filled in for the user when the fault is created and they cannot be set by a user. The Priority, Project, Sub-system, Module and Description fields can all be given values by a user.

When a fault report is in the process of being created, the FR Number field is blank. The Create button can only be clicked when the user has selected a project in the Project field and entered a description in the Description field. When the Create button is clicked, a unique FR number is generated and assigned to the fault report, a fault report is created in the database and the status is set to Raised.

When a user is granted the Analyst role and a fault has a status of Raised or Not Fixed, a user can change the values in the Priority, Project, Sub-system or Module fields if necessary and enter details in the Analysis field. The user can save any changes made to the fault report, without progressing it, by clicking the Save button. The user can progress the fault by clicking the Implement button or the Reject button. In either case, the Analyst field, the Date Analysed field and the Status field will all be automatically updated with appropriate values and the fault report will be saved to the database.

When a user is granted the Implementer role and a fault has a status of Evaluated, the user can enter information in the Reason for Fault and Solution field. The user cannot modify the Priority, Project, Sub-system or Module fields. The Save button can be clicked to save the information to the database without progressing the fault, or alternatively the Test button can be clicked to save the information to the database and progress the fault report to the next status value. In either case, the values in the following fields will be updated automatically: Implementer, Implementation Date and Status.

When a user is granted the Originator role and a fault has a status of Implemented, the user can enter information in the Test Steps and Test Results fields. The user cannot modify the Priority, Project, Sub-system or Module fields. The Save button can be clicked to save the information to the database without progressing the fault, or alternatively the Fixed or Not Fixed buttons can be clicked to save the information to the database and progress the fault report to the next status value. Whichever of the three buttons is clicked, the values in the following fields will be updated automatically: Tester, Test Date and Status.

Screen rules

It is assumed that a user can select an existing fault report in another screen and then enter the screen to be designed in this case study to view the full details of the fault report. Alternatively a user granted the Originator role can enter this screen to create a new fault report. The other screen will be referred to as the main screen, but it will not be designed in this case study.

There are four categories of screen rules: entry and exit events; items with varying behaviour; items with constant behaviour; and screen modes.

Entry and exit events

- The screen can be entered by clicking the New button in the main screen if the user has a role of Originator. This will allow a user to create a new FR.

- The screen can be entered by selecting an existing FR and clicking the View button in the main screen. This will allow a user to view and possibly edit an existing FR.

- The screen can be exited by clicking the Close button.

Items with varying behaviour

Header items

- The **Priority** field is enabled when the FR has a status of *New* and the user has a role of *Originator*, or when the FR has a status of *Raised* or *Not Fixed* and the user has a role of *Analyst*.

- The **Project** field is enabled when the FR has a status of *New* and the user has a role of *Originator*, or when the FR has a status of *Raised* or *Not Fixed* and the user has a role of *Analyst*.
  Note: after a project is selected, it is only possible to select another project – it is not possible to clear the field. This is desired behaviour because the Project field must contain a value when the fault report is saved to the database.

- The **Sub-system** field is enabled when a project has been selected in the Project field and when the FR has a status of *New* and the user has a role of *Originator*, or when a project has been selected in the Project field and when the FR has a status of *Raised* or *Not Fixed* and the user has a role of *Analyst*.
  When a different project is selected in the Project field, the value in the Sub-system field is set to <Unknown> because the range of available sub-systems is determined by the project selected.

- The **Module** field is enabled when a sub-system has been selected in the Sub-system field and when the FR has a status of *New* and the user has a role of *Originator*, or when a sub-system has been selected in the Sub-system field and the FR has a status of *Raised* or *Not Fixed* and the user has a role of *Analyst*.
  When a different project or sub-system is selected, the value in the Module field is set to <Unknown> because the range of available modules is determined by the sub-system selected.

Description tab-card items

- The **Description** field is enabled when the FR has a status of *New* and the user has a role of *Originator*.

- The **Create** button is enabled when the FR has a status of *New*, the user has a role of *Originator*, the Description field contains some text and the Project field contains a value. (The Sub-system and Module fields are not mandatory.)

Analysis tab-card items

- The **Analysis** field is enabled when the FR has a status of *Raised* or *Not Fixed* and the user has a role of *Analyst*.

- The **Save** button is enabled when the FR has a status of *Raised* or *Not Fixed*, the user has a role of *Analyst*, and a change is made to one or more of the following fields: Priority, Project, Sub-system, Module or Analysis. The button is disabled after it is clicked.

- The **Implement** button is enabled when the FR has a status of *Raised* or *Not Fixed* and the user has a role of *Analyst*.

- The **Reject** button is enabled when the FR has a status of *Raised* or *Not Fixed* and the user has a role of *Analyst*.

Implementation tab-card items

- The **Reason for Fault and Solution** field is enabled when the FR has a status of *Evaluated* and the user has a role of *Implementer*.

- The **Save** button is enabled when the FR has a status of *Evaluated*, the user has a role of *Implementer* and the Reason for Fault and Solution field is modified. The button is disabled after it is clicked.

- The **Test** button is enabled when the FR has a status of *Evaluated* and the user has a role of *Implementer*.

Testing tab-card items

- The **Test Steps** field is enabled when the FR has a status of *Implemented* and the user has a role of *Originator*.

- The **Test Results** field is enabled when the FR has a status of *Implemented* and the user has a role of *Originator*.

- The **Save** button is enabled when the FR has a status of *Implemented*, the user has a role of *Originator* and the Test Steps or Test Results fields are changed. The button is disabled after it is clicked.

- The **Fixed** button is enabled when the FR has a status of *Implemented* and the user has a role of *Originator*.

- The **Not Fixed** button is enabled when the FR has a status of *Implemented* and the user has a role of *Originator*.

Items with constant behaviour

Header items

- The **FR Number** field is always disabled. When the status is New the field will be blank. When the Create button is clicked, a unique FR number will be created and displayed in the field.

- The **Status** field is always disabled. The field will display the status of the FR. The status will be updated if the FR is progressed by a user.

- The **Close** button is always enabled.

Description tab-card items

- The **Originator** field is always disabled. When the Create button is clicked the name of the user who has created the FR will be filled in automatically.

- The **Date** field is always disabled. When the Create button is clicked the current date is filled in automatically.

Analysis tab-card items

- The **Analyst** field is always disabled. The name of the user will be filled in automatically when the Save, Implement or Reject buttons are clicked.

- The **Date** field is always disabled. The date will be filled in automatically when the Save, Implement or Reject buttons are clicked.

Implementation tab-card items

- The **Implementer** field is always disabled. The name of the user will be filled in automatically when the Save or Test buttons are clicked.

- The **Date** field is always disabled. The date will be filled in automatically when the Save or Test buttons are clicked.

Testing tab-card items

- The **Tester** field is always disabled. The name of the user will be filled in automatically when the Save, Fixed or Not Fixed buttons are clicked.

- The **Date** field is always disabled. The date will be filled in automatically when the Save, Fixed or Not Fixed buttons are clicked.

Screen modes

Looking at the screen rules for items with varying behaviour, it is apparent that the combination of user role and fault report status determine which user interface objects are enabled and which are disabled (the user roles and status values have been italicized in the screen rules above to emphasize this point). There are five combinations of role and status that make certain objects enabled:

1   If a user has a role of **Originator** and the fault report displayed in the screen has a status of **New** then objects in the **header** and **Description** tab-card are enabled.

2   If a user has a role of **Analyst** and the fault report displayed in the screen has a status of **Raised** then objects in the **header** and **Analysis** tab-card are enabled.

3   If a user has a role of **Analyst** and the fault report displayed in the screen has a status of **Not Fixed** then objects in the **header** and **Analysis** tab-card are enabled.

4   If a user has a role of **Implementer** and the fault report displayed in the screen has a status of **Evaluated** then objects in the **Implementation** tab-card are enabled.

5   If a user has a role of **Originator** and the fault report displayed in the screen has a status of **Implemented** then objects in the **Testing** tab-card are enabled.

Any other combination of user role and fault report status will not allow the user to modify data displayed in the screen. Thus, the screen can be in one of six different modes – the five listed above plus a 'read-only' mode. These modes broadly determine the behaviour of the screen.

Statechart design

The best starting point in the design of the statechart for the screen is to consider the modes identified in the screen rules. It is important to identify modes because they often act as the high-level states in a design. The six modes can be clustered into two groups: the five modes that are related to viewing fault reports that already exist in the database and the mode that is related to creating a new FR (see Figure 11.6).

There are two ways to enter the screen. If a user is granted the Originator role then the New button in the main screen can be clicked. Alternatively, a user can select an existing fault report and click the View button in the main screen. When a user creates a new FR in the database (by clicking the Create button in the Description tab-card) the status of the FR is set to Raised and the details of the FR remain displayed in the screen. Thus, after a user clicks the Create button, the screen behaves as if the user has just selected an existing FR in the main screen and clicked the View button. The two groups of modes form the basis of the screen's high-level statechart shown in Figure 11.7.

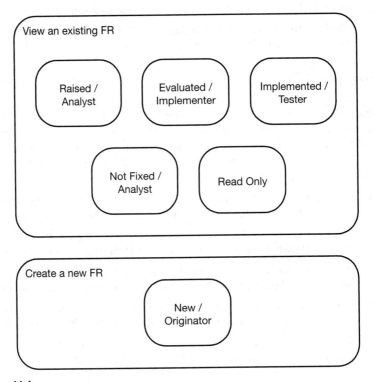

Figure 11.6

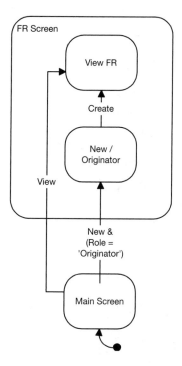

Figure 11.7

If a user is in the process of creating a new FR and clicks the Close button, then an alert message should be displayed reading 'Do you want to abandon creating this FR' with two buttons: OK and Cancel. If the Cancel button is clicked then the user will be able to continue entering the details of the new FR, but if the OK button is clicked then the user will be returned to the main screen (see Figure 11.8).

A user can also click the Close button when viewing an existing FR. If the user has not entered any information in the screen when the Close button is clicked, then the screen will be exited immediately. If the user has entered information in the screen and the Close button is clicked, then the alert message: 'Do you want to save the changes you have made?' will be displayed along with the following buttons: Yes, No and Cancel. Clicking Yes or No will cause the screen to be exited, but clicking Cancel will not. The transition from the View FR state back to the main screen is included in Figure 11.8, but the precise details of the transitions will be delayed until later in the design process.

The View FR state in Figure 11.8 is an abstract view of the five modes identified in Figure 11.6. When a user selects an FR in the main screen and clicks the View button, the fault report is fetched from the database and displayed in the screen. The status of the fault report and the roles granted to the user will determine the mode the screen will operate in initially. The mode will be used to determine which fields the user will be allowed to edit. To model this behaviour in a statechart, a transient state can be used with event arrows containing conditions that check the status of the fault report and the roles granted to the user (see Figure 11.9). Notice that the event arrows leaving the transient state are prioritized to ensure that the Read Only state is only entered as a last resort.

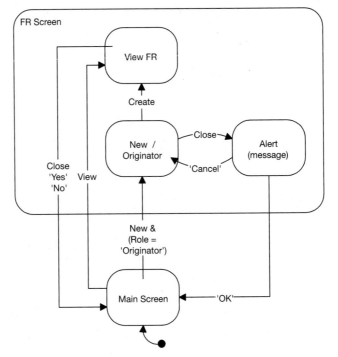

Figure 11.8

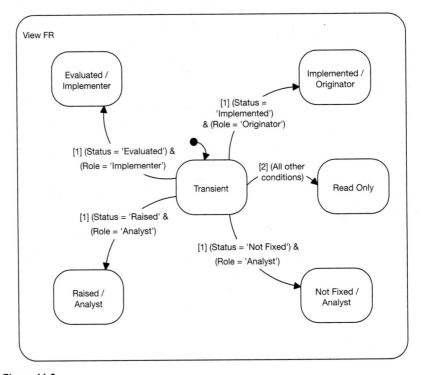

Figure 11.9

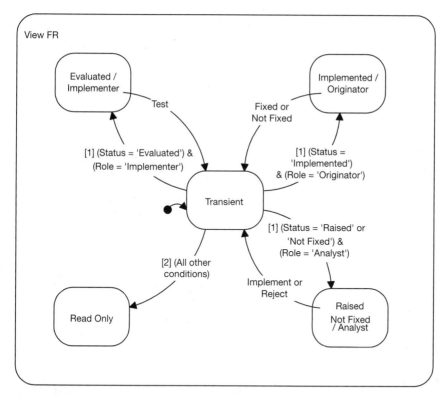

Figure 11.10

When the software is in any of the four states that will allow a user to enter information in the fault report, a user can progress the fault by clicking an appropriate button. For instance, if the software is in the Evaluated / Implementer role then the user will be allowed to click the Test button when the fault has been fixed. Clicking the Test button indicates that the fix is ready to be tested and the status of the FR will be updated to Implemented. If clicking the Test button causes a transition to the transient state (in addition to causing the status value to be updated) then the roles granted to the user and the status of the fault report can be used to determine the next state. The statechart with the events that progress a fault report to the next state in the life-cycle are shown in Figure 11.10.

Notice that the Raised/Analyst and the Not Fixed/Analyst states have been merged into one. When faults with a status of Raised or Not Fixed are displayed in the screen, the user interface objects behave in exactly the same way. When an FR has either status value, an analyst is required to decide whether the fault should be rejected or implemented. Thus the two states can be combined into a single state.

The statechart shown in Figure 11.10 provides a lower-level view of the View FR state shown in Figure 11.8. The two statecharts can be combined to provide a single high-level statechart for the user interface screen (see Figure 11.11). It is important to appreciate that states 3, 4, 5 and 6 each have lower levels of detail which define the precise behaviour of the user interface objects.

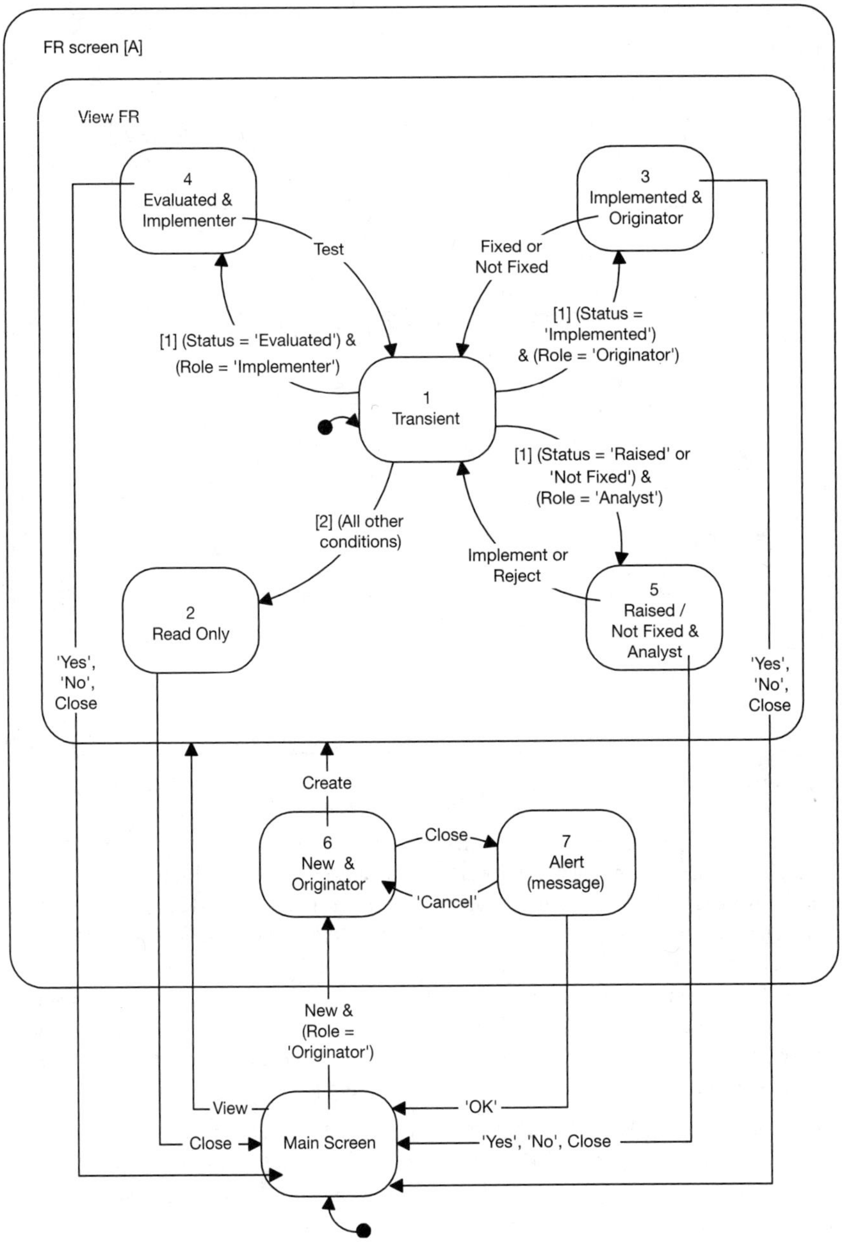

Figure 11.11

State 1 is a transient state. It does not enable or disable any screen items. It is used to switch to the next state after an FR has been progressed. Using this state reduces the number of event arrows required in the diagram.

State 2 is a read-only state. All the screen items are disabled with the exception of the Close button. When the application is in this state, a user can view the details of the FR in all of the tab-cards, but none of the information can be modified.

States 3, 4, 5 and 6 each define certain screen items to be enabled and others to be disabled. For instance, when in state 6 the Description field is enabled but in the other three states it is disabled. Other screen items can be either enabled or disabled as the user interacts with them. For instance, in state 6, if the Project field contains a value then the Sub-system field is enabled, but if the Project field is blank then the Sub-system field is disabled. To control such behaviour, a lower-level statechart is required for each of the states 3, 4, 5 and 6.

State 6: New and Originator

From the screen rules, it is apparent that the following screen items can be enabled when the application is in state 6: Priority, Project, Sub-system, Module, Description and the Create button. The Priority, Project and Description fields are enabled throughout the time the application is in state 6, but the other items switch between enabled and disabled as the user interacts with the screen.

The Sub-system field only becomes enabled in state 6 when a user selects a project. It is not possible for a user to clear the Project field, it is only possible to select a different project. Thus, once the Sub-system field has become enabled, it cannot be disabled. This behaviour is captured in Figure 11.12.

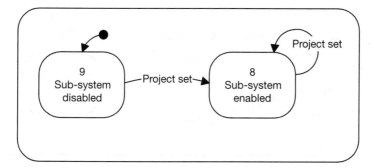

Figure 11.12

The Module field only becomes enabled in state 6 when a user selects a sub-system. If the sub-system is set to Unknown or the Project is changed, then the Module should be disabled again until the Sub-system field is set. The behaviour of the field is modelled by the state-chart in Figure 11.13.

The Create button is enabled in state 6 when a user sets a value in the Project field and enters some text in the Description field. The Create button can only be disabled by deleting the text in the Description field – the value in the Project field cannot be cleared, only modified. When the Create button is clicked, the status is updated to Raised and the fault report is created in the database. The application then enters state 1 – the transient state – in the View FR state. This behaviour is modelled in the statechart in Figure 11.14.

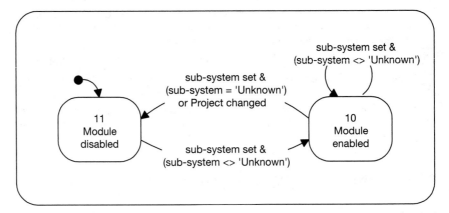

Figure 11.13

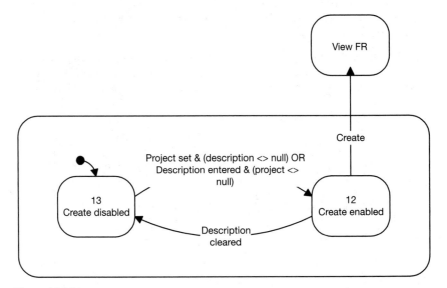

Figure 11.14

The three statecharts can be brought together as concurrent parts of the same statechart (see Figure 11.15). Notice that if the Close button is clicked, then the alert message 'Do you want to abandon creating this FR?' with the buttons OK and Cancel is displayed in state 7. If the user clicks the Cancel button then the history mechanism is used to return to the last states in state 6, otherwise if OK is clicked then the main screen is entered.

The full details of the states, events and actions shown in Figure 11.15 are given in Appendix D.

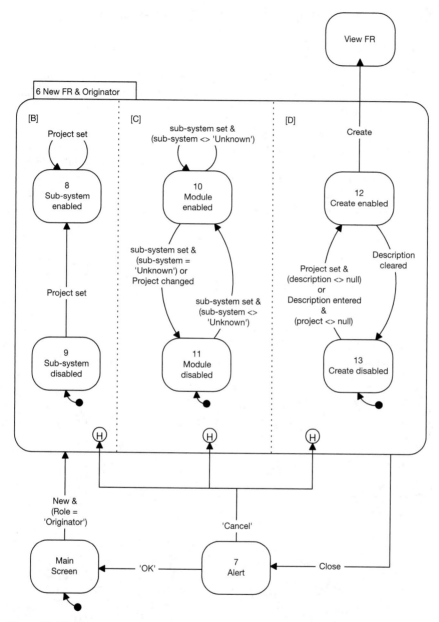

Figure 11.15

State 5: Raised or Not Fixed and Analyst

From the screen rules, the Priority field, Project field, Sub-system field, Module field, Analysis field, Save button, Implement button and Reject button can all be enabled in state 5. The Priority field, Project field, Sub-system field, Analysis field, Implement button and Reject button are always enabled, but the other items can be enabled or disabled depending on the events supplied by the user.

The Module field is disabled if the Sub-system field is set to Unknown, otherwise the Module field is enabled. If the Sub-system field contains a value and the Module field is enabled, then if a user changes the Project field, both the Sub-system and Module fields will be set to Unknown and the Module field will be disabled. This behaviour is modelled by the statechart in Figure 11.16. Notice that the default start state is a transient state because the Sub-system field, for the FR displayed in the screen, may or may not be set to Unknown when it is retrieved from the databases.

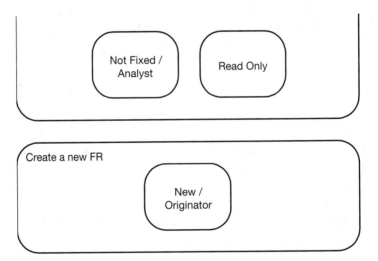

Figure 11.16

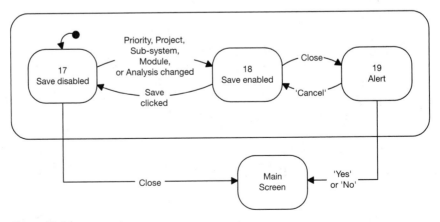

Figure 11.17

The Save button in the Analysis tab-card is enabled in state 5 when a user modifies any of the values in the Priority, Project, Sub-system, Module or Analysis fields. When the Save button is clicked, it becomes disabled again. If the Close button is clicked when there are changes made to the fields but not saved to the database, then an alert message is displayed reading 'Do you want to save the changes you have made?' with three buttons: Yes, No and Cancel. If Yes or No are clicked then the main screen is entered. This behaviour is modelled in the statechart shown in Figure 11.17.

The two statecharts can be brought together as concurrent parts of a statechart that defines the behaviour of the application in state 5 (see Figure 11.18). Notice that if the Implement or Reject buttons are clicked, then any changes made to the fault report are saved to the database, the status value is updated to the appropriate value and then transient state 1 is entered.

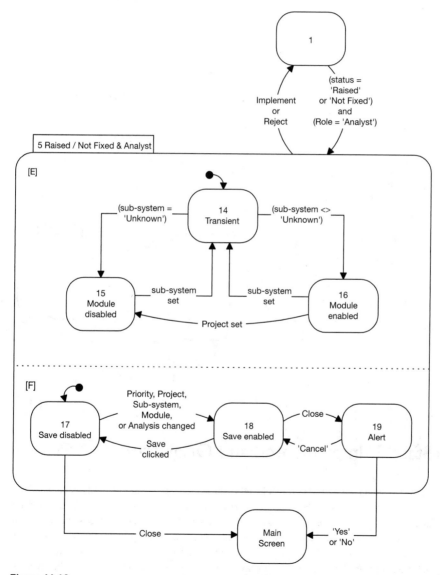

Figure 11.18

State 4: Evaluated and Implementer

In state 4, when the fault report displayed in the screen has a status of Evaluated and the user has the Implementer role granted, the Reason field and Test button are enabled. The Save button on the Implementation tab-card is enabled when the Reason field is changed and it is disabled when the Save button is clicked (see Figure 11.19). If the Close button is clicked with changes not saved to the database then an alert message is displayed giving the user the option to save the changes before entering the main screen. If the Test button is clicked, then any changes made to the fault report are saved to the database, the status is updated to Implemented and transient state 1 is entered.

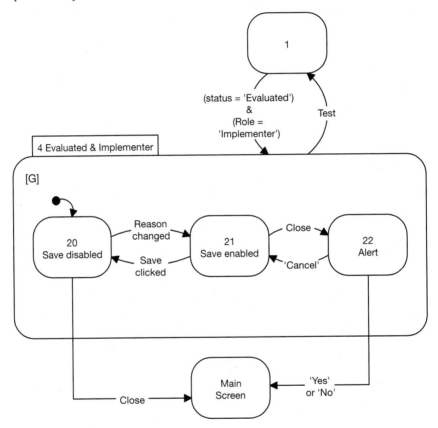

Figure 11.19

State 3: Implemented and Originator

In state 3, when the fault report displayed in the screen has a status of Implemented and the user has the Originator role granted, the Test Steps field, Test Results field, Fixed button and Not Fixed button are enabled. The Save button on the Testing tab-card is enabled when the Test Steps or Test Results fields are changed, and disabled when the Save button is clicked (see Figure 11.20). If the Close button is clicked with changes not saved to the database then an alert message is displayed giving the user the option to save the changes

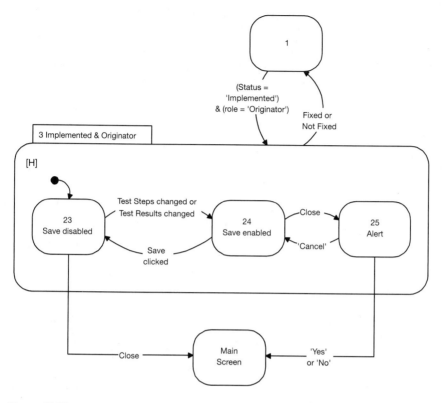

Figure 11.20

before entering the main screen. If the Fixed or Not Fixed buttons are clicked, then any changes made to the fault report are saved to the database, the status is updated accordingly and transient state 1 is entered.

Summary

The statechart that controls the fault reporting application has two levels of detail. The higher-level statechart (Figure 11.11) defines the life-cycle through which an FR can be progressed. The lower-level statecharts define the behaviour of the screen when it displays fault reports at different stages in the life-cycle. The design will allow the software to be changed easily if the behaviour of the screen is made more complex in any stage of the life-cycle, or the life-cycle itself is changed. For instance, the application could be enhanced to make the life-cycle of faults configurable for different projects. In other words, faults raised against different projects could be progressed through different life-cycles. The life-cycle for a project could be set up by the administrator of the application.

To make this change, new high-level states could be added for new roles and status values. The conditions that determine which high-level state is entered from transient state 1 could be changed to take into account the life-cycle being used. This would be a relatively straightforward change to both the design and the code of the high-level statechart, but the design of the lower-level statecharts would not be affected.

Coding the application without a statechart would not provide the same level of flexibility during the maintenance phase of the software. Significant changes to the software, such as making the life-cycle configurable, would be very difficult to achieve.

Chapter 12
Case study 3:
A student database

Introduction

The purpose of this chapter is to use a third case study to demonstrate the statechart approach. The case study makes use of most aspects of the statechart notation and, in particular, it demonstrates how two screens, controlled by separate statecharts, can be designed to interact together. This is an important part of the technique because it allows a number of developers to work simultaneously on different parts of the same user interface.

Readers will notice that one of the screens in this case study has a similar appearance to the screen in the fault reporting application of case study 2. Despite the similarity of the screen layout, the behaviour of the screen and the design of the underlying statechart are considerably different.

High-level requirements and main tasks of the users

This case study is an application that supports the admissions process of A level students in a college of further education. The user interface is not a complete application and future versions are likely to support a greater range of tasks.

The application has been designed to support the working procedures of a real college. Currently, the college manages the admissions process using a spreadsheet, but it requires an application to allow several users to access the information simultaneously and also to improve the quality of the information held by the college. The only people who will use the application will be from a small team of tutors who are responsible for the admissions process, so there will only be one type of user. The main tasks of the users will be as follows:

1   Students apply to the college by submitting paper application forms. The basic details of the student will be entered into the system and an interview date will be set. A letter and address label will be produced using Word and posted to the student.

2   All students are interviewed and further details are entered into the system after the interview. On the basis of the interview, the interviewer can reject the student, make a conditional offer, or make a firm offer. A conditional offer requires the student to achieve the minimum mandatory GCSE grades for entry to the college. A firm offer is made when the student has already achieved the necessary GCSE grades. After the offer has been set in the system, a letter and address label should be produced using Word and the letter posted to the student.

3   On receipt of an offer letter, the student is required to confirm whether they wish to accept or decline the offer. When this confirmation is received by the college, the details should be entered into the system.

4   After the results of the GCSE exams have become available, all students who have accepted a firm or conditional offer must either enrol with the college or withdraw from it. This information should also be entered into the system.

5   The application will be used to monitor the students throughout the time they are at the college. In particular, the college wants to keep a record of the exam results achieved or, alternatively, the point in the course at which students withdraw from studying individual subjects. It should be possible to generate various reports related to exam results and withdrawal rates.

Each application passes through the stages shown in Figure 12.1.

The screens of the user interface

The application will have two screens: a Summary screen and a Details screen. The Summary screen will provide a list of all the students whose details have been added to the system. It will only provide a one-line summary of the information held for each student. The second screen, the Details screen, will be entered from the Summary screen and will provide the user with the complete details of a student selected in the Summary screen. The Details screen will only show the details of one student at a time.

The purpose of having a Summary screen is to allow the users to filter the student records in various ways and then generate reports based on the filtered list. Although this filter and report facility is not available in the first version (that is, the version to be designed in this chapter) a subsequent version is intended to provide such a facility.

The high-level statechart

The starting point with any statechart design is to identify the top-level states. In most cases, these correspond to the main screens in the application. The events that cause navigation between the screens should be identified, but the precise details of those events are not necessary at this stage. For instance, it may be obvious that certain transitions between high-

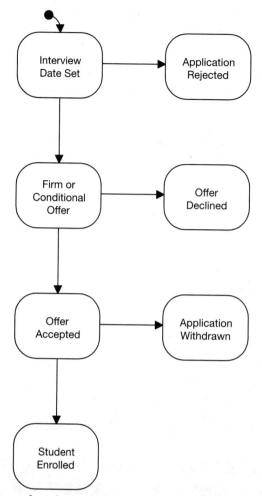

Figure 12.1 The stages of a student application.

level states will only be possible if certain conditions are true. Low-level details such as this can be filled in later. At this point in the design process, we just need to identify the events that will cause the application to move from one high-level state to another.

The high-level states for the student database application are shown in Figure 12.2. The application will start off in the Summary screen which is indicated by the default starting arrow. A user can enter the Details screen by clicking a button labelled New or a button

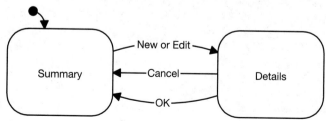

Figure 12.2

labelled Edit. The New button is clicked when a user wants to create a new student record and the Edit button is clicked when a user wants to view and possibly modify an existing student record. Clearly, the software must be designed to ensure that it is only possible to enter the Details screen using the Edit button when a student has been selected in the Summary screen. However, this level of detail is not necessary at this point in the design process and will not be considered until the Summary screen is designed in detail.

The Details screen will contain an OK button and a Cancel button. Clicking either button will cause the Summary screen to be displayed. Again, this is an oversimplification because it will be necessary to perform some data validation when the OK button is clicked. The details of this validation will be considered when the Details screen is designed later in the process.

Having identified the high-level states, the next task is to consider each of the two states in more detail. The Summary screen will be designed first, since this is the screen that is first entered when the application is started.

The Summary screen

The Summary screen contains a scrolling list that is used to display one-line summaries of each student record entered in the system (see Figure 12.3). The list displays the name of the student, the A level subjects that the student will be studying and status information related to the admissions process. (The admissions process and the meaning of the offer, acceptance and enrolment statuses will become apparent when the Details screen is designed.) A user can highlight a particular student record by clicking the record in the list with the mouse pointer. Only one student record can be highlighted at a time.

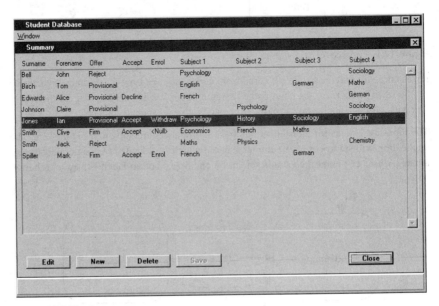

Figure 12.3 The Summary screen.

There are five buttons in the screen and the purpose of each is described below.

When the **Edit** button is clicked, the Details screen is displayed in place of the Summary screen and it will contain all the details of the student record currently highlighted in the Summary screen.

When the **New** button is clicked, this also causes the Details screen to be displayed, but the fields in the screen will be blank and ready for a user to create a new student record.

When the **Delete** button is clicked, the student record highlighted in the Summary screen will be deleted.

Any changes made to the student records using the Edit, New or Delete buttons are not permanent changes to the underlying database until they have been explicitly saved. The purpose of the **Save** button is to allow a user to save the work they have done and make those changes visible to other users of the system. (When a user modifies, creates or deletes student records, the necessary changes are made to the underlying database tables, but those changes are not permanent changes. An application can be designed either to issue a commit command which will make any changes made to the database permanent, or a rollback command which will undo any changes made to the database since the last commit command was issued. The purpose of the Save button is to issue a commit command to the database, to make the changes that have been made to database records permanent.)

The **Close** button is used to exit the application. If changes have been made to the student records, but have not been saved using the Save button, then the user will be given the opportunity to save these changes to the database before exiting the application.

Screen rules

The first step to designing a statechart for the Summary screen is to identify the screen rules. There are four categories of rules: user interface objects with constant behaviour; user interface objects with varying behaviour; entry and exit events; and screen modes.

User interface objects with constant behaviour

- The **scrolling list** has constant behaviour. A user can click a student record and that student will be highlighted. Only one row in the list can be selected at a time. The default behaviour of a scrolling list does not need to be modified for the application.

- The **New** button causes the Details screen to be displayed and allows a student record to be created. The button is enabled all the time and its behaviour does not vary.

User interface objects with varying behaviour

- When the **Edit** button is clicked the Details screen is displayed and details of the student highlighted in the Summary screen are displayed in it. The Edit button is enabled when student records are displayed in the Summary screen scrolling list and is disabled when there are no student records in the scrolling list.
  Note: this rule is based on the assumption that a record will always be highlighted if there are one or more records in the scrolling list. In other words, it relies on the default behaviour of the scrolling list object which ensures that a record is always highlighted when there are records in the list.

- The **Delete** button deletes the student record that is currently highlighted in the scrolling list. The Delete button is enabled when student records are displayed in the scrolling list and is disabled when there are no student records in the scrolling list.

- The **Save** button is used to commit changes made to the student records by a user. The Save button is disabled when the application is first started. The button becomes enabled when the Delete button is clicked or the OK button is clicked in the Details screen. After the user clicks the Save button, the button is disabled again.

- The **Close** button is used to exit the application. If the user has not made any changes to the student records, or changes have been made but they have been saved to the database, then the application is closed immediately when the Close button is clicked. If the user has made changes to the student records but has not clicked the Save button, then when the Close button is clicked a modal alert message will be displayed reading: 'Do you want to save the work you have done?' along with three buttons: Yes, No and Cancel.

Entry and exit events

- The screen is entered when the application is started.
- The screen is entered when the OK or Cancel buttons in the Details screen are clicked.
- The screen can be exited when the Close button is clicked.
- The screen is exited when the New button is clicked.
- The screen is exited when the Edit button is clicked.

Screen modes

Screen modes are concerned with the screen behaving in different ways depending on some condition such as the type of data displayed, the privilege of the user using the screen and so on. There are no such modes associated with the Summary screen.

Statechart design

Having identified the screen rules the next step is to start designing a statechart. The best starting point is to consider the modes that the screen can be in. However, in the case of the Summary screen, there are no such modes, so we will move on to consider the objects with varying behaviour.

From the screen rules, it is clear that the behaviour of the Edit and Delete buttons is determined by whether a student is selected in the scrolling list or not. If a student is selected, then both buttons are enabled. If a student is not selected then both buttons are disabled. Before this behaviour is specified in a statechart, it is necessary to understand the default behaviour of a scrolling list object. After data is first fetched into the list, the first record is highlighted by default. As the user clicks records, the scrolling list object ensures that one and only one record is highlighted at a time. It is not possible to highlight a blank row if there are records in the list. If there are no records in the list, then the first (blank) row is highlighted and the user cannot highlight any other row.

When the application is started and the Summary screen is entered, all the student records will be fetched from the database and displayed in the scrolling list. If there are no student records in the database, then the Delete and Edit buttons should be disabled. If there are records in the database then the Delete and Edit buttons should be enabled. This behaviour can be modelled by using a transient state as shown in Figure 12.4. On starting the application, the data is fetched from the database into the scrolling list and then state 1 is entered. The conditions on the arrows leaving state 1 are used to determine whether records are displayed in the scrolling list or not. If no student records are fetched from the database then state 2 is entered. If one or more student records are fetched from the database then state 3 is entered. In state 2 the Edit and Delete buttons are disabled and in state 3 the Edit and Delete buttons are enabled. (Note: this is indicated in the diagram by labels such as 'Edit (e)' which indicates the Edit button is enabled and 'Edit (d)' which indicates the Edit button is disabled.)

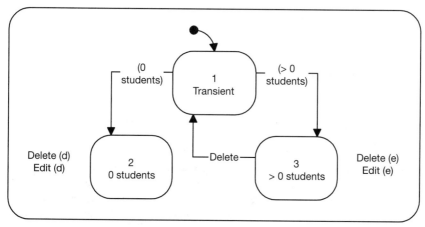

Figure 12.4

The statechart in Figure 12.4 also models what happens when the Delete button is clicked. The Delete button is enabled in state 3 and when it is clicked by a user the currently highlighted record in the scrolling list is deleted both from the screen and the database. The deleted record may have been the only record in the scrolling list. If it was the only record in the list, then the application would have to enter state 2, otherwise it would stay in state 3. The easiest way to model this behaviour is to cause the application to enter the transient state again (state 1) when the Delete button is clicked. The action associated with the Delete event causes the student record to be deleted and the conditions associated with state 1 then determine whether there are any student records left in the scrolling list. The statechart will enter either state 2 or state 3 as appropriate. The event–action table for the statechart is given in Table 12.1.

Note that it is possible for the Delete event not to make use of the transient state 1. Instead, two event arrows could be added. The first would be from state 3 to state 2 and would have a condition checking whether the current record is the only record in the list. That is, the label would be: Delete & (1 student in the scrolling list). The second event arrow would start and end at state 3 and would have a condition checking whether there is more than one record in the list. That is, the label would be: Delete & (> 1 student in the scrolling list). Two event arrows are necessary because both would have the action to delete the record associated with them.

We now return to the screen rules for objects with varying behaviour. It is apparent that the Save button is enabled and disabled based on whether the user has made changes to the student

Table 12.1 The event–action table for the statechart in Figure 12.4.

Current state	Event	Actions	Next state
A			A
–	Start application	Display the Summary screen; Fetch all the student records from the database and display them in the Summary screen scrolling list;	1
1	(0 student records in the scrolling list)		2
1	(> 0 student records in the scrolling list)		3
3	Delete button clicked	Delete the currently highlighted student record from the screen and from the database;	1

records. This can be modelled with two states: a state in which changes have been made to the student records and a state in which changes have not been made to the student records. The application will enter the 'Changes have been made to the student records' state when either the Delete button in the Summary screen is clicked, or the OK button in the Details screen is clicked. When the Save button is clicked, the changes made to the student records will be committed in the database and the application will return to the 'Changes have not been made to the student records' state. This behaviour is modelled by the statechart in Figure 12.5. The statechart starts in state 4, because a user will not have modified any student records when the application is first started.

Notice that the Delete event in this statechart is not intended to cause the highlighted student record to be deleted. The event that causes the record to be deleted is in the previous

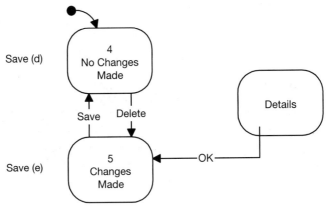

Figure 12.5

Table 12.2 The event–action table for the statechart in Figure 12.5.

Current state	Event	Actions	Next state
5	Save button clicked	Commit changes to the database;	4
4	Delete button clicked		5

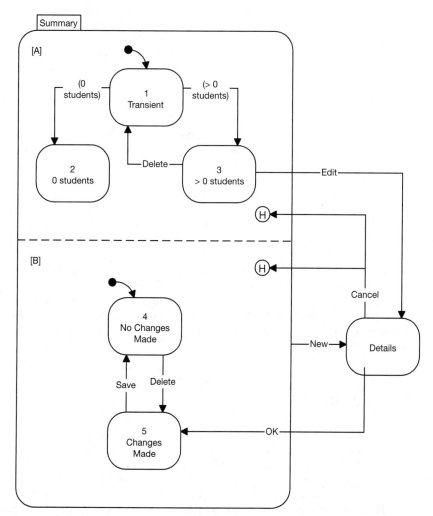

Figure 12.6

statechart in Figure 12.4. The Delete event in Figure 12.5 is a concurrent transition with no actions associated with it (see Table 12.2). It is used to signal that changes have been made to the student records and so the Save button should be enabled.

We now have two statecharts that need to be combined into a single statechart for the summary screen. The two statecharts operate almost independently of each other and so they are best kept separated in concurrent parts of the same statechart (see Figure 12.6).

Notice that events that cause entry to and exit from the Details screen have been included. The Details screen can be entered by clicking the New button in any state (in the screen rules this was identified as an object that does not vary in behaviour). Thus, the New event is attached to the outer state of the Summary screen statechart. The Edit button can only be clicked when it is enabled and it is only enabled in state 3: thus the Edit event from the Summary screen to the Details screen starts in state 3. When the user clicks the Cancel button in the Details screen, any changes made to the student record in the Details screen are not updated in the database and the application returns to the last Summary screen state it was in. Since there are two parts to the Summary screen statechart, the history symbol appears twice. Note that when the OK button is clicked in the Details screen, the application moves to states 1 and 5 in the Summary screen. There is not an arrow to the top part of the statechart, but state 1 is entered because of the default start arrow. Entering state 1 will cause the latest data to be fetched from the database and so the Summary screen will be updated to reflect the changes made in the Details screen.

The only screen rule that has not been addressed is the one related to closing the application by clicking the Close button. The response of the application to this event is determined by whether the screen contains data that has not been saved to the database. That is, if the state-chart is in state 4 when the Close button is clicked, then the application is closed immediately, but if the statechart is in state 5 when the Close button is clicked, then an alert message is displayed which reads: 'Do you want to save the changes you have made?'. The message is displayed with three buttons: Yes, No and Cancel. Clicking the Yes button will cause the changes made to the student records to be committed and then the application will close. Clicking the No button will cause the changes made to the student records to be rolled back (undone) and then the application will close. Clicking the Cancel button will not cause the application to close and the changes made to the student records will be left unchanged in the database. The statechart that captures this behaviour is shown in Figure 12.7 and the event–action table for the Close event is given in Table 12.3. Notice that buttons that appear in alert message windows are distinguished from screen buttons by being surrounded by single quotes.

The Details screen

The Details screen allows a user either to create a new student record or to edit an existing student record selected in the Summary screen. The Details screen contains all the details related to one student and because of the volume of this information, the screen makes use of tab-cards. The OK and Cancel buttons are at the bottom of the screen and are always visible. The information about a student has been grouped into four related areas: A Levels, GCSEs, Address and Interview.

The A Levels tab-card

The A Levels tab-card (see Figure 12.8) is used to display the A level subjects that the student will be studying at the college. The timetable at the college is based on a simple block structure. There are four blocks and each block contains a range of subjects. The subjects in each block are all taught at the same time, so a student may choose one subject from each block. It is expected that each student will study at least two A levels, but the software should not impose this minimum. The college will not allow a student to study more than four A level subjects.

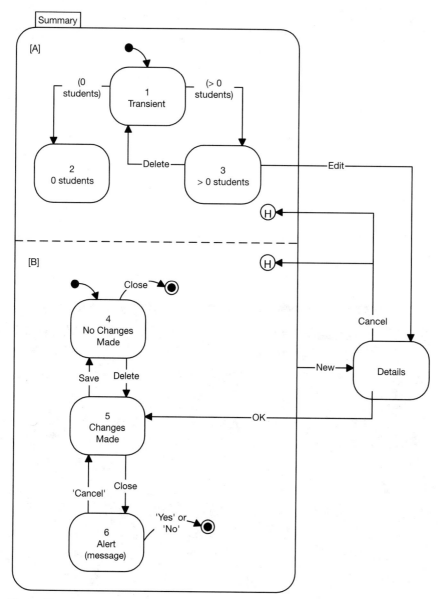

Figure 12.7

Table 12.3 The event–action table for the Close event in Figure 12.7

Current state		Event	Actions	Next state	
A	B			A	B
	4	Close	Close the application		–
	5	'Close' button clicked	State 6 alert message parameter: 'Do you want to save the work you have done?'		6

Table 12.3 (Cont'd) The event–action table for the Close event in Figure 12.7

Current state		Event	Actions	Next state	
A	B			A	B
	6	'Cancel' button clicked in the alert message window displayed in stage 6			5
	6	'Yes' button clicked in the alert message window displayed in state 6	Commit changes to the database; Close the application;		–
	6	'No' button clicked in the alert message window displayed in state 6	Rollback changes to the database; Close the application;		–

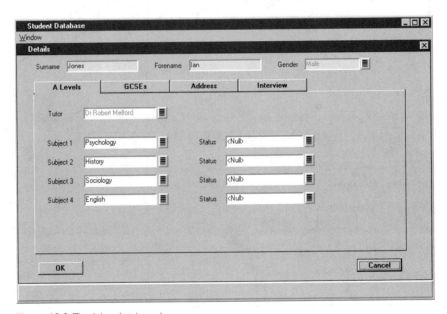

Figure 12.8 The A Levels tab-card.

Adjacent to each subject field is a status field. While a student is studying a subject, the status value is null. If the student withdraws from studying the subject then the status indicates which year of study the student withdraws from the subject (that is, either year 1 or year 2). After taking the A level exams, the A level grade achieved in the subject will be recorded in the status field.

The A levels tab-card also contains the name of a tutor. All students who enrol at the college are assigned a tutor.

The GCSEs tab-card

The GCSEs tab-card is used to record the GCSE subjects that the student has studied before enrolling at the college and the grade achieved in each of them (see Figure 12.9). The tab-card is also used to record the student's previous school and the dates the student started and finished at that school.

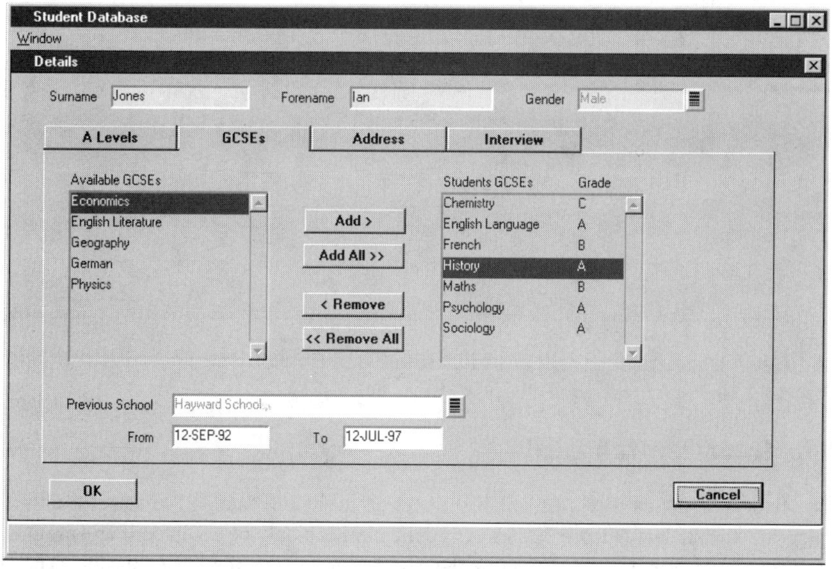

Figure 12.9 The GCSEs tab-card.

When a student's GCSE exam results are available, the subjects and grades achieved by the student are entered into the system using this tab-card. The tab-card contains two lists. The list on the left is a list of all the possible GCSE subjects a student can study and the list on the right shows the GCSE subjects the student has studied. A user can move subjects back and forth between the two lists by using the Add, Add All, Remove and Remove All buttons. Clicking the Add button will cause the currently highlighted subject in the list on the left to be moved to the list on the right. Clicking the Remove button will cause the currently highlighted subject in the list on the right to be moved to the list on the left. The Add All and Remove All buttons can be used to move all the subjects from one list to the other. A grade can be typed in the column to the right of each subject in the list on the right of the screen.

The Address tab-card

The Address tab-card is used to enter the details of the student's address and telephone number (see Figure 12.10). There are three mandatory fields – the House Number, the Street Name and the Town. This information is mandatory because it is needed to create an address label when letters are sent to the students.

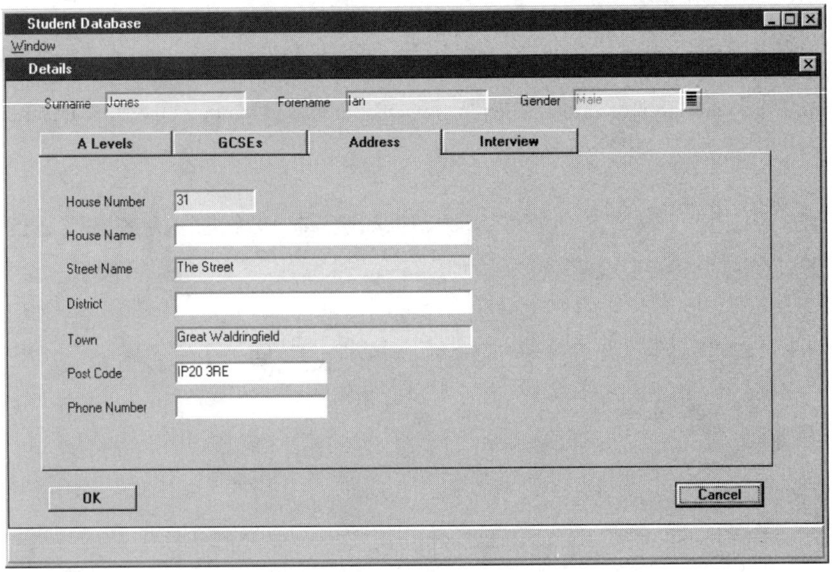

Figure 12.10 The Address tab-card.

The Interview tab-card

The Interview tab-card is used initially to set an interview date and to select a tutor to interview the student (Figure 12.11). An application can only be accepted if an enrolment fee is enclosed with it. A letter inviting the student for an interview (and the address label) can be generated by clicking the Letter button at the top of the screen. The letter appears in Word based on the information entered by the user. The letter can be amended if necessary before it is printed. When the interview letter is sent to the student, a receipt for the enrolment fee is enclosed with the letter. The enrolment receipt number must be entered in the field in the Interview tab-card before the student record can be created.

After a student is interviewed, any additional information about the student that the interviewer feels should be recorded can be entered in the Comments field. The interviewer can Reject a student, make a Provisional offer, or make a Firm offer. If the student has not yet taken the GCSE exams, then a Provisional offer can be made that requires the student to achieve the minimum entry standard of the college (currently five grade C's including Maths and English – but this should not be imposed by the software). If the student has already taken GCSE exams and the results are judged to be sufficient for entry to the college, then a Firm offer can be made to the student. If the student is not considered suitable for the college, then the student is Rejected. After setting the Offer status, the user can click the Letter button adjacent to the field. A standard letter appropriate for the Offer status will appear in Word.

After receiving a Firm or Provisional offer, a student is required either to Accept or Reject the offer. The decision made by the student is entered in the Acceptance status field.

After the GCSE results are available, all students that have accepted Firm or Provisional offers are required to confirm whether they will be studying at the college. The Enrolment status is set to either Enrol or Withdraw as appropriate.

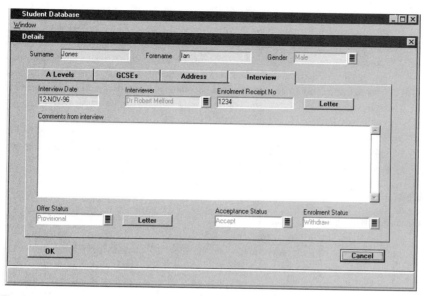

Figure 12.11 The Interview tab-card.

Screen rules

The tab-card group in the Details screen is a user interface object and, like any other object, it has certain default behaviour. The statechart that will be designed to control the Details screen does not have to control the behaviour of the tab-card object. The tab-card object can be created and other user interface objects can be placed on the four tab-cards just as objects would normally be placed on canvases. The objects placed on the tab-cards will appear and disappear as the user selects different tabs. Note that if the tab-cards were enabled and disabled at different points when the application is used then the statechart would be designed to control that behaviour.

Screen modes

The screen only operates in one mode.

Entry and exit events

- The screen can be entered by clicking the Edit button in the Summary screen. This will cause the fields in the Details screen to display the details of the student record currently highlighted in the Summary screen.

- The screen can be entered by clicking the New button in the Summary screen. This will cause the fields in the Details screen to be cleared in readiness for a user to create a new student record.

- The screen can be exited by clicking the Cancel button. This will cause any information entered or modified in the Details screen to be discarded and the data in the underlying database will not be modified.

- The screen can be exited by clicking the OK button. When this is clicked the application must ensure that certain mandatory fields contain values. To help the user, the mandatory fields are yellow and they are: Surname, Forename, Gender, House Number, Street Name, Town, Interview Date, Interviewer and Enrolment Receipt Number. If one or more of the mandatory fields do not contain values then an appropriate alert message must be displayed. After the user acknowledges the message, the screen will not be exited and the user will be able to enter more information in the screen. If all the mandatory fields contain values then, on clicking the OK button, the data in the Details screen will be entered into the database (without being permanently committed at this stage). If the New button was clicked on entry to the screen, then a new student record will be created in the database. If the Edit button was clicked on entry to the screen, then the existing student record will be updated in the database.

User interface objects with constant behaviour

The statechart design is only concerned with user interface objects that have varying behaviour. Many of the objects in the screen are passive fields – they are there to receive values from the user but they do not perform any actions when the user interacts with them. For instance, the fields for the surname, forename and gender are passive fields. The statechart does not have to control the behaviour of such fields, but the user interaction design should ensure that they are enabled, can only receive values of the appropriate type (such as numbers, dates or characters), and list fields have the appropriate values for the user to choose from.

User interface objects with varying behaviour

- The A levels tab-card is used for recording the A level subjects the student will study at the college. Each subject has a status associated with it. (The value in the status field can be one of: A, B, C, D, E, Fail, Withdrawn in year 1, Withdrawn in year 2 or null.) If a subject field is set to null, then the corresponding status field should be set to null and disabled. If a user selects a subject then the corresponding status field should be enabled.

- In the GCSEs tab-card, the four buttons used for moving subjects back and forth between the two lists must be enabled and disabled at the appropriate points. If there are no subjects in the list on the left then the Add and Add All buttons must be disabled. If there are no subjects in the list on the right then the Remove and Remove All buttons must be disabled. In all other circumstances, the buttons should be enabled.

- In the Interview tab-card, the application must ensure that the Offer status, the Acceptance status and the Enrolment status fields are given values in that order. An Acceptance status cannot be set if the Offer status is set to Rejected. An Enrolment status cannot be set if the Acceptance status is set to Decline. The application must not allow the Acceptance and Enrolment statuses to be set at the same time the Offer status is set, because a rejection or offer letter must be sent to the student first. That is, after the Offer status is set, the user must exit the screen and enter it again before being able to set the Acceptance and Enrolment statuses.

Details screen statechart design

From the screen rules, it is evident that there are four independent parts to the Details screen behaviour that need to be designed in a statechart:

1   The subject and status fields in the A levels tab-card.

2   The two lists in the GCSEs tab-card and the buttons for moving subjects between the lists.

3   The Offer, Acceptance and Enrolment status fields.

4   Exiting the screen and the validation that must be performed.

Each of these will be considered in turn before being brought together as a single statechart for the Details screen.

A level subjects

Each A level subject field has a status field associated with it. If the subject field is null then it would not make sense to allow a user to set values in the corresponding status field. Therefore, if the subject field is set to null, then the application should set the status field to null and disable it. If a user then selects a subject in the subject field, then the status field should be enabled. Figure 12.12 shows a simple statechart that models this behaviour.

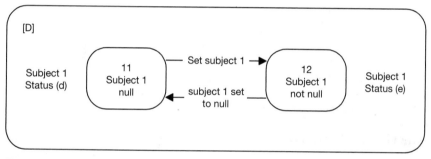

Figure 12.12

A user may enter the Details screen either to create a new student record or to edit an existing one. If a new student record is being created then state 11 will be entered because the subject and status fields will both be null. If an existing record is being edited then the software may enter state 11 or state 12, depending on whether the subject field contains a value after the data for the student has been fetched from the database. A transient state is required, to allow the data to be fetched before entering state 11 or 12 (see Figure 12.13 and Table 12.4). The default start arrow indicates that state 10 is entered regardless of whether the Edit or New button is clicked in the Summary screen. If the Edit button is clicked in the Summary screen then the student record is fetched from the database before state 10 is entered. Alternatively, if the New button is clicked in the Summary screen then the fields in the Details screen are cleared before state 10 is entered.[1] If the subject 1 field is null then state 11 is entered, otherwise state 12 is entered.

There are four A level subject fields and a similar statechart is required for each of them. The fields do not have to work together and so each statechart can be an

---

1.   The actions that will cause the data to be fetched or the screen items to be cleared are associated with the Edit and New buttons being clicked. These events will be modelled in another part of the statechart.

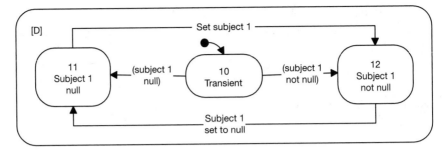

Figure 12.13

Table 12.4 The event–action table for the statechart in Figure 12.13

Current state	Event	Actions	Next State
10	(Subject 1 field = null)		11
10	(Subject 1 field ≠ null)		12
11	A value is set in subject 1 field		12
12	Subject 1 field set to null	Set subject 1 status field to null;	11

independent concurrent part (see Figure 12.14). On entry to the Details screen, the transient states 10, 13, 16 and 19 are entered and the values contained in the A level subject fields determine the next states.

The GCSEs tab-card

The GCSEs tab-card contains two lists: a list of all the possible GCSE subjects and a list of the GCSEs that the student has studied. A user can type the grade achieved by the student in each of the subjects in a column to the right of the subject name in the second list.

Four buttons are provided for moving subjects from one list to the other. At any given time, a subject can appear in only one of the lists. Hence, as one list fills up, the other gradually becomes empty. When one list is empty the buttons that allow a user to move GCSEs from that list should be disabled. For instance, if the list on the left of the screen becomes empty, then the Add and Add All buttons should be disabled. Similarly, if the list on the right of the screen becomes empty, then the Remove and Remove All buttons should be disabled.

From the above description of the buttons, it is clear that the state of the lists determines the state of the buttons. Figure 12.15 shows the four states the two lists can be in and the corresponding state of the buttons ('e' for enabled and 'd' for disabled). Note that the diagram refers to the list on the left of the screen as the 'available' list and the list on the right of the screen as the 'selected' list.

The diagram shows that if there are no GCSEs in either list then all four buttons are disabled (state 22). If there are GCSEs in both lists then all four buttons are enabled (state 25). If there are GCSEs in the available list and none in the selected list, then the Add and Add All buttons are enabled and the Remove and Remove All buttons are disabled (state 23). Finally, if there are no GCSEs in the available list but some in the

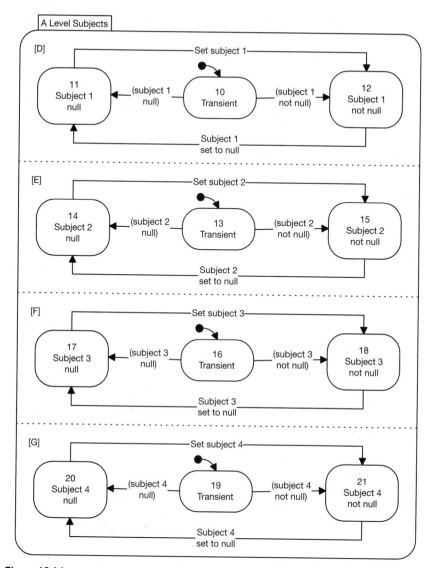

Figure 12.14

selected list, then the Add and Add All buttons are disabled and the Remove and Remove All buttons are enabled (state 24).

As a user interacts with the buttons and moves GCSEs from one list to the other, the application may move from one state to another. The shift from one state to another occurs either when a list becomes empty or when an empty list receives a GCSE. The conditions that will cause such transitions are captured in Figure 12.16. Notice that state 22 is isolated from the other states – there are no transitions entering or exiting it. If there are no GCSEs in either list then the software will always be in state 22. If there are GCSEs in the lists, then it is not possible to remove GCSEs from both lists and so state 22 will not be reached.

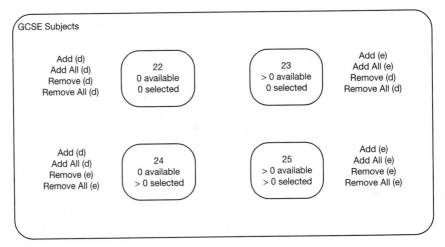

Figure 12.15

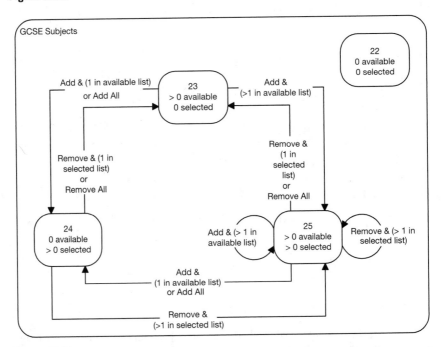

Figure 12.16

When the Details screen is entered, the appropriate state needs to be entered. The initial state could be any one of the four states and therefore a transient state is required (see Figure 12.17). Although this statechart models the required behaviour of the four buttons in the GCSEs tab-card, it is not particularly easy to understand. The events and conditions clutter the diagram unnecessarily.

A more elegant solution is given in Figure 12.18. With this design, the software initially enters state 26 – a transient state. The conditions on the arrows exiting this state test whether the lists are empty or not. The results of these tests determine the next state. Each

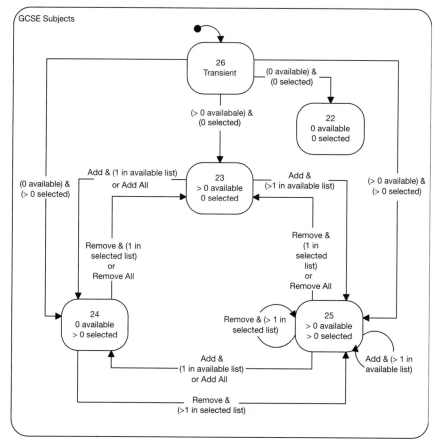

Figure 12.17

time a user clicks one of the four buttons for moving GCSEs between the lists, the software enters the transient state 26 before immediately moving on to the next state. For instance, if the software is in state 25 and the user clicks the Remove button then this event causes the currently selected GCSE subject in the selected list to be moved to the available list. The software then moves to state 26. If the user has just removed the last GCSE from the selected list, then the selected list will be empty and state 23 will be entered. This design is superior because it easy to understand through using a smaller number of event arrows with simpler conditions on the arrows.

Notice that many of the entries in the event–action table for this statechart are very similar. For example, the 'Add button clicked' events which cause transitions 23 to 26 and 25 to 26, both have the same actions and the same end state. An important principle of the technique is to keep such transitions separate from each other – even though it means duplicating code. It is vital that individual events can be identified and changed in isolation from other events if the software is to be maintainable in the long term.

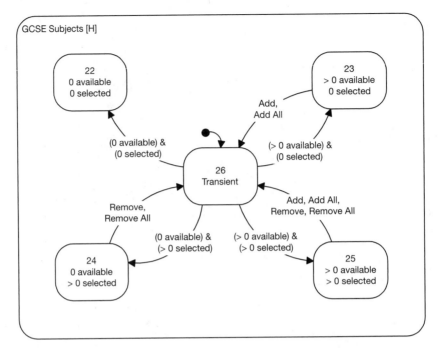

GCSE Subjects [H]

22
0 available
0 selected

23
> 0 available
0 selected

Add,
Add All

(0 available) &
(0 selected)

(> 0 available) &
(0 selected)

26
Transient

Remove,
Remove All

Add, Add All,
Remove, Remove All

(0 available) &
(> 0 selected)

(> 0 available) &
(> 0 selected)

24
0 available
> 0 selected

25
> 0 available
> 0 selected

Figure 12.18

The Offer, Acceptance and Enrolment status fields

There are three phases to enrolling a student in the college. After a student is interviewed, he or she can either be Rejected or be made a Firm or Provisional offer. If an offer is made, a student must either Accept or Decline the offer. If the offer is Accepted, then after the GCSE exam results are available, the student is required either to enrol at the college or withdraw from it.

To support this process, three fields have been included in the user interface. The first is the Offer status which can be set to Reject, Firm or Provisional. The second field is the Acceptance status which can be set to Accept or Decline. And the third field is the Enrolment status which can be set to Enrol or Withdraw. Why three fields? The first two are necessary because if a student accepts an offer, the college wants to know how many Firm and how many Provisional offers have been accepted. The third field is necessary because the college wants an accurate record of how many students withdraw after accepting an offer (this information helps them determine how many offers to make in subsequent years). Despite the apparent simplicity of these user interface objects, the way they work together is not trivial.

The Offer status is the first status that will be set by a user, so we will start the design process with that field. The statechart in Figure 12.19 shows two states. The 'Offer status is null' state represents the application when the Offer status is set to null. If the Offer status is null, then the Letter button is disabled. The 'Offer status set' state represents the application when the Offer status has been set to one of the values: Firm, Provisional or Reject. In this state, the Letter button is enabled and when the user clicks this button, a standard letter based on the offer status will appear in Word. After setting the Offer status, if the user then sets the status back to null then the Letter button will be disabled again.

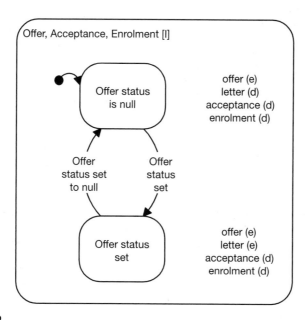

Figure 12.19

Notice that the Acceptance and Enrolment status fields remain disabled throughout this interaction. Given that the letter must be sent to the student and a reply must be received, it would not make sense to allow the user to set either the Acceptance status or the Enrolment status at this stage. The application makes the user leave the screen after setting the Offer status and then re-enter the screen before the other two statuses can be set (to avoid them being set erroneously). Thus, when the Details screen is entered, whether the offer status is set or not will determine whether the user will be able to set the Acceptance and Enrolment statuses. The statechart in Figure 12.20 uses a transient state to model this behaviour.

On entry to the screen, state 27 is entered. If the Offer status is null then state 28 is entered (which was described in Figure 12.19). If the Offer status is set to Rejected then state 30 is entered. In this state, the Acceptance and Enrolment statuses are disabled because the student has been rejected and therefore it would not make sense to allow them to be set. Note that the Offer status field and the Letter button are both enabled in this state – mistakes do happen and the software should not prevent a user from changing the Offer status or sending another letter.

If the Offer status is set to Firm or Provisional then the application moves from state 27 to state 29. In this state, the Offer status field, the Letter button and the Acceptance status field are all enabled. The value contained in the Acceptance status field determines whether the Enrolment status field is enabled or not. If the Acceptance status is set to Decline then the Enrolment field is disabled. If the Acceptance status is set to Accept, then the Enrolment status is enabled. In state 29, there is a lower level of detail (see Figure 12.21). Thus, when the application enters state 29, it also enters state 36 at the lower level of detail. State 36 is a transient state and the value of the Acceptance status determines which of states 34 or 35 is entered.

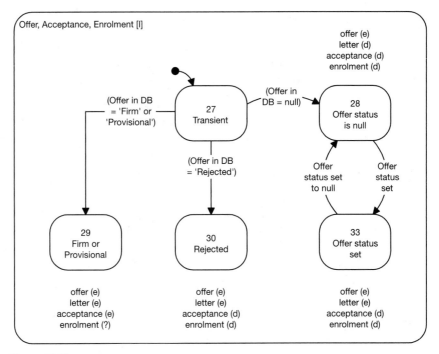

Figure 12.20

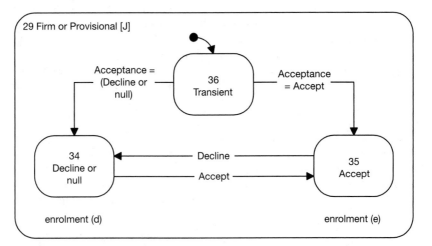

Figure 12.21

When the software is in state 29 or 30, it is possible for the user to modify the Offer status. Figure 12.22 models what happens if the Offer status is modified.

There are two possibilities: the Offer status could be changed to a different value to that which is set in the database, or the Offer status could be set to null. If the Offer status is changed from the database value, then state 31 is entered. If the Offer status is set to null then state 32 is entered. On moving to either state, the Acceptance and Enrolment statuses

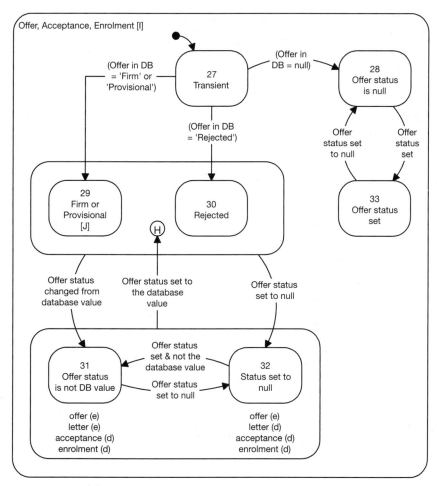

Figure 12.22

should be set to null and in those states the statuses are disabled because a new offer is being made. Notice that states 31 and 32 are very similar to states 33 and 28.

When in state 32, if the Offer status is set to a value that does not match the value held in the database, then state 31 is entered. When in states 31 or 32, if the Offer status is set back to the value in the database then state 29 or state 30 is entered (whichever was last entered).

Entering and exiting the Details screen

The Details screen can be entered by clicking either the Edit or the New button in the Summary screen. If the Edit button is clicked, then the details of the student currently highlighted in the Summary screen are displayed in the Details screen. When the Details screen is exited by clicking the OK button, the existing information in the database is updated with the new information from the Details screen. If the New button is clicked in the Summary screen, then the fields in the Details screen are cleared and a user can enter the details of a new student. When the screen is exited by pressing the OK button, a new student record is created in the database using the information in the Details screen.

The Details screen behaves in the same way regardless of whether the user is creating a new student record or editing an existing one. The only difference is when the screen is first entered and when it is exited by clicking the OK button. Thus, it is necessary for the application to keep track of whether a new record is being created or whether an existing one is being edited, so that the appropriate actions can be performed when the OK button is clicked. It is therefore necessary to have two states, as shown in Figure 12.23 and Table 12.5.

The design in Figure 12.23 is too simplistic because one of the screen rules says that software must check whether certain fields contain values before the screen can be exited by clicking the OK button. This can be achieved by using prioritized events and a parame-

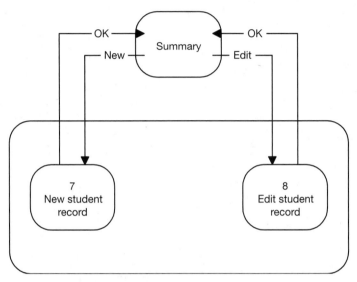

Figure 12.23

Table 12.5

Current state	Event	Actions	Next state	
C			A	B
7	[11] OK button clicked	Create a new student record in the database using the data in the Details screen; Clear the Details screen; Refresh the Summary screen; Highlight the student record just created;	1	5
8	[11] OK button clicked	Update the existing student record in the database for the student currently displayed in the screen; Clear the details screen; Refresh the Summary screen, Highlight the student record just edited;	1	5

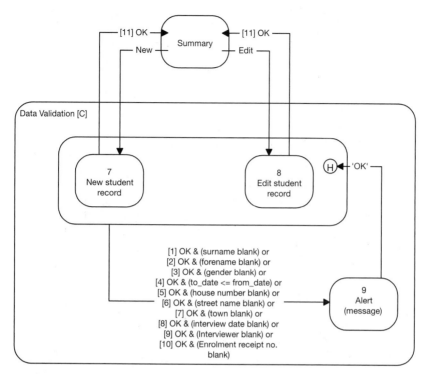

Figure 12.24

terized alert state (see Figure 12.24). When the user clicks the OK button, a number of fields may be blank. By prioritizing the events, only one transition will occur and so the determinism of the statechart is preserved. For instance, if the House Number field and the Interview date fields are blank when the OK button is clicked, then the transition related to the House Number being blank will occur because this transition has a higher priority than the one related to the interview date being blank. In other words, the cursor will be placed in the House Number field and the message 'A house number must be entered before the record can be created' will be passed as a parameter to state 9. The lowest priority transitions are those that return to the Summary screen. These will only occur if all the mandatory fields have values and the 'From' date is before the 'To' date in the GCSEs tab-card.

The Details screen – bringing it all together

The Details screen is clearly composed of four independent parts. These can all be brought together as independent concurrent parts in a single statechart. The Details screen can be represented by the simple high-level statechart shown in Figure 12.25. The details of each of the parts can be considered without a detailed understanding of the other parts.

Summary

The student database application has demonstrated how control can be passed one statechart to another as a user navigates between screens. It has also demonstrated how depth and concurrency can be used effectively to divide an application into simple parts.

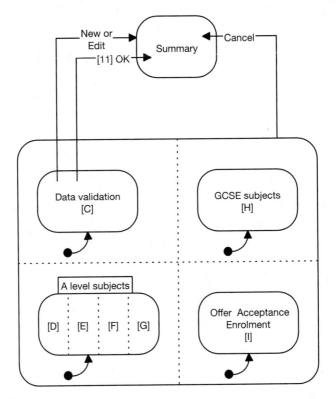

Figure 12.25

The application is not particularly complicated, but the three main advantages of using a statechart to define the behaviour of the application are as follows. Firstly, the statechart provides a precise specification of the behaviour of the user interface – one that is far more concise and far less ambiguous than any natural language equivalent. Secondly, the statechart allows the user interface to be tested quickly and thoroughly (see Chapter 14). Thirdly, the user interface may change in the future and although it may seem simple now, it could easily become significantly more complicated. Even if the future changes are not very large, the very fact that the user interface is precisely specified will allow changes to be made easily.

Part 4
Coding, testing and evaluation

Chapter 13
Coding a statechart

Statecharts can be coded in a number of different ways. This chapter presents a simple technique that results in code that is easy to understand. There are tools available for designing statecharts which allow code to be generated automatically from designs. Although there may be advantages to using such tools, they are not essential. Coding a statechart is a simple process that can be completed very quickly once the design has been finalized.

Throughout this chapter, examples of code will be taken from the student database case study presented in Chapter 12. The code examples have been taken directly from an implementation of the design and modified to avoid irrelevant, language-specific implementation details.

State variables and state hierarchies

It is easy to code a state transition diagram because there is only one current state to keep track of. The current state is stored in a variable which is updated as state transitions occur. Keeping track of the current state of a statechart is not quite as simple because a statechart can have a number of levels of detail and it can also have a number of concurrent parts. For instance, in the statechart shown in Figure 13.1, six state variables are needed to keep track of the current state. At the highest level in the state hierarchy, the statechart can be in state 1, 2 or 3 and this is tracked by state variable A (which is indicated by the letter A in square brackets in the top left hand corner). If the statechart is in state 1 then, at the next level down in the state hierarchy, the statechart must be in either state 4 or state 5 and this is tracked by state variable B. In contrast, state 6 has three concurrent parts and the current state within each state needs to be tracked by a variable. Thus, when the statechart is in state 2 at the highest level and state 6 at the next level down, the current state will be defined by state variables A, C, D, E and F.

In general, a state variable is required for each state that has a lower level of detail below it. For instance, state 1 uses state variable B to track whether the statechart is in state 4 or state 5 when it is in state 1. State 4 does not have a lower level of detail below it and so clearly it does not require a state variable.

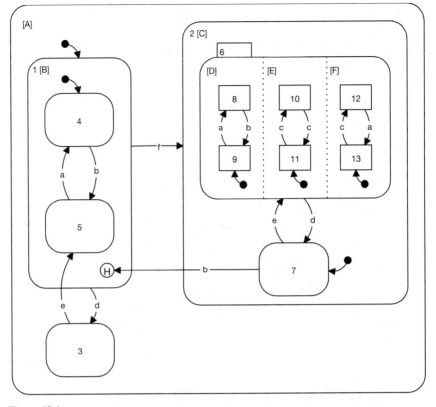

Figure 13.1

Control objects, user interface objects and event handlers

A control object controls and co-ordinates the behaviour of a set of user interface objects. Each user interface object is usually only controlled by one control object. Each control object has a public and a private part. The public part contains a set of procedures which correspond to events that can be supplied to user interface objects which the control object is responsible for. Thus, when a user supplies an event to a user interface object, the event handler for that event simply calls a corresponding procedure belonging to the control object. No other code is contained in the event handlers.

Each control object has a set of state variables which it uses to keep track of the current state of the statechart. The state variables should be hidden from other objects and so they are kept in the private part of the control objects.

A control object also has a set of procedures that define the attributes of user interface objects in different states. There is one state procedure for each state the control object can be in. When a user event causes a state transition to occur in the statechart, the state procedure that corresponds to the destination state is executed. Each state procedure sets the attribute values of certain user interface objects and also updates the appropriate state variable to the current state. The majority of state procedures appear in the private part of control objects. State procedures that appear in the public part of a control object are the ones that can be called by other control objects when control of the application is passed from one control object to another. In other words, the state procedures that appear in the public part of control objects are for those states that are destination states in the event–action tables for the interface between control objects.

Defining the states

In general, when a state is entered, the attributes of user interface objects are modified. Objects can be enabled or disabled, made to move, change size, change colour, disappear, appear and so on. For instance, in the student database case study, when state 29 is entered the Offer Letter button in the Details screen is enabled. Figure 13.2 shows the state procedure for state 29. The procedure updates state variable I to 29 on entry to the procedure and then enables the Offer Letter button.

```
procedure go_state_29 is
    button_pressed number;
begin
    state_variable_I := 29;
    set_item_property('details.offer_status', enabled, true)
    set_item_property('details.bt_offer_letter', enabled, true);
    set_item_property('details.acceptance_status', enabled, true)
end;
```

Figure 13.2

An important feature of a statechart design is that state procedures always set the same attributes to the same values. In other words there should be no conditional statements which could cause different attributes to be set. For instance, if a state procedure contains a conditional statement such as the one contained in Figure 13.3, then there is a problem in the design of the statechart. The attributes of objects should always be set to the same values in a state.

```
procedure go_state_48 is
    button_pressed number;
begin
    state_variable_X := 48;
    if (status = 'Firm') then
        set_item_property('details.bt_offer_letter', enabled, true);
    else
        set_item_property('details.bt_offer_letter', enabled, false);
    end if;
end;
```

Figure 13.3

Transient states

A transient state does not modify the attributes of any user interface objects. A transient state is implemented as a state procedure that updates the appropriate state variable and then tests the conditions that appear on the event arrows that leave the state. For instance, Figure 13.4 is an example of a transient state from the Details screen of the student database case study. The conditions tested in the if statement correspond to the conditions that appear on the event arrows that leave the state in the statechart.

```
procedure go_state_36 is
begin
    state_variable_J := 36;

    if (:details.acceptance_status = 'Accept') then
        go_state_35;
    elsif (:details.acceptance_status = ('Decline') or
        (:details.acceptance_status = '<Null>' then
        go_state_34;
    end if;
end;
```

Figure 13.4

Events, states and conditions

When a user supplies an event to a user interface object, the event handler is made to call a corresponding procedure in the control object. The procedure in the control object uses the current state of the statechart to determine which state transition should occur and thus which actions should be executed. For instance, in the student database case study, when a user clicks the Close button in the Summary screen the application can be in one of two states: No Changes Made (state 4) or Changes Made but not saved (state 5). The when_button_pressed event handler associated with the Close button calls the procedure shown in Figure 13.5.

From the code it is evident that the Close button can be used in two distinct contexts. Importantly, the actions that are executed in these two contexts are clearly identifiable and they are kept separate from each other. If the same event can occur in two different contexts and the resulting actions are identical, it is still strongly advised that the code for the two events are kept separate. By being able to identify the different contexts in which an event can occur, it is possible to update the actions in isolation without fear of introducing unwanted side-effects in the code when the same event occurs in some other context.

When a transition occurs to a state that has a lower level of detail, the code must call the state procedures at all levels in the state hierarchy. For instance, in the Details screen of the student database, state 29 has a lower level of detail. When the transition from transient state 27 to state 29 occurs, a call must be made to both the go_state_29 and the go_state_36

```
when_button_pressed_bt_close
begin

    if (state_variable_B = 4) then -- no changes need saving
        exit_form(no_validate);
    elsif (state_variable_B = 5) then -- changes outstanding that may
    need saving
        go_state_06('Do you want to save the work you have done?');
    end if;
end;
```

Figure 13.5

procedures (see Figure 13.6). State 36 is the default start state at the lower level of detail within state 29. On entry to state 29, state variable I is updated and on entry to state 36, state variable J is updated.

```
procedure go_state_27 is
    current_offer_status char(20);
begin
    state_variable_I := 27;

    current_offer_status := get_offer_status_from_database;

    if (current_offer_status = '<Null>') then
        go_state_28;

    elsif (current_offer_status = ('Firm')
        (current_offer_status = ('Provisional') then
        go_state_29;
        go_state_36;

    elsif (current_offer_status = 'Rejected') then
        go_state_30;

    end if;
end;
```

Figure 13.6

Alert states

It is recommended that all alert states have a parameter for the message that is displayed in the state. When the transition to an alert state occurs, the code that calls the state procedure passes the message to be displayed as a parameter. For instance, in the student database when a user clicks the Close button in the Summary screen, if the user has made changes but not saved them then the application enters alert state 6 (see Figure 13.7).

```
procedure go_state_06(p_alert_message char) is
    button_pressed char(10);
begin
    state_variable_B := 6;

    button_pressed := display_alert('Warning',p_alert_message,'Yes',
    'No','Cancel');

    if (button_pressed = 'Yes') then
        commit; -- make the changes made to the database permanent
        close_application;
    elsif (button_pressed = 'No') then
        rollback; -- undo the changes made to the database
        close_application;
    elsif (button_pressed = 'Cancel') then
        go_state_05;
    end if;
end;
```

Figure 13.7

In this procedure, after state variable B has been updated, the modal alert message shown in Figure 13.8 will be displayed. The user's response to this alert message will determine which state the screen enters next. If the user clicks the Yes button then any changes made by the user to the records in the database will be committed and then the application is closed. If the user clicks No, then any changes made to the database (since the last save point) are undone before the application is closed. If the user clicks the Cancel button then state 5 is entered and no actions are executed.

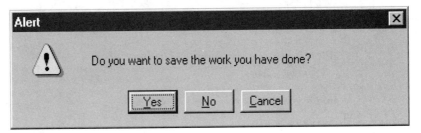

Figure 13.8

Prioritized events

The next state that a statechart enters can be determined by a combination of a user event, the current state and a condition. The condition should be directly related to the state that the event arrow leads to. Several transitions with the same event but different conditions can all leave the same state. When the event occurs, if more than one of the conditions evaluates to true then the behaviour of the statechart will not be deterministic. Non-determinism can be

avoided by prioritizing the events arrows that leave a state. For instance, in the Details
screen in the student database case study, state 7 has many events leaving it with conditions
that could all evaluate to true at the same time. The events have a priority number associated with them (shown in square brackets). The priority number simply determines the
order in which the conditions are evaluated in the conditional statement of the procedure
called by the event handler (see Figure 13.9).

```
declare
      current_student_id students.student_id%type;
begin

   if (state_variable_C in (7,8)) then
      state_variable_c_history := state_variable_C;

      if (:details.surname is null) then   -- [Priority 1]
         go_item('details.surname');
         go_state_09('The student's surname must be entered before ' ||
                  'the record can be created');

      elsif (:details.forename is null) then   -- [Priority 2]
         go_item('details.forename');
         go_state_09('The student's forename must be entered before ' ||
                  'the record can be created');

            .
            .
            .

      elsif (:details.enrolment_receipt_no is null) then   -- [Priority 10]
         go_item('details.enrolment_receipt_no');
         go_state_09('The receipt number for the enrolment fee must ' ||
                  'be entered before the record can be created');

      else -- [Priority 11]
         if (state_variable_C = 7) then   -- New student record
            create_new_student_record;
            display_summary_screen;

            go_state_01;
            go_state_05;

         elsif (state_variable_C = 8) then   -- Modifying existing student record
            update_student_record;
            display_summary_screen;
            go_state_01;
            go_state_05;
         end if;
      end if;
   end if;
end;
```

Figure 13.9

History mechanism

The history mechanism is used to return to the last state entered in a particular group of states. The simplest way to code this is for any event leaving the group of states to store the current state in a variable in the control object. On returning to the group of states, the value of the variable can be used to determine the next state. For instance, in the student database case study, if a user returns to the Summary screen from the Details screen by clicking the Cancel button, then either state 4 or state 5 is entered depending on which was last entered. There are two events that cause the software to move from the Summary screen statechart to the Details screen statechart: the Edit button being clicked and the Add button being clicked. The code that is executed when these events occur is given in Figures 13.10 and 13.11. Notice that, in both cases, the current value of state variable B is stored in the B_history variable. If the user returns to the Summary screen by clicking the Cancel button in the Details screen, then the B_history variable is used to determine the next state (see Figure 13.12).

```
when_button_pressed_bt_edit
begin
    if (state_variable_B in (4,5)) then
            state_variable_B_history := state_variable_B;
            display_details_screen;
            fetch_student_record_from_database;

            go_state_08;
            go_state_10;
            go_state_13;
            go_state_16;
            go_state_19;
            go_state_26;
            go_state_27;
    end if;
end;
```

Figure 13.10

Some readers may have noticed that state variable B is not used in the Details screen and therefore there is no need to store the value of the state variable in a history variable because the value of the state variable will be preserved. Storing the state variable in an explicit history variable is recommended because it is clear in the code that the state value is intended to be preserved.

Concurrency

Statecharts can have a number of independent parts that run together at the same time. Such independent concurrent parts are controlled by separate state variables. For instance, the

```
when_button_pressed_bt_new
begin
        if (state_variable_B in (4,5)) then
            state_variable_B_history := state_variable_B;
            display_details_screen;
            clear_details_screen;

            go_state_07;
            go_state_10;
            go_state_13;
            go_state_16;
            go_state_19;
            go_state_26;
            go_state_27;
        end if;
    end;
```

Figure 13.11

```
when_button_pressed_bt_cancel
begin
        if (state_variable_B_history = 4) then
            clear_details_screen;
            display_summary_screen;
            sc_summary.go_state_01;
            sc_summary.go_state_04;

        elsif (state_variable_B_history = 5) then
            clear_details_screen;
            display_summary_screen;
            sc_summary.go_state_01;
            sc_summary.go_state_05;

        end if;
    end;
```

Figure 13.12

Summary screen in the student database has two concurrent parts. One part is controlled by state variable A and the other by state variable B. When the application is started, both the go_state_01 and go_state_04 procedures are called in order to start the two concurrent parts of the statechart. As events occur, the transitions in the two parts occur independently of each other.

It is possible for an event to trigger a transition in more than one concurrent part of a statechart. For instance, in the Summary screen of the student database, when the statechart is in states 3 and 4 and the user clicks the Delete button, a transition occurs in both parts: state 3 to state 1 and state 4 to state 5. The procedure that is called when the Delete button is clicked is shown in Figure 13.13. Notice that there are two distinct parts to this procedure which correspond to the two concurrent events.

Clearly, it is not possible for the events actually to occur simultaneously, but they are assumed to be concurrent in the sense that it does not matter which event occurs first. In

```
when_button_pressed_bt_delete
begin
    if (state_variable_A = 3) then
        delete_current_record;
        go_state_01;
    end if;

    if (state_variable_B = 4) then
        go_state_05;
    end if;

end;
```

Figure 13.13

other words, it is possible to change the order in which the conditional statements appear in the procedure in Figure 13.13 without affecting the behaviour of the code.

Notice that the action which deletes the student record is associated with only one of the events. It is important that the delete action is associated with the event that causes a transition to state 1, because state 1 is a transient state that should be entered after the student record is deleted. If the delete action was associated with the other event instead (see Figure 13.14), then the software would not work correctly. In this instance, state 1 would be entered before the record had been deleted. The code could be made to work by changing the order in which the conditional statements occur, but this means that the two concurrent parts of the statechart are relying on transitions occurring in a particular order.

```
when_button_pressed_bt_delete
begin
    if (state_variable_A = 3) then
        go_state_01;
    end if;

    if (state_variable_B = 4) then
        delete_current_record;
        go_state_05;
    end if;
end;
```

Figure 13.14

Adding code to help testing and debugging

The advantage of using a statechart to control a user interface is that distinct contexts in which events can occur are easily identifiable. To take full advantage of the statechart approach, it is strongly recommended that debugging code is included in all user interfaces as a matter of course. Such code is invaluable when the software is being unit tested. The performance overhead of including debugging code is negligible, but if it is considered to be a problem then it can be commented out after unit testing has been completed.

A debug window can be included in the software which shows the value of each state variable and each history variable used in the statechart. The code that is executed when the application is started can be modified to cause such a debug window to appear in addition to the main window of the application. For instance, the code in Figure 13.15 is executed when the student database application is started. The first three lines of code cause the debug window shown in Figure 13.16 to be displayed. These lines of code can be commented out after the code has been unit tested.

```
when_application_started
begin
        show_window('wi_debug');
        show_canvas('cv_debug');
        :debug.rbg_mode := 'Step';

        display_summary_screen;
        fetch_student_records_from_database;
        go_state_01;
        go_state_04;
end;
```

Figure 13.15

The state procedures need to be modified to make use of the debug window. When a state procedure is executed, a state variable is updated. The state procedures can be modified to cause the corresponding text item to be updated in the debug window. In this way the current values of the state variables are visible as the application is executed.

There is a slight drawback with this approach. Many transitions can occur as a result of a single user event and transient states can be passed through without a unit tester having time to see the transition in the debug window. It can be difficult to keep track of which transitions are occurring. It is therefore recommended that code is added to the start of each state procedure that will cause an alert message to appear when the procedure is executed (see Figure 13.17). This message simply indicates that a state transition is about to occur and which state variable will be changed. The code that causes such an alert message to be displayed is given in Figure 13.18. Since such messages can be irritating, they can be switched on and off by clicking the Step and Continuous radio buttons in the debug window. The alert messages are only displayed if the Step radio button is clicked.

Being able to switch between a continuous mode and a step mode during the execution of the software is very useful. Rarely will developers want to wade through a sequence of alert messages for every single state transition. It is more likely that they will want to get to the point which is causing problems and then step through the code transition by transition.

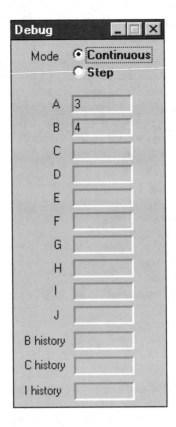

Figure 13.16

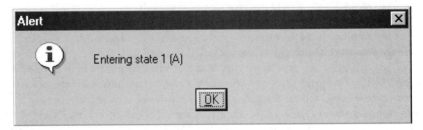

Figure 13.17

Error handling

Exception handlers should be written throughout the code to avoid the software failing because of unexpected conditions. This is especially true for database applications. If an error occurs that cannot be recovered from, then the application should be shut down in a controlled way. In particular the values of the current state variables should be written to an error log before the application is closed down. Closing the application down because

```
procedure go_state_01 is
    button_pressed number;
begin
    if (:debug.rbg_mode = 'Step') then
        button_pressed := display_alert(1,'Information', 'Entering state 1 (A)');
    end if;
    :debug.A := 1;

    state_variable_A := 1;

    if (:summary.student_id is null) then
        sc_summary.go_state_02;
    elsif (:summary.student_id is not null) then
        sc_summary.go_state_03;
    end if;
end;
```

Figure 13.18

of an error should be a last resort and should very rarely happen once real users are using the software. However, during integration and system testing, serious problems can and do occur. Having a log of the precise state of the application at the point of failure can make tracking down errors much easier than normal.

The steps for coding a statechart

Coding a statechart is a very simple process. There are four main tasks which should be carried out in the following order:

1   Create the user interface objects (ideally this should be done by an interaction designer).

2   Create the state variables.

3   Create the state procedures (the go_state_XX procedures).

4   Implement the state transitions defined in the event–action tables of the statechart.

Chapter 14
Testing statecharts

Software testing, of whatever type, is *not* concerned with demonstrating that a program does what it is supposed to do. It is concerned with executing a program with the intention of finding errors. It is about finding errors in the logic of the software, in the functions of the software, in the usability of the software and in the translation of requirements into code.

This chapter is *not* concerned with validating software against its requirements and it is *not* concerned with finding problems in the usability of the software. Such testing is important and must be performed, but before either can occur, it is necessary to find and correct errors in the control software of a user interface. In other words, it is first necessary to ensure the right actions are executed in response to events supplied by the user and that the events a user can supply to a user interface will not cause errors in the application.

This chapter is focused on testing that is not normally performed for user interface software developed using a bottom-up approach. It is about testing the user interface control software using test cases based on the structure of the code. Without a statechart design, it is difficult to identify logical paths through the code and it is even more difficult to verify whether or not the paths are exercised when the software is executed.

When the control software of a user interface is designed and coded based on a statechart, the quality of the unit testing can be significantly higher than when using a bottom-up approach. A statechart allows test cases to be designed that will exercise each event in each distinct context. The thoroughness of testing that is possible ensures that many of the errors in the software can be found during unit testing rather than in subsequent system testing.

The objective of this chapter is to consider ways of testing user interfaces controlled by statecharts. The purpose of the testing techniques presented is to find errors in the control software during unit testing. It is still necessary to perform other types of testing such as usability testing, integration testing and system testing.

White box and black box testing

The key to good testing is to design test cases that have a high probability of finding errors and thus it is important for the test cases to be created in a systematic way. There are two broad approaches to creating test cases: white box testing and black box testing. White box testing is concerned with generating test cases based on the internal structure of the software; it is about exercising the logical paths through the software. Black box testing is concerned with generating test cases based on the functions that the software should perform; the test cases are not concerned with the internal paths through the software. Black box testing subjects a system to inputs and the outputs are verified for conformance to the specification of the software.

Both black box and white box testing are essential. Both are effective and both have limitations. Unit testing tends to be based on structural testing and system testing tends to be based on black box testing. Unit testing is usually performed by the developers of the system who understand the way it is implemented. They can use white box techniques to exercise the software and can avoid wasting time executing test cases that have little chance of finding errors. System testing is best performed by independent testers using black box techniques. Independent testers are more likely to find missing functions and incorrect interpretations of requirements. In short, both black box and white box techniques should be used to maximize the chances of catching as many errors as possible.

It may seem that very thorough white box testing would discover all the errors in a program. However, for non-trivial software, exhaustive testing is infeasible because it would require every statement and every possible path to be executed. In practice, this is impossible because of loops that can be executed any number of times. Even small programs that have fixed size loops can have very large numbers of test cases. Complete testing is therefore impossible and so testing must be based on a subset of all the possible test cases. One of the goals of testing is to identify the tests that have the highest probability of discovering errors. In other words, it is concerned with identifying a small number of test cases that have the highest probability of discovering previously unknown errors.

Testing user interface software using white box techniques is not easy when a bottom-up approach is used because the code in event handlers is not self-contained since they make use of global information, as was discussed in Chapter 3. For instance, one event handler may enable a button, another may disable the same button and yet another may use the state of that button (either enabled or disabled) to determine which lines of code to execute. In order to create good white box test cases, it is necessary to understand how all the event handlers work together as an application. Testing event handlers in isolation from each other is not particularly useful and proves very little. Understanding how the event handlers work together and then specifying the test cases in a concise and meaningful way is not really viable for user interface software constructed using a bottom-up approach. Most developers recognize this and resort to using black box testing techniques when unit testing the software. The problem with this is that unit testing then tends to be duplicated in system testing. More seriously, the unit testing is not as thorough as it should be. Most errors in software lie in parts of the code that are not exercised frequently, for instance those parts that are executed in exceptional circumstances such as when there is no data in certain database tables. White box testing tends to identify exceptional circumstances and test cases are designed specifically to exercise the software in those circumstances. Without using white box techniques, it is unlikely that thorough coverage of the code will be achieved.

When a user interface is constructed using a statechart, the statechart provides a very clear view of the structure of the code and therefore provides an ideal basis for structural testing. The developer does not have to be concerned with understanding the code itself because the statechart provides an accurate view of the code's structure. Therefore white box test cases can be generated using the statechart and specified in terms of events, conditions and states. The resulting test specifications are quick and easy to generate, they are very concise and yet they provide very thorough coverage of the control code.

Testing criteria for statechart events

Path testing is the basis of all white box testing. In a statechart, a path is a sequence of state-to-state transitions invoked by a sequence of events. The objective of white box testing is to execute enough different paths to find where the actual structure of the software does not match the intended structure. What follows in this section is based on Glenford Myers' thorough treatment of white box testing techniques (Myers, 1979).

When testing a state transition diagram, a reasonable testing strategy would be to exercise each transition at least once. However, for a statechart, such a strategy would be quite weak because transitions can be dependent on conditions as well as events. For instance, consider the simple transitions in Figure 14.1. To ensure that both transitions are exercised, two test cases could be specified:

Test case 1: event E occurs when a = 1 and b = 6
Test case 2: event E occurs when a = 0 and b = 7

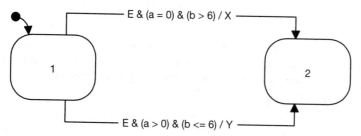

Figure 14.1

If the statechart is implemented correctly, then the first test case will cause transition 1 to 2 and action Y to occur, and the second test case will cause transition 1 to 2 and event X to occur. Now these might seem quite reasonable test cases – not only is each transition tested, but each possible outcome for each condition is also exercised. For instance, the condition (a = 0) is evaluated to true and false by the test cases. Likewise, each of the other three conditions is also evaluated to true and false by the two test cases.

The problem with this test strategy is that it is geared towards demonstrating that the transitions occur correctly. The test cases have not been designed to find faults in the transitions. For instance, if the statechart in Figure 14.1 was actually implemented as the statechart in Figure 14.2, neither of the test cases would reveal the error. Both would cause the same transitions and the same actions as the statechart in Figure 14.1.[1]

1.   One of the transitions in Figure 14.2 has been changed from its equivalent in Figure 14.1 by the addition of two parentheses and the logical operator being changed from an And to an Or. This might seem an unlikely error to occur in the code. However, the two additional parentheses would not be necessary in the code, because the event itself would not be part of the conditional statement which would be just 'if (a = 0) or (b > 6) then …'. In other words, the error in the code would simply be that the wrong logical operator had been used.

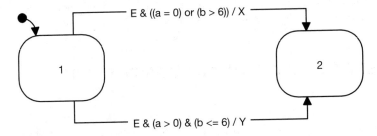

Figure 14.2

In order to test thoroughly the conditions associated with a transition, it is necessary to create test cases that exercise all the possible combinations of condition outcomes in each transition. That is, each condition must be evaluated to either true or false and all the possible combinations of true and false outcomes must be exercised. This is a standard white-box technique called multiple-condition coverage. For example, for the statechart in Figure 14.1, there are four possible combinations of condition outcomes for each of the two transitions and these can be achieved through using the values of a and b shown below:

1	$a = 0, b > 6$	5	$a <= 0, b > 6$
2	$a <> 0, b > 6$	6	$a > 0, b > 6$
3	$a = 0, b <= 6$	7	$a <= 0, b <= 6$
4	$a <> 0, b <= 6$	8	$a > 0, b <= 6$

There are eight possible combinations of condition outcomes to be covered by the test cases, but this does not necessarily mean that eight separate test cases are necessary. For instance, the following four test cases will cover the eight combinations:

Test case 3: event E occurs when $a = 0$ and $b = 7$ (covers 1 and 5)
Test case 4: event E occurs when $a = 1$ and $b = 7$ (covers 2 and 6)
Test case 5: event E occurs when $a = 0$ and $b = 6$ (covers 3 and 7)
Test case 6: event E occurs when $a = 1$ and $b = 6$ (covers 4 and 8)

When test cases 3 to 6 are run, the following transitions and actions should occur if the statechart in Figure 14.1 is coded correctly:

Test case 3: transition 1 to 2 and action X
Test case 4: no transition and no action
Test case 5: no transition and no action
Test case 6: transition 1 to 2 and action Y

However, if the statechart is coded as in Figure 14.2, then the following actions will occur:

Test case 3: transition 1 to 2 and action X
Test case 4: transition 1 to 2 and action X
Test case 5: no transition and no action
Test case 6: transition 1 to 2 and action Y

Clearly, for the statechart in Figure 14.2, test case 4 causes a transition to occur when the expected result is for there to be no transition. Therefore the error in the logic of the conditions has been found by the test cases.

To summarize, it is not sufficient simply to exercise each possible transition in a statechart if the transitions contain conditions. Instead, the test cases must exercise all combinations of condition outcomes associated with each transition. If a transition does not contain any conditions, then it is sufficient for the test cases to exercise the transition just once.

Testing statecharts

This section identifies the basic principles of testing a statechart and offers some pragmatic suggestions to help make testing easier. It then goes on to consider specific statechart features and how best to test them to maximize the chances of finding errors.

Principles

1   **Test to find errors in the design and the implementation** It is important for statecharts to be tested to find errors in the design of the statechart and not just in the code. There is little to be gained from finding errors in the implementation of a statechart whose design simply does not achieve what it is supposed to achieve. Many design errors can be found by inspecting the statechart before testing is started. Throughout the software design and test case design processes, it is recommended that statecharts are thoroughly inspected using the guidelines in Chapter 9.

2   **The state transitions should be made visible during testing** When a user interacts with a user interface, the states of a statechart are hidden. However, during unit testing, it is essential that the states and state transitions are made visible to allow testers to find errors in the software. In Chapter 13, it was recommended that test support code was added to the software in order to make testing and debugging easy. The debugging code should make the current state of the application visible at all times by displaying the values of the state variables in a separate window. In addition, the window allowed a tester to step through the transitions or run through them continuously. If the transitions are stepped through, then each transition causes an alert message to be displayed which names the state being entered. This can be useful when testing transient states or when testing events that cause 'simultaneous' transitions in several concurrent parts.

3   **Check the actions carefully** When testing it is important to carefully check that each action that should occur in response to an event actually does occur. Note also, the converse should also be checked: if no actions are to be executed, then try and check that none are and also check that no extra actions are executed. Checking that nothing extra occurs is difficult and is more easily checked in code reviews. However, it should still be borne in mind during unit testing.

4   **Check the states carefully** In addition to looking for errors in the transitions to states, check also that the state actually represents what it is supposed to represent. For instance, if a particular button is supposed to be disabled in a given state, then check that it is actually disabled. Check that the state controls only the user interface objects that it is supposed to control.

5   **Check for dead states** Ensure there are no dead states, or sets of dead states. When a dead state is entered, it cannot be exited. When a set of dead states is en-

tered, it may be possible to move between states in the set, but it is not possible to enter any state outside the set. To find dead states, test cases should end at an end state.

6   **Ensure events that are not supposed to be possible, *really* cannot happen** In general, if it is not possible for a user to supply a particular event in a state then the state will do something to prevent a user thinking it is possible. For example, a user interface object may be made to disappear or it may be disabled in certain states. This may not always be true of course, for example an object may be enabled to allow a user to click it, but is necessary to check that no transitions are caused if a user double-clicks the object, or holds the mouse button down on the object and so on.

Pragmatics

1   **Generating test cases** All test cases should be generated from the design of the statechart and not the code. The design represents what the software should be doing and the code represents what software is actually doing. A lot of effort could be put into writing tools that automatically generate test cases from statechart designs. Although in principle I am not against such tools, bear in mind that there may be errors in the design of the statechart itself and not just errors in the implementation of the statechart. The point is to find errors in the software – both design errors and code errors. The point is not simply to demonstrate that all states can be reached and that there are no dead states. The statechart still has to be carefully checked even if test cases are generated automatically. I have never used a tool to generate test cases, because it is quick and easy to generate them from the event–action tables. The amount of time that would be saved is minimal given that more time is spent carrying out the test cases than is spent creating them.

A quick way of generating test cases based on the event–action tables is as follows:

a   Take a copy of the event–action table and delete the actions.[2]

b   Find the 'start' event and move this to a new table (for example, the event 'Screen entered' may cause the transition: start → 1).

c   Now find an event in the event–action table that has a current state that matches the next state of the previous transition and move this event to the test case table. (For example, the destination state of the previous transition was 1, therefore a transition 'New button clicked' which causes the transition: 1 → 3 could be added to the table.)

d   Repeat the previous step until an end state is reached or there are no events left in the table.

e   If there are still rows in the event–action table then start a new test case.

Note: It is unlikely that you will be able to test each event only once. Therefore it may be necessary to take a copy of an event from one of the test case tables once the events in the event–action table start to reduce.

---

2.   I recommend deleting the actions on the grounds that it is best to avoid duplicating information for ease of maintenance. If more than one set of information has to be updated when the software is corrected or enhanced, the more likely it is for the sets of information gradually to become inconsistent.

The tests cases generated using the above process do not take into account the conditions associated with events. It will be necessary to enhance the test cases generated with tests that exercise all possible combinations of condition outcomes.

2   **What to record in test cases** In theory, the outcome of a test case should be predicted and documented before the test is run. However, to adopt such an approach is often not possible in the real world because there is simply not enough time to keep detailed test cases up to date. Instead, the aim should be to create test cases that can be updated or rewritten quickly if a major change to the design is made. It is therefore recommended that each step in a test case records the start state, the event, the conditions and the expected next state. The test cases should be used in conjunction with the event–action tables and the statechart diagrams when the testing is carried out. The diagram will give a good view of the paths that need to be executed and, more importantly, it will help you spot any missing transitions (something that is more difficult to achieve when working from the event–action tables alone). The event–action tables are important because they give the precise actions that should be executed in response to a specific event.

In short, spend more time thinking of good test cases (that is, those with a high probability of finding an error) and actually carrying out the testing, rather than writing test cases in unnecessary detail.

3   **Carrying out the tests** When executing test cases, have a diagram of the statechart to hand and use a highlighter pen to mark each event that is executed. In doing so, you will be confident that every event has been exercised at least once.

Depth

When using superstates to group states and reduce the number of event arrows, ensure that the event is tested for each state in the group. For instance, for the state chart in Figure 14.3, it is necessary to test each of the transitions $2 \rightarrow 1, 3 \rightarrow 1$, and $4 \rightarrow 1$ even though there is only a single event arrow from those states.

History

When the history mechanism is used for a group of states, for each arrow that leaves the group, it is necessary to check whether the last state is remembered correctly. For each arrow that enters the group, it is necessary to check that the last state is entered successfully and that the default start state is entered if the group has not been entered before.

Thus, for the statechart in Figure 14.3 it is necessary to exercise the following transitions:

$1 \rightarrow 3$ (3 is the default start state when there is no history),
$2 \rightarrow 1$ and $1 \rightarrow 2$,
$3 \rightarrow 1$ and $1 \rightarrow 3$,
$4 \rightarrow 1$ and $1 \rightarrow 4$

Concurrency

Consider the statechart in Figure 14.4. There are three concurrent state diagrams (A, B and C). The state of the statechart as a whole is defined by the three state variables A, B and C.

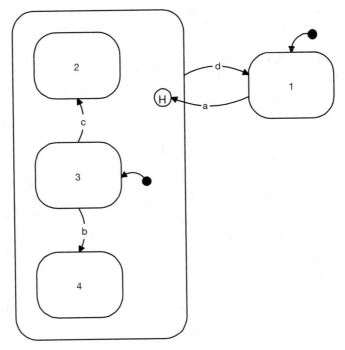

Figure 14.3

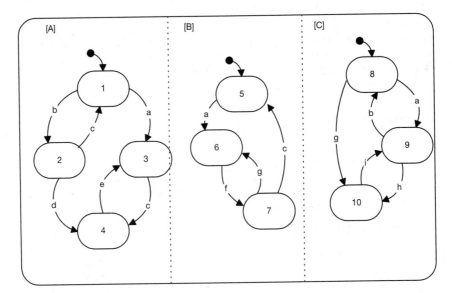

Figure 14.4

For instance, the default start state is [1,5,8]. There are only 10 states in the statechart but, because there are three concurrent parts, the number of possible state combinations is 36 (that is, $4 \times 3 \times 3$). Effectively, this means the statechart can be in one of 36 states at any given moment.

Now let's consider the number of events in the statechart. There are nine distinct events (a through to i). If each of these nine events were to be executed in all 36 states then this would give 324 test cases (9×36). Each of those test cases would name the state before the event, the event and the expected state after the event is executed. For instance, one of the tests would be: [3,7,10] event c → [4, 5, 10].

Testing the concurrent parts of a statechart in this way is not a particularly pragmatic approach. It is not necessary to test every event in every possible state combination. It is better to reduce the number of test cases by testing each concurrent part independently. In a good design, the concurrent parts should be controlling different user interface objects and there should be few if any dependencies between the concurrent parts. However, where a single event causes simultaneous transitions in a number of concurrent parts, test cases should be exercised to find errors in such transitions. Remember also that just because concurrent parts are meant to be independent, this doesn't necessarily mean they are. Always check that events only cause transitions in the parts they should do.

Code reviews

It is important that code is reviewed as well as tested. In a code review, the reviewers read the statechart designs and corresponding code in advance of the review meeting. During the meeting, the author of the code usually talks the reviewers through the code and the reviewers identify errors as the review proceeds. Reviewing statechart designs and code is much easier than reviewing user interface code written using the bottom-up approach because the statechart provides an abstract view of the software. Without such an abstract view, understanding how all the different fragments of code work together as a whole can be a time consuming process. It can be even more time consuming trying to understand the different contexts in which an event may occur.

When reviewing a statechart design and code, bear the following points in mind:

- Check that only the specified actions are executed in response to an event.
- Check that the actions executed in response to an event in a particular context are always the same. There should not be conditional statements in the code unless those conditions are associated with the event in the statechart.
- Check that the states only set the attributes of objects that they are supposed to set. Ensure that there is no action code slipped into the state procedures unless the states have been defined to execute such code.

Regression testing

Regression testing is performed after changes are made to the software, to find any new errors introduced into the code by the changes made. When user interface software based on a statechart is modified, the changes can always be related to particular transitions in the statechart. Thus, it is easy to identify suitable test cases to execute when regression testing.

When a statechart design is modified, the chances of introducing an unwanted side-effect are significantly reduced because it is possible to identify events and contexts precisely and modify them in isolation to closely related events and contexts.

Summary

Most user interface software is tested using black box testing techniques. In other words, the test cases are derived from what the software is supposed to achieve and not from the structure of the code. Many test cases exercise the mainstream paths through the software. It is the obscure paths that are often not exercised because they are only used in exceptional circumstances. Testing of user interface software is often based on random test cases that have little chance of finding errors because they are not designed to do so. The testing that is typically performed cannot be certain whether every statement has been executed once, let alone whether every combination of conditions has been executed in every decision.

Statecharts allow structural (white box) testing to be performed because they provide the necessary view of the code that can be used to derive the test cases. Without a statechart, it would be very difficult to generate structural tests.

This chapter has focused heavily on unit testing based on statecharts. It is important that other unit testing is carried out, such as finding errors in screen labels and help text, finding errors in the length of data, type of data and format of data that can be entered by users and so on. The intention of this chapter was not to provide a complete guide to testing user interfaces, but simply to provide a guide to testing user interfaces based on statecharts.

Chapter 15
Evaluation

Two distinct types of work are required to produce a good user interface: user interaction design and user interface construction. This book has been entirely concerned with a technique for constructing user interfaces with statecharts. A statechart provides the solid foundations for effective coding, testing and maintenance of a user interface. The alternative, constructing a user interface using a bottom-up approach, is like constructing a multi-storey building without foundations. At first the building may seem acceptable, but as the number of storeys increases the lack of foundations will rapidly become apparent. The same is true of software constructed without a solid design. The software may seem acceptable initially, but as it is enhanced the stability of the product will rapidly deteriorate.

There are many advantages to using the statechart approach and this chapter will identify some of them. It will also provide answers to questions that are often asked by people who are new to the approach.

Does the technique work?

The most commonly asked questions are: Does the technique work? Has it been used on real projects? Why are statecharts not widely used? This section provides some answers to these questions.

Have statecharts been used on real user interface projects?

I have experience of using statecharts on two major projects that ran for a period of four years. The projects were not case studies set up to evaluate the approach. They were real projects, with real budgets, real deadlines and real users. Neither project was developed entirely with statecharts. So useful comparisons could be made between the bottom-up approaches and the statechart approach. I must stress, I am not a researcher, I am a practitioner. By using the technique on real projects, the following can be said:

- The technique has resulted in software that can withstand the pressure of changing requirements – not contrived changes, but real changes demanded by users.

- The technique is scalable – it has been used on large, complex user interface modules.

- The technique is not a theory looking for a case study – it is a proven solution.

- The emphasis has been on applying the technique rather than developing a tool to support it. Too often researchers discover a problem and rush out to write a tool that will solve the problem. However, it is much better to understand the problem in detail, apply potential solutions to real projects and evaluate those solutions before getting involved in writing tools.

- The technique is concerned with applying an established notation and not with defining yet another notation (or worse, a variation on a notation).

Observations from real projects

An experienced statechart designer can construct user interface modules quicker with the statechart approach than with a bottom-up approach. This is mainly because the designer can reuse existing design techniques from other modules.

It was noticeable that in the early stages of the construction of a module, the statechart approach seemed to be slower that the bottom-up approach. This was because the design process generally took more than half the time available for constructing and unit testing a module. However, the coding and testing of a statechart is a quick and easy process and so significantly less time is spent on those tasks. Developers using the bottom-up approach seemed to finish coding quickly, but then spent a lot of time testing and debugging the software.

The bug rates were significantly lower in modules designed with statecharts than in modules developed with a bottom-up approach. The number of bugs found during the system testing of a statechart module was between 10 and 20% of the number of bugs found in similar modules constructed using the bottom-up approach. Significantly, most of the bugs found in statechart modules were related to errors in the actions associated with events or errors in the attributes of screen items, rather than errors in the design of the statechart itself.

It is difficult to measure maintainability, but it is worth making the following points. Changes made to statechart modules were much quicker and easier to make than changes to other modules. The maintainability of statechart-constructed modules remained constant. There was no deterioration in the quality of the code, despite several significant changes to the designs. Three modules that were constructed using a bottom-up approach were rewritten using the statechart approach because the required user interface was too complicated to develop. No statechart module needed to be rewritten.

Code reviews for the modules constructed using a bottom-up approach were difficult and time consuming. Design and code reviews of the statechart modules were quick and effective because the software could be understood by the reviewers.

There was no perceptible difference in the user interaction design of the two types of user interface modules. Only the developers were aware of the fundamental differences in the way the modules were constructed. System testers and users did not observe any differences in the modules, except for there being fewer bugs in the statechart modules and a general feeling that those modules were more reliable.

Can statecharts be used for RAD and DSDM projects?

I am in favour of increasing the development speed by using evolutionary prototyping techniques such as Rapid Application Development (RAD) (Martin, 1991) and the Dynamic Systems Development Method (DSDM) (for example, Stapleton, 1997). The evolutionary approach avoids writing large requirements and design documents, and instead focuses on producing a prototype and evolving that prototype based on feedback. This can be a good approach to user interface construction, especially if the early prototypes are paper based.

The problem with many evolutionary prototypes is that they are put together quickly and they are not designed to withstand the pressure of changing requirements. Another problem commonly raised against the evolutionary approach is related to testing. How can the resulting software be tested if there is no definition of what the software is supposed to be doing? The answer to this question is always less than convincing because there *is* no specification against which the software can be tested.

The statechart approach offers a solution to both these problems. Firstly, a statechart design ensures a user interface is maintainable in the long term. A statechart user interface module is much easier to change and enhance than a module constructed using a bottom-up approach. When evolving software, the goal must be to design software that can be repeatedly enhanced. Constructing software that cannot survive the first bout of change requests is a waste of time and effort. User interfaces constructed with statecharts will make DSDM and RAD more likely to succeed.

Secondly, a statechart design provides a precise specification of the software which can be used during unit testing. The role of a tester is to find faults in the statechart design, or in the translation of the statechart into code. Certainly a statechart does not specify the business requirements, but then the role of the tester is to find errors in the software. Testing software to ensure it supports user tasks or meets business needs is the responsibility of the users and the customers.

DSDM or RAD techniques recognize that large natural language documents slow projects down because they are often incomplete, inconsistent, ambiguous and difficult to maintain. To achieve truly rapid development, natural language documents should be avoided. In contrast, statecharts are concise, precise and have very well-defined semantics. The statechart approach is fast and results in high-quality software (that is, a low number of bugs and excellent long-term maintainability). Statecharts will not slow down a DSDM project – they will allow higher quality software to be delivered quicker than when using a bottom-up approach.

Why is everyone not using statecharts?

Statecharts have been around since 1987 and the notation is part of both the Object Modelling Technique (OMT) (Rumbaugh et al., 1991) and the United Modelling Language (UML) (for example, Fowler and Scott, 1997). However, if statecharts are as powerful as I say they are, why are they not widely used? There are several books that recommend the use of statecharts, and most present them in a similar way: a presentation of the notation, claims about how much better they are than state transition diagrams, and finally a small example to show how they can be used. Unfortunately, the examples are usually based on mechanical or electrical devices such as traffic lights, digital watches, the gears on a car and so on. Such examples may help readers understand the notation, but they do nothing to help readers apply the notation to the design problems they face – many developers design and develop business systems that are entirely software based.

A significant problem is the lack of advice on how to code them. A notation is not useful if it is not obvious how to convert it into code. Although coding a statechart is straightforward, because of the complexity of the diagrams, it may seem more difficult than it actually is.

Statecharts are not widely used for user interfaces because it is not obvious that such interfaces can be designed in this way. Most programming manuals are geared towards the event–action paradigm. Very little is written in manuals about how to determine the contexts in which events occur. This is an unmentioned problem that developers are left to solve for themselves. There is a general perception that user interface construction is easy because of the powerful development tools that are available. The fact is, user interface tools do not solve all the problems and the cost of maintaining user interface code can be huge.

The roles of user interaction designers and software developers

There are three things that are certain with any software development project:

1   A complete and consistent set of requirements will not be captured before the design and coding starts.

2   The requirements will change during the lifetime of the project.

3   The user interface is more likely to change than any other part of the system.

For these reasons, the worst thing that any project can do is attempt to write a natural language specification for a user interface. Such an approach would be a waste of time and effort because the document would be out of date almost the moment it is written and it would be a full-time job trying to keep it up to date.

With the statechart approach, natural language specifications are not written. The user interaction designer works closely with users and requirements analysts to design a user interface that meets the needs of the users and supports the business processes of the system. Having designed and refined the user interface, the designer should then put the design directly into a development tool from sketches of the screens made on paper. The designer does not have to write any code – just ensure that the user interface objects have their attributes set to appropriate values. The interaction designer must then communicate the detailed behaviour of the user interface to developers who are responsible for designing a statechart that captures the required behaviour. After developers translate the statechart into code and test the software, the user interface designer can then evaluate the user interface with real users and make modifications to the design if necessary.

By adopting this approach, time is not wasted writing documents that serve no purpose. If a large document is written by a designer, then few developers will read it in detail – they will look at the screen layouts and not spend sufficient time reading the written details of the interaction design.

Adopting this approach will highlight any gaps in the interaction design. For instance, statecharts tend to make developers think in terms of what happens in exception conditions such as when there is no data to display in a screen. The source of user interface problems is when a developer thinks entirely in terms of how the software should work under normal circumstances and fails to identify all the exceptional circumstances. Making a user interface work under normal conditions is easy, but making it work under all conditions is much more difficult. A statechart helps focus the mind on what the exceptional conditions are.

Most interaction designers will not be comfortable with the thought of specifying a user interface with a statechart. It is, after all, a software engineering skill rather than a user interaction design skill. It is therefore realistic to expect developers to work closely with interaction designers to capture the behaviour of a user interface in a statechart. It is important for interaction designers to be able to understand a statechart, but it is not necessary for them to be able to construct one. Note that users and customers should never be exposed to statecharts. Statecharts are a language of communication between interaction designers, developers and testers. An interaction designer should translate the behaviour defined in a statechart into plain, spoken language when discussing a user interface with users. Just like when I buy a car, I want to know how fast it can go and not how the car is designed to achieve that speed. Users of a user interface want to know what the user interface will do and not how it will be achieved.

Advantages of the statechart approach

This section lists the many benefits that the statechart approach can bring to user interface construction.

General

A low number of bugs

In general, software constructed with a statechart is of significantly higher quality than software constructed using a bottom-up approach. Typically, few bugs are found after unit testing has been completed.

A language independent notation

A statechart design can be coded in any programming language or development tool. Clearly, the language or development tool must be capable of implementing the actions specified in the design. In general, if a particular behaviour can be coded using a bottom-up approach, then it can be designed using a statechart.

Complicated user interfaces can be developed with ease

Very complicated screens are significantly quicker and easier to develop and maintain if a statechart design is used. A bottom-up approach is only viable for simple user interfaces. For complex user interfaces, statecharts are essential.

The speed of user interface development is not reduced

An experienced statechart designer can construct a user interface faster than an experienced developer can construct a similar interface using a bottom-up approach. The statechart approach is faster because developers are not left trying to fix minor bugs in the software. When a statechart design is coded, bugs can be fixed quickly because the code is easy to understand in conjunction with the statechart.

The performance of the software is not affected

The performance of user interfaces constructed using statecharts is no slower than if a bottom-up approach had been used. User interface code based on a statechart usually contains more conditional statements than an interface constructed using a bottom-up approach. However, the performance of a user interface is usually affected more by the network performance between a client and server. Having extra conditional statements in the code will not have any significant impact on the performance of the software.

User interface components

The statechart approach is intended to co-ordinate the behaviour of user interface objects. A user interface cannot be constructed from components without the need to write application code; the components still have to be co-ordinated to work together with other objects. Components themselves can be complex entities and would benefit from being designed with statecharts.

Statecharts are easier to understand than code alone

Most people prefer to communicate their ideas using drawings because pictures are often faster to create and easier to understand than the words for the same information. Statecharts allow engineers to communicate the precise control of a user interface with a drawing, rather than with code or a natural language specification.

Design

The designs are precise and consistent

Statechart designs define precisely how a user interface will work before any code is written. The designs can be reviewed by other developers and changes can be made before the code is written.

A problem with many user interfaces is that several developers work on different parts of the same user interface. The result can be differences in user interface styles. Using statecharts will reduce the possibility of such differences in style because the designs can be reviewed to ensure consistency before the coding starts. Furthermore, similar screens can reuse existing designs. If the statecharts are consistent, then the user interface will be more consistent.

The designs are modular

Statechart user interface designs have a natural modular structure. Several developers can work on different modules of the same user interface at the same time.

The designs are compact

A statechart does not design every aspect of a user interface. Much of the behaviour of an interface is defined by the objects used to construct it. Statecharts are only used to co-ordinate the behaviour of user interface objects so that they work together as an application.

Most statechart designs can be drawn so that each part of the design can fit on a single piece of paper. The notation is very good for dividing a design into several parts and viewing the software at different levels of detail.

The designs are kept up to date

It is easier to modify the design of a statechart and then modify the code, than it is to modify the code directly. Thus designs are likely to be kept in step with the code. If the code is generated automatically from the designs, then there would be no problem of keeping design and code in step.

The designs can be reused

Most user interfaces can be split into a relatively small set of screen types. (Most are designed to have a consistent look and feel.) Thus, a developer can reuse designs for similar screens. Once a core set of screen types has been developed, similar screens can be developed extremely quickly.

Reusing control code developed using a bottom-up approach is usually not possible. It is more likely that a developer will look at the techniques used to construct the existing code, but the code itself is not usually reusable.

Coding

Simple and consistent code

A statechart can be coded very quickly and easily because ad hoc programming techniques are not used. No matter how complicated the statechart is, the code itself will always remain simple.

No requirements work during the coding phase

The statechart designs do not leave any ambiguities for developers to resolve when coding. For instance, it is usually left to the developer to decide the behaviour of a user interface when no data is available in a screen. When such behaviour is not specified, the resulting user interface is usually inconsistent if a number of people are developing it.

The code is easy to debug

Debugging statechart code during unit testing is very easy because debugging code can be added to during the coding process. Such code allows the current state to be displayed as a user interacts with the screens. When a user event occurs, it is easy to identify exactly which lines of coded are executed in response to that event. This cannot be achieved easily with a bottom-up approach, because the context in which an event occurs is usually difficult to identify.

Code walk-throughs

Code walk-throughs of statechart user interfaces are very productive because developers can understand what they are reviewing. Without a statechart design, developers do not have the time to understand and review event-driven code in sufficient detail to find faults in the code.

Testing

Unit testing is thorough

Statecharts allow a tester to test each distinct user event at least once. It is also possible to test all the combinations of condition outcomes associated with events. More significantly, this level of testing can be achieved very quickly. The tests are good, because they have a high probability of finding errors.

When the bottom-up approach is used, it is very difficult to achieve and demonstrate that each line of code has been executed at least once. To test all the conditions in the application would take a very long time. Most unit testing is black box testing with very little white box testing. The standard of unit testing is usually very low.

Regression testing is efficient and effective

When a user interface is changed, a statechart design ensures that any ripple effect is minimized. A full re-test is rarely required for most changes. However, if a significant change is made to the statechart (for instance, a number of states are added or deleted) then new test cases can be produced and used very quickly.

The unit test documents written for user interface software constructed using a bottom-up approach are not usually kept up to date after they are written. The effort required to keep such documents in step with the code cannot usually be justified because the tests specified in them are not usually very effective.

The unit test cases are compact

The test cases for a statechart are very thorough and yet very compact. The tests are largely generated from the event–action tables of the statechart.

For a user interface constructed using the bottom-up approach, the test cases are usually written in a natural language and so they are very large, as well as being ineffective. The test cases are usually based on a natural language specification that has many problems itself.

Maintenance

Faults can be traced easily

If a fault occurs in a statechart module, it is easy to locate the precise lines of code which caused the fault because the state information and the event which caused the error can be written to an error log. It is usually easy to understand why the fault occurred and how to fix it.

Changes are local in effect

A statechart design identifies each distinct context in which an event can occur. If the actions that are executed in response to an event in a particular context are changed, then the actions executed in response to that event in all the other contexts will not be affected. Thus, statecharts dramatically reduce the likelihood of introducing unwanted side-effects when the software is changed.

Very big changes to a user interface are relatively easy to achieve

It is usually easy to make big changes to the way a user interface behaves if it is designed with a statechart. This is because changes can be planned in the statechart design before the corresponding changes are made to the code.

With a bottom-up approach, large changes are extremely difficult to achieve because when the software is changed the impact of those changes cannot be predicted.

It is easy to maintain unfamiliar software

Writing user interface code is easy. Writing user interface code that can repeatedly be enhanced by different people over a long period of time, is very difficult. The code that results from a bottom-up approach is difficult to understand by anyone other than the person who developed it. Even the original developer can struggle to understand the code and make significant changes to it. The intricate dependencies between event handlers usually only become apparent when the code is changed and errors are introduced.

A statechart provides an abstract view of the software which allows developers to gain a detailed understanding of it very quickly. It is easier to understand another person's statechart design than it is to understand the code written using a bottom-up approach. When changes are made to the design, each event in the event–action table can be precisely identified in the code. Modifying the actions associated with one event will not affect the behaviour of the same event in a different context

Estimates are more accurate

When a user interface is constructed using a bottom-up approach, estimating the cost of modifying the code is difficult because unwanted side-effects can make a seemingly simple change very difficult to achieve.

When a statechart approach is used, side-effects are not a significant problem. It is easy to understand how big a change will be and how long it is likely to take to achieve.

Some possible limitations of the statechart approach

Translating a statechart to code is boring

Designing a statechart is an interesting challenge, but translating a design into code is not. Good tool support would solve this problem.

The code may not adhere to the design

Developers who maintain the software must understand the statechart notation. To be blunt, it would be insane to modify the code in a way that did not adhere to the statechart design because this would be reverting to a bottom-up approach. Modifying the code and not the design would be analogous to a developer not adhering to the principles of information hiding when maintaining software that makes use of information hiding. It is not possible to stop a developer from making stupid decisions, but if a tool was used to generate the code from a design, then this problem would be removed.

The code can be indecipherable to people not familiar with the design notation

The code will make little sense to anyone without the design. This is not necessarily a disadvantage because it may deter developers making changes to something they don't understand.

The method will take a reasonable amount of time to learn

Statecharts are an intuitive extension to state transition diagrams and so anyone with basic design skills will have no problem learning the statechart notation. However, learning how to apply the notation to solve design problems is much more difficult. I hope this book will go some way to overcoming this problem.

Developers, particularly weak developers, may resist using the technique because of its rigour

Statechart user interface designs may seem a little unnatural compared to a bottom-up approach. However, any time-served developer knows that coding without a design always results in complex code that is difficult to understand and maintain. User interface code is no different.

User interface development tools of the future

A statechart design tool is not essential to design statecharts to control user interfaces. A good drawing tool is sufficient. All the statecharts in this book have been drawn using a basic drawing tool which allows templates of the statechart symbols (states, history symbol, default start symbol and so on) to be created. Using standard templates can help make the designs look consistent.

The current range of development tools could easily be enhanced to make statechart construction an integral part of the tools. In addition to the components of a development identified in Chapter 2, a statechart design tool could be included with the development tools. Developers could then construct user interfaces based on statecharts, rather than writing code directly in the event handlers.

For instance, a statechart design tool could be developed which would allow developers to specify how each state affects the attributes of objects. A developer could click on a state and the details of that state could appear in a window which would show which attributes of which objects were affected by the state. If a state has a lower level of detail, then double-clicking the state could cause the lower-level statechart to be displayed.

Similarly, if a user double-clicked an event arrow in such a tool, then the appropriate entry in the event–action table could be displayed. Developers would specify the events, conditions and actions for an event arrow in the table. The entries in the table could be compiled and the code could then be generated automatically from the statechart.

Such a tool is not difficult to achieve. Existing development tools could easily be enhanced to provide support for statechart designs.

Appendix A
Errors in the calculator application in Chapter 3

The following are errors found in the calculator example given in Chapter 3, which was constructed using a bottom-up approach. The column on the left of each table gives the sequence of user events required to reproduce the fault. The column on the right of each table gives the values displayed in the Readout field after the event is supplied.

Error 1

User event	Displayed in the Readout field
Start application	0.
6	6.
/	6.
−	−
=	−
6	−6.
=	

On clicking the equals button, the application crashes with a runtime error caused by a type mismatch.

Error 2

User event	Displayed in the Readout field
Start application	0.
2	2.
−	2.
−	−
−	−
2	−2.
−	

On clicking the minus button, the application crashes with a runtime error caused by a type mismatch.

Error 3

User event	Displayed in the Readout field
Start application	0.
6	6.
–	6.
–	–
%	

On clicking the percent button, the application crashes with a runtime error caused by a type mismatch.

Error 4

User event	Displayed in the Readout field
Start application	0.
5	5.
+	5.
CE	0.
7	7.
=	12.

The cancel entry event had no effect, even though it appeared to cancel the 5 from the Readout field.

Error 5

User event	Displayed in the Readout field
Start application	0.
3	3.
0	30.
+	30.
3	3.
0	30.
=	60.
%	0.6
×	36.

Clicking the multiply button at this point should not cause the value 36 to appear.

Error 6

User event	Displayed in the Readout field
Start application	0.
3	3.
0	30.
%	0.3
5	5.
0	50.
=	0

A user may be expecting to see 30% of 50, but the calculator does not return this answer.

Error 7

User event	Displayed in the Readout field
Start application	0.
5	5.
0	50.
%	0.5
−	0.1
=	−0.05

Clicking the minus button should not cause 0.1 to appear.

Error 8

User event	Displayed in the Readout field
Start application	0.
5	5.
0	50.
+	50.
2	2.
5	25.
%	0.25
=	12.5

Note: This behaviour is seen with any other operator in place of the + operator.

Error 9

User event	Displayed in the Readout field
Start application	0.
5	5.
0	50.
+	50.
5	5.
0	50.
%	0.5
%	0.005
=	0.005

From this point on, the calculator will not perform any operations unless the cancel button is clicked.

Error 10

User event	Displayed in the Readout field
Start application	0.
5	5.
0	50.
%	0.5
%	0.005
+	0.
3	3.
=	3.

The addition of 0.005 and 3 does not occur correctly.

Appendix B
The calculator

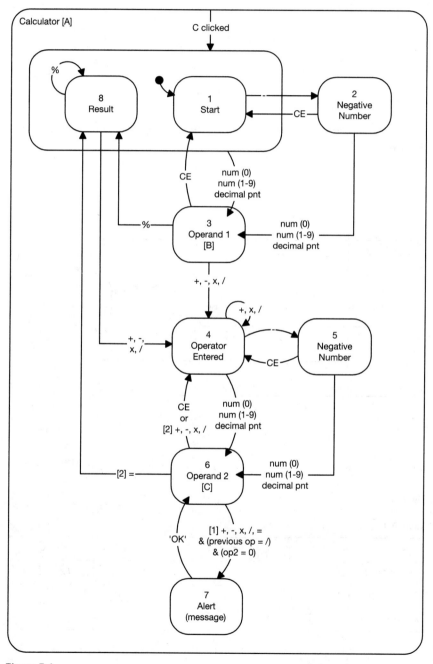

Figure B.1

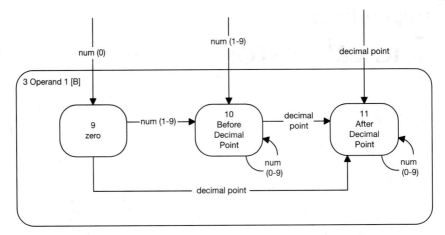

Figure B.2

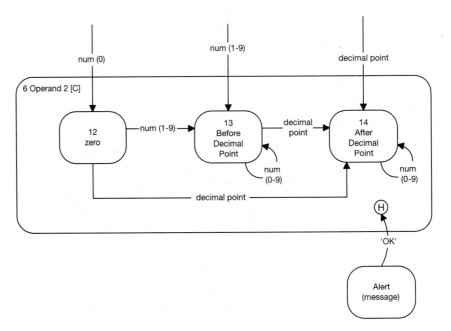

Figure B.3

Table B.1

User interface object		A								B			C	
	1	2	3	4	5	6	7	8	9	10	11	12	13	14
CE (Cancel Entry)	d	e	e	d	e	e	–	d	–	–	–	–	–	–
%button	d	d	e	d	d	d	–	e	–	–	–	–	–	–

Table B.2

Current state A	B	C	Event	Actions	Next state A	B	C
–	–	–	start application	Readout := '0.'; calc.put_operand1 (null); calc.put_operand2 (null); calc.put_operator (null);	1	0	0
%			Cancel (C) button clicked	Readout := '0.'; calc.put_operand1 (null); calc.put_operand2 (null); calc.put_operator (null);	1	0	0
1, 8			num(0) clicked	Readout := '0.';	3	9	
1, 8			num(1–9) clicked	Readout := label of the clicked button || '.';	3	10	
1,8			decimal point clicked	Readout := '0.';	3	11	
1			– button clicked	Readout := '–';	2		
2			Cancel Entry (CE) button clicked	Readout := '0.';	1		
2			num(0) clicked	Readout := '–0.';	3	9	
2			num(1–9) clicked	Readout := Readout || label of the clicked button || '.';	3	10	
2			decimal point clicked	Readout := '–0.';	3	11	
3			Cancel Entry (CE) button clicked	Readout := '0.';	1	0	
3	9		num(1–9) clicked	Readout := Readout with zero and decimal point removed || label of the clicked button || '.';	3	10	
3	9		decimal point clicked	-- no action (the decimal point is already displayed)	3	11	
3	10		num(0-9) clicked	Readout :=Readout with deicmal point removed || label of the clicked button || '.';	3	10	
3	10		decimal point clicked	-- no action (the decimal point is already displayed)	3	11	
3	11		num(0-9) clicked	Readout := Readout with decimal point || label of the clicked button;	3	11	
3			percent button clicked	Readout := Readout/100; calc.put_operand1 (readout);	8	0	

Table B.2 (Cont'd)

Current state			Event	Actions	Next state		
A	B	C			A	B	C
3			One of the following buttons clicked: +, −, ×, /	calc.put_operand1 (Readout) calc.put_operator (label of the clicked button)	4	0	
4			One of the following buttons clicked: +, ×, /	calc.put_operator (label of the clicked button)	4		
4			− button clicked	Readout := '−';	5		
4			num(0) clicked	Readout := '0.';	6		12
4			num(1–9) clicked	Readout := label of the clicked button || '.';	6		13
4			decimal point clicked	Readout := '0.';	6		14
5			Cancel Entry (CE) button clicked	Readout := '0.';	4		
5			num(0) clicked	Readout := '−0';	6		12
5			num(1–9) clicked	Readout := Readout || label of the clicked button || '.';	6		13
5			decimal point clicked	Readout := '−0.';	6		14
6			Cancel Entry (CE) button clicked	Readout := '0.';	4		0
6			Priority [2] One of the following buttons clicked: +, −, ×, /	calc.put_operand2 (Readout) Readout := evaluate (calc.get_operand1, calc.get_operator, calc.get_operand2); calc.put_operand1 (Readout) calc.put_operator (label of the clicked button) calc.put_operand2 (null);	4		0
6	12		num(1–9) clicked	Readout := Readout with zero and decimal point removed || label of the clicked button || '.';	6		13
6	12		decimal point clicked	-- no action (the decimal point is already displayed);	6		14
6	13		num(0-9) clicked	Readout := Readout with decimal point removed || label of the clicked button || '.';	6		13
6	13		decimal point clicked	-- no action (the decimal point is already displayed)	6		14

Table B.2 (Cont'd)

Current state			Event	Actions	Next state		
A	B	C			A	B	C
6		14	num(0–9) clicked	Readout := Readout with decimal point || label of the clicked button;	6		14
6			Priority [1] One of the following buttons clicked: +, –, ×, / and (previous operator = /) and (Readout = 0)	message parameter for state 7 = 'Cannot divide by zero'	7		
6			Priority [1] = button clicked and (previous operator = /) and (Readout = 0)	message parameter for state 7 = 'Cannot divide by zero'	7		
6			Priority [2] = button clicked	calc.put_operand2 (Readout) Readout := evaulate(calc.get_operand1, calc.get_operator, clac.get_operand2); calc.put_operand1 (Readout) calc.put_operand2 (null); callc.put)operator (null);	8		0
7			'OK' clicked in response to the alert message displayed in state 7	-- no action	6		Hist (C)
8			percent button clicked	Readout := Readout/100; calc.put_operand1(Readout);	8		
8			One of the following buttons clicked: +, –, ×, /	calc.put_operator (label of the clicked button	4		

Appendix C
The CD player

Table C.1

User interface object or attribute	1	2	3	4	5	6	7	8	9
Play	d	d	–	e	d	e	e	–	–
Pause	d	d	–	d	e	e	e	–	–
Stop	d	d	–	d	e	e	e	–	–
Previous Track	d	d	–	e	e	e	e	–	–
Reverse	d	d	–	e	e	e	e	–	–
Forward	d	d	–	e	e	e	e	–	–
Next Track	d	d	–	e	e	e	e	–	–
Eject	e	e	–	e	e	e	e	–	–
Time field	v	v	–	v	v	v	I	v	v
Track field	v	v	–	v	v	v	I	v	v
Play balloon help	Play	Play	–	Play	Play	Resume	Resume	Play	Play
Pause balloon help	Pause	Pause	–	Pause	Pause	Resume	Resume	Pause	Pause
Eject balloon help	Eject	Close	–	Eject	Eject	Eject	Eject	Eject	Eject

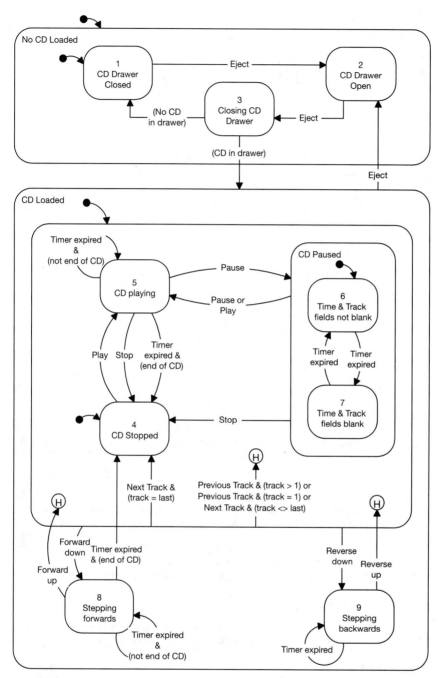

Figure C.1

Table C.2 Event–action table for the CD player statechart.

Current state A	Event	Actions	Next state A
Start	Application started	cd_player.close_drawer; Time_field := 0; Track_field := 0;	1
1	Eject button clicked	cd_player.open_drawer;	2
2	Eject button clicked	cd_player.close_drawer	3
3	(cd_player.cd_loaded = false)	none	1
3	(cd_player.cd_loaded = true	none	4

4	Play button clicked	track_field := 1;
		cd_player.play(track_field, time_field);
		create_timer('play_timer, 1');
			5

4, 5, 6, 7, 8, 9	Eject button clicked	cd_player.stop; cd_player.open_drawer; Time_field := 0; Track_field := 0;	2
4, 5, 6, 7	Next Track & (cd_player.last_track = true)	cd_player.stop; Time_field := 0; Track_field := 0;	4
4, 5, 6, 7	Next Track & (cd_player.last_track = false)	cd_player.next_track; Time_field := cd_player.current_time; Track_field := cd_player.current_track;	H(4, 5, 6, 7)
4, 5, 6, 7	Previous Track & (cd_player.current_track = 1)	cd_player.go_track(1); Time_field :=cd_player.current_time; Track_field := cd_player.current_track	H(4, 5, 6, 7)
4, 5, 6, 7	Previous Track & (cd_player.current_track > 1)	cd_player.previous_track; Time_field := cd_player.current_time; Track_field := cd_player.current_track;	H(4, 5, 6, 7)
4, 5, 6, 7	Forward down	cd_player.forward_one_sec; create_timer('forward_timer', 0.1); Time_field := cd_player.current_time; Track_field := cd_player.current_track;	8
8	Forward up	none	H (4, 5, 6, 7)
4, 5, 6, 7	Reverse down	cd_player.back_one_sec; create_timer('reverse_timer', 0.1); Time_field := cd_player.current_time; Track_field := cd_player.current_track	9

Table C.2 (Cont'd) Event–action table for the CD player statechart.

Current state A	Event	Actions	Next state A
9	Reverse up	none	H (4, 5, 6, 7)
9	reverse_timer expired	cd_player.back_one_sec; create_timer('reverse_timer', 0.1); Time_field := cd_player.current_time; Track field := cd_player.current_track;	9
5	Stop	cd_player.stop; Time_field := 0; Track_field := 0;	4
5	play_timer expired & (end of CD)	cd_player.stop; Time_field := 0; Track_field := 0;	4
5	play_timer expired & (not end of CD)	Time_field := cd_player.current_time; Track_field := cd_player.current_track;	5
5	Pause	cd_player.pause; create_timer('pause_timer', 1);	6
6	pause_timer expired	create_timer('pause_timer', 1);	7
6, 7	Play	cd_player.play(track_field, time_field); create_timer('play_timer, 1');	5
6, 7	Pause	cd_player.play(track_field, time_field; create_timer('play_timer, 1');	5
6, 7	Stop	cd_player.stop; Time_field := 0; Track_field :=0;	4
7	pause_timer expired	create_timer('pause_timer', 1);	6
8	forward_timer expired & (cd_player.end_of_cd = true)	cd_player.stop; Time_field := 0; Track_field := 0;	4
8	forward_timer expired & (cd_player.end_of_cd = false)	create_timer('forward_timer', 0.1); Time_field := cd_player.current_time; Track_field := cd_player.current_track;	8
9	reverse_timer expired	create_timer('reverse_timer',0.1);	9

Appendix D
Case study 2: A fault reporting application

The high-level statechart

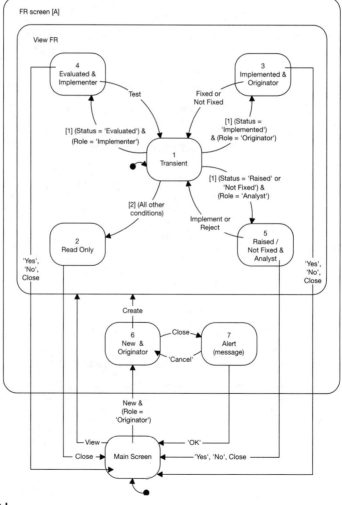

Figure D.1

Table D.1

Screen area	Screen item	A 1	A 2
Header items	All items	—	d
Description tab-card	All items	—	d
Analysis tab-card	All items	—	d
Implementation tab-card	All items	-	d
Testing tab-card	All items	-	d
	Close button	—	e

Table D.2

Current state A	Event	Action	Next state A
—	View button clicked in the main screen & (an FR has been selected in the main screen)		1
2	Close	Clear the FR screen; Return to the Main screen;	0
1	[Priority 2]		2

New FR (state 6)

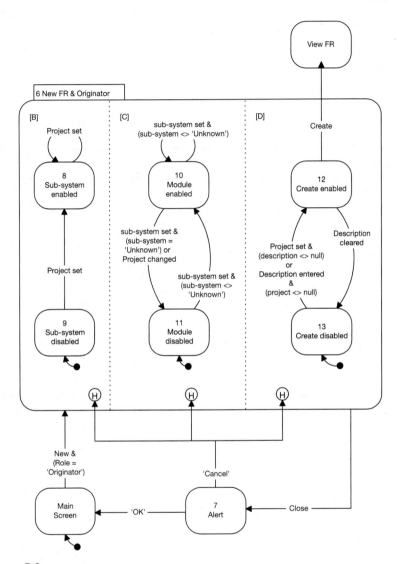

Figure D.2

Table D.3

Screen area	Screen item	A 6	7	B 8	9	C 10	11	D 12	13
Header	FR Number	d	–	–	–	–	–	–	–
Header	Status	d	–	–	–	–	–	–	–
Header	Priority	e	–	–	–	–	–	–	–
Header	Project	e	–	–	–	–	–	–	–
Header	Sub-system	–	–	e	d	–	–	–	–
Header	Module	–	–	–	–	e	d	–	–
Description tab-card	Originator	d	–	–	–	–	–	–	–
Description tab-card	Date	d	–	–	–	–	–	–	–
Description tab-card	Description	e	–	–	–	–	–	–	–
Description tab-card	Create button	–	–	–	–	–	–	e	d
Analysis tab-card	All items	d	–	–	–	–	–	–	–
Implementation tab-card	All items	d	–	–	–	–	–	–	–
Testing tab-card	All items	d	–	–	–	–	–	–	–
	Close button	e	–	–	–	–	–	–	–

Table D.4

Current state A	B	C	D	Event	Actions	Next state A	B	C	D
–	–	–	–	New button clicked in the Main screen & (Role = Implementer)	FR = null; Status = New; Priority = Low; Project = null; Sub-system ='<Unknown>'; Module ='<Unknown>'; Display the FR screen; Display the Description tab-card;	6	9	11	13
6	8			Project selected	Sub-system ='<Unknown>';	6	8		
6	9			Project selected		6	8		
6		10		Sub-system selected & (sub-system <> '<Unknown>')	Module ='<Unknown>	6	'	10	
6		10		Sub-system selected & (sub-system = <Unknown>)		6		11	
6		10		Project selected	Module ='<Unknown>'	6		11	
6		11		Sub-system selected & (sub-system <> <Unknown>)		6		10	

Table D.4 (Cont'd)

Current state	Event	Actions	Next state			
6	12 Create button clicked	Generate an FR number; Set the status = 'Raised'; Set Originator to the user's name; Set Date raised to the current date; Commit the FR to the database;	1	0	0	0
6	12 Description field cleared		6			13
6	13 Project selected & (description field is not null)		6			12
6	13 Description entered & (project is not null)		6			12
6	Close clicked	State 7 alert message parameter: 'Do you want to abandon creating this FR?'	7			
7	'OK' clicked in response to the alert displayed in state 7	Clear the FR screen; Display the Main screen;	0			
7	'Cancel' clicked in response to the alert displayed in state 7		6			

Raised/Not Fixed (state 5)

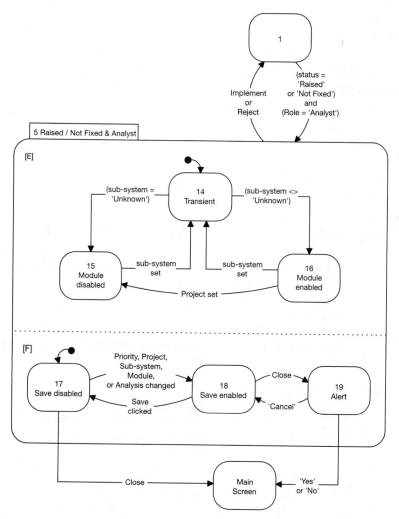

Figure D.3

Table D.5

Screen area	Screen item	A	E			F		
		5	14	15	16	17	18	19
Header	FR Number	d	—	—	—	—	—	—
Header	Status	d	—	—	—	—	—	—
Header	Priority	e	—	—	—	—	—	—
Header	Project	e	—	—	—	—	—	—
Header	Sub-system	e	—	—	—	—	—	—

Table D.5 (Cont'd)

Screen area	Screen item	A	E			F		
		5	14	15	16	17	18	19
Header	Module	—	—	d	e	—	—	—
Description tab-card	All items	d	—	—	—	—	—	—
Analysis tab-card	Analyst	d	—	—	—	—	—	—
Analysis tab-card	Date Analysed	d	—	—	—	—	—	—
Analysis tab-card	Analysis	e	—	—	—	—	—	—
Analysis tab-card	Save button	—	—	—	—	d	e	—
Analysis tab-card	Implement button	e	—	—	—	—	—	—
Analysis tab-card	Reject button	e	—	—	—	—	—	—
Implementation tab-card	All items	d	—	—	—	—	—	—
Testing tab-card	All items	d	—	—	—	—	—	—
	Close	e	—	—	—	—	—	—

Table D.6

Current state			Event	Actions	Next state		
A	E	F			A	E	F
1			[Priority 2] (Status = 'Raised') & (Role = 'Analyst')) or ((Status = 'Not Fixed')) & (Role = 'Analyst'))		5	14	17
5			Implement clicked	Set the Analyst field to the user's name; Set the Analysis Date to the current date; Set the status = 'Implemented'; Commit the FR to the database;	1	0	0
5			Reject clicked	Set the Analyst field to the user's name; Set the Analysis Date to the current date; Set the status = 'Rejected'; Commit the FR to the database;	1	0	0
5	14		(Sub-system = '<Unknown>')		5	15	
5	15		(Sub-system <> '<Unknown>')		5	16	
5	15		Sub-system set	Module = '<Unknown>';	5	14	
5	15		Sub-system set	Module = '<Unknown>';	5	14	
5	16		Project selected	Sub-system = '<Unknown>'; Module = '<Unknown>';	5	15	
5		17	Close clicked	Clear the screen	0	0	0
5		17	Priority changed		5		18

Table D.6 (Cont'd)

Current state	Event		Actions	Next state	
5	17	Project changed		5	18
5	17	Sub-system changed		5	18
5	17	Module changed		5	18
5	17	Analysis changed		5	18
5	18	Save button on the Analysis tab-card clicked	Set the Analyst field to the user's name;	5	17
5	18	Close clicked	Set the Analysis Date to the current date; Commit the FR to the database; State 19 alert message parameter: 'Do you want to save the changes you have made?'	5	19
5	19	'Yes' clicked in response to the alert displayed in state 18	Set the Analyst field to the user's name; Set the Analysis Date to the current date; Commit the FR to the database;	0 0	0
5	19	'No' clicked in response to the alert displayed in state 18	Clear the screen;	0 0	0
5	19	'Cancel' clicked in response to the alert displayed in state		5	18

Evaluated (state 4)

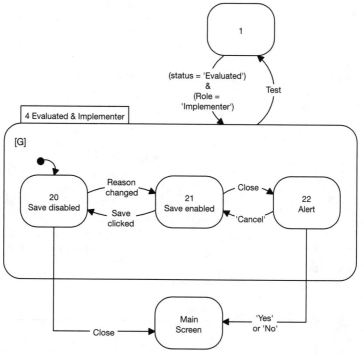

Figure D.4

Table D.7

		A		G	
Screen area	Screen item	4	20	21	22
Header	All items	d	–	–	–
Description tab-card	All items	d	–	–	–
Implementation tab-card	Implementer	d	–	–	–
Implementation tab-card	Implementation date	d	–	–	–
Implementation tab-card	Reason field	e	–	–	–
Implementation tab-card	Save button	–	d	e	–
Implementation tab-card	Test button	e	–	–	–
Analysis tab-card	All items	d	–	–	–
Testing tab-card	All items	d	–	–	–
	Close button	e	–	–	–

Table D.8

Current state		Event	Actions	Next state	
A	G			A	G
1	0	[Priority 2] (Status = 'Evaluated') & (Role = 'Implementer')		4	20
4	–	Test button clicked	Set the Implementer field to the user's name; Set the Development Date to the current date; Set the Status = 'Implemented'; Commit the FR to the database;	1	0
4	20	Close clicked	Clear the screen;	0	0
4	20	Reason/Solution field changed		4	21
4	21	Save button clicked on the Implementation tab-card	Set the Implementer field to the user's name; Set the Development Date to the current date; Commit the FR to the database	4	20
4	21	Close clicked	State 22 alert message parameter: 'Do you want to save the changes you have made?'	4	22
4	22	'Cancel' clicked in response to the alert displayed in state 21		4	21

Table D.8 (Cont'd)

Current state		Event	Actions	Next state	
A	G			A	G
4	22	'Yes' clicked in response to the alert displayed in state 21	Set the Implementer field to the user's name; Set the Development Date to the current date; Commit the FR to the database;	0	0
4	22	'No' clicked in response to the alert displayed in state 21	Clear the screen;	0	0

Implemented (state 3)

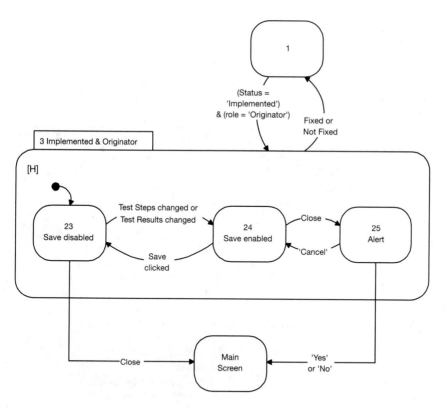

Figure D.5

Table D.9

Screen area	Screen item	A 3	23	H 24	25
Header	All items	d	–	–	–
Description tab-card	All items	d	–	–	–
Analysis tab-card	All items	d	–	–	–
Implementation tab-card	All items	d	–	–	–
Testing tab-card	Tester	d	–	–	–
Testing tab-card	Test Date	d	–	–	–
Testing tab-card	Test Steps	e	–	–	–
Testing tab-card	Test Results	e	–	–	–
Testing tab-card	Save button	–	d	e	–
Testing tab-card	Fixed button	e	–	–	–
Testing tab-card	Not Fixed Button	e	–	–	–
	Close Button	e	–	–	–

Table D.10

Current state A	H	Event	Actions	Next state A	H
1	0	[Priority 2] (Status = 'Implemented') & (Role = 'Originator')		3	23
3		Fixed button clicked	Set the Tester field to the user's name; Set the Testing Date to the current date; Set the Status = 'Fixed'; Commit the FR to the database;	1	0
3		Not Fixed button clicked	Set the Tester field to the user's name; Set the Testing Date to the current date; Set the Status = 'Not Fixed'; Commit the FR to the database;	1	0
3	23	Close clicked	Clear the screen	0	0
3	23	Test Steps field changed		3	24
3	23	Test Results field changed		3	24

Table D.10 (Cont'd)

Current state		Event	Actions	Next state	
3	24	Save button clicked on the Testing tab-card	Set the Tester field to the user's name; Set the Testing Date to the current date; Commit the FR to the database;	3	23
3	23	Close clicked	State 25 alert message parameter: 'Do you want to save the changes you have made?'	3	25
3	25	'Yes' clicked in response to the alert displayed in state 24	Set the Tester field to the user's name; Set the Testing Date to the current date; Commit the FR to the database;	0	0
3	25	'No' clicked in response to the alert displayed in state 24	Clear the screen;	0	0
3	25	'Cancel' clicked in response to the alert displayed in state 24		3	24

Appendix E
Case study 3: A student database

The high-level statechart

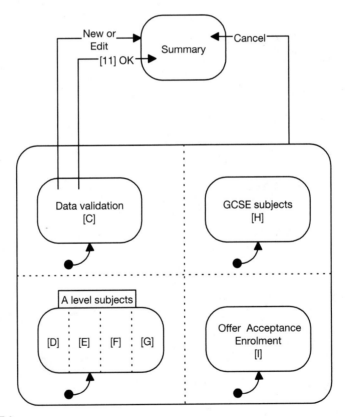

Figure E.1

CASE STUDY 3: A STUDENT DATABASE   237

Table E.1 Summary to Details interface table.

Current state		Event	Actions	Next state						
A	B			C	D	E	F	G	H	I
1,2,3	4,5	New button clicked	Display the Details screen; Clear the Details screen; Display the A levels tab-card;	7	10	13	16	19	26	27
3		Edit button clicked	Display the Details screen; Populate the details block with the student record highlighted in the Summary screen; Display the A levels tab-card;	8	10	13	16	19	26	27

Table E.2 Details to Summary interface event–action table.

Current state							Event	Actions	Next state	
C	D	E	F	G	H	I			A	B
%	%	%	%	%	%	%	Cancel button clicked	Display the Summary screen;	I	Hist
7							[11] OK button clicked	Create a new student record in the database using the data in the Details screen; Clear the Details screen; Refresh the Summary screen; Highlight the student record just created;	I	5
8							[11] OK button clicked	Update the existing student record in the database for the student currently displayed in the screen; Clear the Details screen; Refresh the Summary screen; Highlight the student record just edited;	I	5

The Summary screen

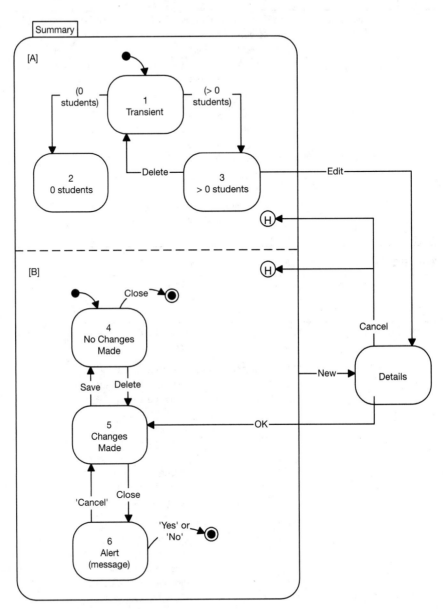

Figure E.2

Table E.2

		A				B	
User interface object	1	2	3	4	5	6
View	–	d	e	–	–	–
New	–	e	e	–	–	–
Edit	–	d	e	–	–	–
Delete	–	d	e			–
Save	–	–	–	d	e	–
Close	–	e	e	e	e	–

Table E.3

Current state		Event	Actions	Next state	
A	B			A	B
–	–	Start application	Display the Summary screen; Fetch all student records from the database into the Summary screen scrolling list;	1	4
1		(0 student records in the scrolling list)		2	
1		(> 0 student records in the scrolling list)		3	
3		Delete button clicked	Delete the currently highlighted student record from the screen and from the database;	1	
	4	Close	Close the application;		–
	4	Delete button clicked			5
	5	Save button clicked	Commit changes to the database;		4
	5	Close button clicked	State 6 alert message parameter: 'Do you want to save the work you have done?'		6
	6	'Cancel' button clicked in the alert message window displayed in state 6			5

Table E.3 (Cont'd)

Current state	Event	Actions	Next state
6	'Yes' button clicked in the alert message window displayed in state 6	Commit changes to the database; Close the application;	–
6	'No' button clicked in the alert message window displayed in state 6	Rollback changes to the database; Close the application;	–

The Details screen

Data validation

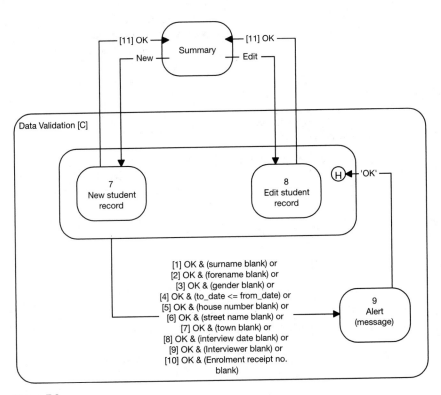

Figure E.3

Table E.5

Current state	Event	Actions	Next state
7 or 8	[1] OK button clicked And (surname field is blank)	Put the cursor in the surname field; State 9 alert message parameter: 'The student's surname must be entered before the record can be created';	9
7 or 8	[2] OK button clicked And (forename field is blank)	Put the cursor in the forename field; State 9 alert message parameter: 'The student's forename must be entered before the record can be created';	9
7 or 8	[3] OK button clicked And (gender field is blank)	Put the cursor in the gender field; State 9 alert message parameter: 'The student's gender must be entered before the record can be created';	9
7 or 8	[4] OK button clicked And (to_date field precedes or is equal to the from_date field)	Put the cursor in the from_date field; State 9 alert message parameter: 'The from and to dates do not seem to be correct';	9
7 or 8	[5] OK button clicked And (house number field is blank)	Put the cursor in the house number field; State 9 alert message parameter: 'A house number must be entered before the record can be created';	9
7 or 8	[6] OK button clicked And (street name field is blank)	Put the cursor in the street name field; State 9 alert message parameter: 'A street name must be entered before the record can be created';	9
7 or 8	[7] OK button clicked And (town field is blank)	Put the cursor in the town field; State 9 alert message parameter: 'A town must be entered before the record can be created';	9
7 or 8	[8] OK button clicked And (interview date field is blank)	Put the cursor in the interview date field; State 9 alert message parameter: 'An interview date for the student must be entered before the record can be created';	9
7 or 8	[9] OK button clicked And (interviewer field is blank)	Put the cursor in the interviewer field; State 9 alert message parameter: 'The name of an interviewer must be entered before the record can be created';	9
7 or 8	[10] OK button clicked And (enrolment receipt no. field is blank)	Put the cursor in the enrolment receipt no. field; State 9 alert message parameter: 'The receipt number for the enrolment fee must be entered before the record can be created';	9
9	'OK' button clicked		History (7, 8)

A level subjects

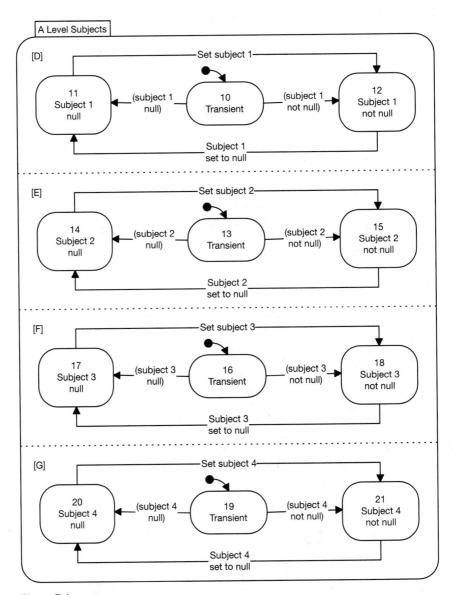

Figure E.4

Table E.6a

		D	
User interface object	*10*	*11*	*12*
Subject 1	-	e	e
Subject 1 status	-	d	e

Table E.6b

User interface object	E		
	13	14	15
Subject 2	-	e	e
Subject 2 status	-	d	e

Table E.6c

User interface object	F		
	16	17	18
Subject 3	-	e	e
Subject 3 status	-	d	e

Table E.6d

User interface object	G		
	19	20	21
Subject 4	-	e	e
Subject 4 status	-	d	e

Table E.7a

Current state D	Event	Actions	Next state D
10	(Subject 1 field = null)		11
10	(Subject 1 field ≠ null)		12
11	A value is set in subject 1 field		12
12	Subject 1 field set to null	Set subject 1 status field to null;	11

Table E.7b

Current state E	Event	Actions	Next state E
13	(Subject 2 field = null)		14
13	(Subject 2 field ≠ null)		15
14	A value is set in subject 2 field		15
15	Subject 2 field set to null	Set subject 2 status field to null;	14

Table E.7c

244	Event	Actions	Next state F
16	(Subject 3 field = null)		17
16	(Subject 3 field ≠ null)		18
17	A value is set in subject 3 field		18
18	Subject 3 field set to null	Set subject 3 status field to null;	17

Table E.7d

Current state G	Event	Actions	Next state G
19	(Subject 4 field = null)		20
19	(Subject 4 field ≠ null)		21
20	A value is set in subject 4 field		21
21	Subject 4 field set to null	Set subject 4 status field to null;	20

GCSE subjects

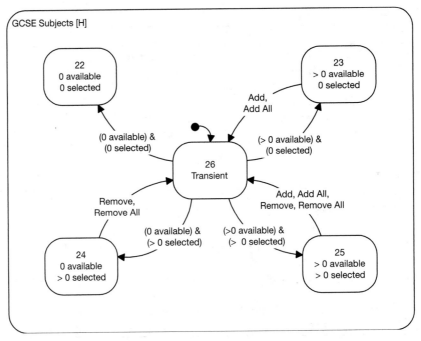

Figure E.5

Table E.8

User interface object	H				
	22	23	24	25	26
Add	d	e	d	e	-
Add All	d	e	d	e	-
Remove	d	d	e	e	-
Remove All	d	d	e	e	-

Table E.9

Current state (H)	Event	Actions	Next state (H)
26	(0 records in available list) And (0 record in selected list)		22
26	(> 0 records in available list) And (0 record in selected list)		23
26	(0 records in available list) And (> 0 record in selected list)		24
26	(> 0 records in available list) And (> 0 record in selected list)		25
23	Add	Add the highlighted record in the available list to the selected list; Remove the highlighted record from the available list;	26
23	Add All	Add all the records in the available list to the selected list; Remove all the records from the available list;	26
24	Remove	Add the highlighted record in the selected list to the available list; Remove the highlighted record from the selected list;	26
24	Remove All	Add all the records in the selected list to the available list; Remove all the records from the selected list;	26
25	Add	Add the highlighted record in the available list to the selected list; Remove the highlighted record from the available list;	26
25	Add All	Add all the records in the available list to the selected list; Remove all the records from the available list;	26

Table E.9 (Cont'd)

Current state (H)	Event	Actions	Next state (H)
25	Remove	Add the highlighted record in the selected list to the available list; Remove the highlighted record from the selected list;	26
25	Remove All	Add all the records in the selected list to the available list; Remove all the records from the selected list;	26

Offer, Acceptance and Enrolment

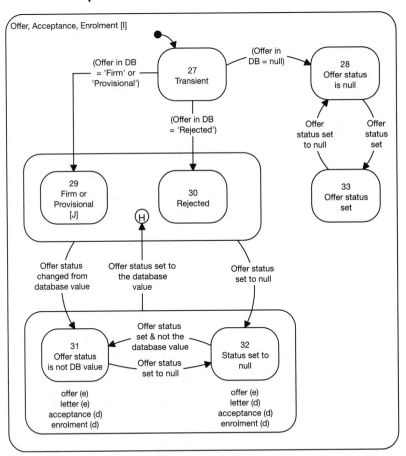

Figure E.6

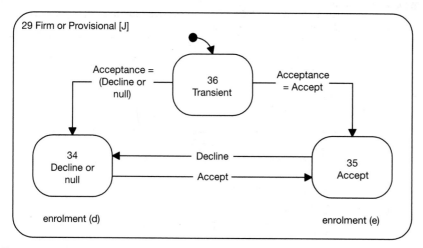

Figure E.7

Table E.10

User interface object	27	28	29	30	31	32	33	34	35	36
Offer Status	-	e	e	e	e	e	e	-	-	-
Offer Letter button	-	d	e	e	e	d	e	-	-	-
Acceptance Status	-	d	e	d	d	d	d	-	-	-
Enrol Status	-	d	-	d	d	d	d	d	e	-

The columns 27–33 are grouped under **I**, and columns 34–36 under **J**.

Table E.11

Previous state I	J	Event	Actions	Next state I	J
27		(Offer status in the database is null for the student)		28	
27		(Offer status in the database is set to 'Firm' or 'Provisional' for the student)		29	36
27		(Offer status in the database is set to 'Rejected' for the student)		30	
28		Offer status set And (offer status <> null)		33	

Table E.11 (Cont'd)

Previous state		Event	Actions	Next state	
I	J			I	J
33		Offer status set And (offer status = null)		28	
29, 30		Offer status updated And (the offer status displayed in the screen <> the offer status in the database for the student) And (offer status <> null)	Set Acceptance Status field to null; Set Enrolment Status field to null; Clear letter sent date field; -- because a new offer is being set	31	
29, 30		Offer status updated And (the offer status displayed in the screen <> the offer status in the database for the student) And (offer status = null)	Set Acceptance Status field to null; Set Enrolment Status field to null; Clear letter sent date field; -- because a new offer is being set	32	
31, 32		Offer status updated And (the offer status displayed in the screen = the offer status in the database for the student) & (previous state = 29)	Set Acceptance Status field to null; Set Enrolment Status field to null; Clear letter sent date field; -- because a new offer is being set	29	36
31, 32		Offer status updated And (the offer status displayed in the screen = the offer status in the database for the student) & (previous state = 30)	Set Acceptance Status field to null; Set Enrolment Status field to null; Clear letter sent date field; -- because a new offer is being set	30	

Table E.11 (Cont'd)

Previous state		Event	Actions	Next state	
I	J			I	J
31		Offer status updated And (the offer status displayed in the screen <> the offer status in the database for the student) And (offer status = null)	Set Acceptance Status field to null; Set Enrolment Status field to null; Clear letter sent date field; -- because a new offer is being set	32	
32		Offer status updated And (the offer status displayed in the screen <> the offer status in the database for the student) And (offer status <> null)	Set Acceptance Status field to null; Set Enrolment Status field to null; Clear letter sent date field; -- because a new offer is being set	31	
	36	(Acceptance Status field = 'Accept')			35
	36	(Acceptance Status field = 'Decline' or null)			34
	35	Acceptance Status set to 'Decline' or null	Set Enrolment Status field to null; -- avoids status conflicts such as Decline and Enrol		34
	34	Acceptance Status set to 'Accept'	Set Enrolment Status field to null; -- avoids status conflicts such as Accept and Withdraw		35

References

Davis A. (1990). *Software Requirements: Analysis and Specification*. Prentice-Hall

Fowler M. and Scott K. (1997). *UML Distilled*. Addison-Wesley

Harel D. (1987). Statecharts: a visual formalism for complex systems. *Science of Computer Programming*, **8**(3), 231–74

Jacobson I., Christerson M., Jonsson P. and Overgaard G. (1993). *Object-Oriented Software Engineering*. Addison-Wesley

Martin J. (1991). *Rapid Application Development*. Macmillan

Martin J. and McClure C. (1985). *Diagramming Techniques for Analysts and Programmers*. Prentice-Hall

Myers G. (1979). *The Art of Software Testing*. John Wiley

Rumbaugh J., Blaha M., Premerlani W., Eddy F. and Lorenson W. (1991). *Object-Oriented Modelling and Design*. Prentice-Hall

Stapleton J. (1997). *Dynamic Systems Development Method*. Addison-Wesley

Index